The End of My Soap Opera Life :-)

Book Two: A Change in Perception

SAM

Dedicated to the One within us that prompts our memory to recall heaven on earth. This shift increases as we forget the patterns of exclusion and move forward in time to its end.

Acknowledgements

Gratitude fills me with ever-increasing recognition of the Divine Source of *All the Good There Is*, the entity many people call God. Knowledge of the One, prompting me to share experiences as more people open their minds to reveal the Truth within, fuels thoughts.

A Change in Perception would not exist without the help of many people. Sources listed in the bibliography helped to shape this book. I am eternally grateful for them. Everyone noted within these pages taught me valuable lessons. Family, friends, and spiritual teachers met through classes, workshops, seminars, and conferences influenced thoughts. Sincere thanks also go to Cheryl M. Gorder of Eagle Spirit Publishing for helping with editing and publication in 2009.

Contents

Preface

Most people thought I went crazy when my son Daniel passed out of physical form. Some people still believe I live in the twilight zone. Journals, poems, family pictures, videos, and class work assignments document a full and colorful life. *A Change in Perception* incorporates these elements and shows how my viewpoint changed over the year 2005. It offers insight to personal experiences by seeing them in another way and reveals my journey of ascension (rising of Christ Consciousness).

Daniel's continuing evolution drastically changed my perception of life. His essence prompted new thoughts, thereby giving me the key to a new understanding. A renewed thirst for information about life after death, initiated after a near-death experience at age sixteen, became unquenchable. It grew slowly due to Daniel's spirit guidance, on websites to follow, and quickly progressed while guided to books and classes. Increasing awareness of the power of thought spurred the realization that it's possible to reshape life. New experiences led to insights, which changed my point of view and perception of events.

Because my journey starts with a change in thought patterns, it's useful to point out misperceptions. *Italics* identify notes, related to beliefs, when writing the book. They describe lessons learned, revelations concerning life situations, my current state of mind, or messages received while writing.

The first book of this series (*Death of the Sun*) contains a bibliography of resources that guided me early in the mourning process. Although the book is useful – for people interested in learning about power games, and those unaware of gifts from the Otherside (such as spirit orbs and after death communication) – I rarely recommend it now, for it's an emotional roller coaster ride. You see, I write at the level of awareness that I'm currently in. And that level seems to change as rapidly as life conditions. As I continue to understand new ways of thinking, my thought process changes, and I no longer relate to old ways of opinion.

I knew Daniel's Palm Sunday passing was a wake-up call, within a few months, but still was not sure what "wake-up" means. Words such as consciousness and ascension were not in my vocabulary making it all the more difficult to understand what was occurring within. It was finally time to reconnect with Source, to move beyond ego and fears, and blindly trust that there's more to life than consciously imagined.

The year 2005 brought with it another life, a turning point. Juggling business meetings between watching grandchildren was no longer an issue. Volunteer days ended as I withdrew from the national, state, and local activities that once meant so much. They no longer mattered. Daniel's death, which I referred to as a passing, gave birth to issues outside of ordinary experience. In time, I learned this was necessary for my consciousness to evolve.

Thoughts do indeed shape our world. Daniel's guidance from the Otherside planted seeds to change my thoughts to ones of increasing positivity and spiritual growth. The progression accelerated with recognition of the need for change. Life was no longer comfortable and it was time to do the work of my soul. It was vital to let go of the world, as I saw it, and begin to improve living conditions, before doing what I came to do.

In 2005, it was time to stop constant talking and start listening to my Higher Self. It was time to learn how to control emotions, to stop reacting and adding negative thoughts to mass consciousness. I begin changing reality by transforming ideas and beliefs and soon realize that all things are possible, all things thought projections. Using free will to change circumstances, my quality of life begins to improve.

Self-Mastery becomes a subconscious goal as I learn how to master emotions, thoughts, desires, and feelings.

Neale Donald Walsh, author of the *Conversations with God* book series, and many other books, notes a change in perspective makes it possible for us to change everything. Perspective creates perception, which forms beliefs. What we believe generates our behavior and subsequently our experience. Experience creates the reality of our life.

Thoughts affect the entire world so changing the way we think also changes the world. After more than four years, I see how mis-thought detrimentally affected the growth of my soul. Watching and judging others fostered separation. It was easy to pay more attention to the behavior of others than to my own actions. Concentrating on what other people did, or how they acted, left little time to think about fixing my own life.

My journey of self-discovery really accelerated when I realized we see what is in ourselves when we judge others. I soon realized it was time to change thoughts. There's a long way to go before recognizing myself as a lightworker, a wayshower here on earth to help others learn the truth of their being. But by the end of the year, I'm closer to changing everything about who I thought was 'me.'

:-)

Chapter One

A New Year

All that we see or seem is but a dream within a dream. Edgar Allen Poe - A Dream Within A Dream

New Years Day is a rude awakening as my fat, hung over body rolls out of Rebecca's bed. My head aches terribly. I again swear to stop drinking after picking up the camera to see if there are any surprises. My daughter's scowl reveals her hangover when the camera displays our New Year's Eve photos. I defiantly take one picture of Rebecca's pretty, heart-shaped face before putting the camera away. The morning remains uneventful. Rebecca fixes us brunch and, after eating, I leave for home to sleep again.

Momma's birthday is the next day so I telephone her in the evening to see what she wants to do. Momma lives with Terry, my younger brother. Terry says she's sick and not ready to celebrate.

Momma is ready three days later when I arrive to take her to the park so she can feed her beloved ducks. Several more pounds grace her five-foot frame. Tight fitting clothes reveal rolls of fat, leaving little to the imagination.

"I don't need any more clothes," she says insistently after opening the box with the coral-striped sweater. "I've got enough clothes to open a store."

It's useless to argue with legally blind Momma. She doesn't see that her clothes are ill fitting and in disrepair, just like mine. Momma's clothes and obesity bother me much more than they concern her. The doctor's remark after weighing her on the last visit comes to mind.

"Whoa Momma, you're up past 180 pounds. It's time to lose some weight."

Momma remains unconcerned for food is her only friend. Food now seems to be my only friend too but ego tells me the 165 pounds on my 5'2" frame is just fine.

We live in the third dimension, a place of consciousness where the illusion of linear time exists. This environment promotes the feeling of separation to avoid self-improvement. Fear, conflict, resistance, and despair increase as I focus on judging others. Allowing ego to concentrate on Momma is much easier than changing myself.

Ego is that arrogant part of us that says, "I'm okay but you are not." It lives by comparisons, which it uses to separate us from others, but it cannot survive without judgment. We identify mis-thought by the way we feel. If our mood is depressed, anxious, or anything but wholly joyous, we have reacted with a lack of love and ego rules our world. We become one with God, Universal Energy, Spirit, Source, Cosmic, whatever term you care to use, by recognizing mis-thought and deciding otherwise. Ego's rule is over when our collective consciousness unites.

A field of unlimited, unified energy surrounds us. However, in the process of creating various life forms, individual souls separated from the higher vibration. Focusing on our creations, we became trapped in the physical and lost our connection with Source. This led to the concepts of duality and karma, cause and effect, as a means to eliminate, eventually, the artificial concepts of good and evil.

Old souls in this environment often manifest certain health conditions to teach and learn valuable lessons. They may choose to have weight issues, or other handicaps, presenting others and themselves with lessons, such as an opportunity to love unconditionally despite appearances. Loving oneself is vital so that we may learn to love others unconditionally.

Momma slowly climbs into my white, 1997 Nissan Sentra for the two mile drive to the park. It's a beautiful day and I'm happy for we have not been there in months. After laboriously pulling herself out of the car, Momma walks with me to the first exercise station, sits down, and begins to toss breadcrumbs. At first, only a few ducks come to eat but many more arrive while I take pictures. Fat black ducks, and white birds with long beaks, called egrets, surround Momma by the time her bread bag is empty. They leave the area as soon as the bread is gone.

I watch the ducks thinking of vacation as they waddle into the lake for a swim. As always, thoughts turn to Daniel, my spirit son. Depression rises within, to turn blue skies to gray, while remembering his much-missed presence during family racquetball games held several feet away. Still missing him, I sigh and herd Momma into the car, ignoring her senseless, constant chatter, while listening to my own.

As we drive, ego takes control and locks me, once again, into the earth's negative, distortional, thought form, the past. I drop Momma off quickly now envisioning 2004 as the worse year of my life. World and life changes, that mattered very little after Daniel's passing, now consume me, even though I know he doesn't want me to be sad over his physical loss.

Daniel's essence led me to information on death and dying less than two months after he passed to the Otherside. Popular website data helped me come to terms with his passing but I quickly forgot most information. Now the instant knowing, upon reading of contracts, surfaces. Souls agree to contracts, carried out in physicality, when they need to learn from the same lesson. The thought fails to comfort me.

Early days of grief filled with a knowing that Daniel's soul planned his transition, to help others access higher consciousness. My soul planned this life carefully to nurture a higher perspective after his physical death. But now ego rules for I'm stuck in the past and lost in a sea of judgment. It's impossible to enjoy the present. The more I think about the past the angrier, and more fearful, I become. Completely caught up in the illusion of this world, I quickly forget that my soul attracted lessons to learn, and karma to transmute, on the way to getting closer to Higher Self, the God within.

Living in the past, with the company of judgment, guilt, and fear increases depression and leads to even greater disharmony and disunity. The discord creates artificial boundaries, which maintain our self-imposed prison and stifle spiritual growth.

Our souls consciously plan all experiences before birth to help with spiritual growth. As souls, we plan our earth death just as carefully as we plan our life. Many souls choose a transition that will achieve maximum impact on those it leaves behind. The time and place of physical death is part of the agreement made before incarnation.

The experience of tragedy teaches sympathy and compassion and is the working-out of cause and effect. We learn to change the cause as we experience the effects. I stifled my spiritual growth, for many years, by using the gift of free will to react negatively to opportunities. My soul chose to experience the tragedy of losing a son to transmute negative karma, created in a past life in Egypt. In that life, I turned away from God becoming bitter and disillusioned after losing a child. In this life, my soul chose to balance out that energy and further spiritual growth in others and myself.

The telepathy I continue to share with Daniel resurfaces upon arriving home. His essence guides me to turn off trusted, television news programs and pay no attention to world events. Following the wisdom of positive words that come to mind makes me happier. I unconsciously bless people at the end of emails without realizing it until someone points it out. Eventually, I'll learn that when we bless others we are really blessing ourselves. This applies to berating or praising others, for what we see in others is what we see in ourselves, and we strengthen what we share.

It feels good to give hope to others in the darker days of winter as various health conditions demand excessive amounts of time. Daniel's essence leads me to spiritual information about good karma that I joyously email to friends who respond positively.

Business sales slowly increase as friends help by promoting my work in hiv nutrition. But unmet expenses for the corporation, began as a mission in 1996, plague me. Health issues forced me to resign to working from home in 1997 but the small business now flops like a fish out of water. It feels like someone pulled a rug out from under me as everything counted on in the past quickly disappears.

Family members seem to be sliding deeper into poverty and dependence on others. After becoming accustomed to life without his ex-wife and son, Terry now deals with multiple sclerosis and a part time job. Younger sister Ruth and daughter Rebecca are plagued with other genetic health issues. James, my husband of eighteen years, although healthy, remains out of work with no job prospects in sight. I wonder what will happen next.

Human thoughts draw to us what we dwell on. I didn't know I was the creator of my own circumstances, nor, did I realize all the disruptions were symptoms of ascension. The ascension process takes us through many life changes, including health issues and changes in employment, as we let go and undo to return to the perfect state we arrived in when our souls were first created.

Souls may choose to be in families who have bodies with certain genetic factors. They choose a physical form that has a potential for a specific disease to help with the spiritual growth of self and others. Some may live with a condition from birth, while others may use it as a release valve, designed to react when certain elements in their life get to a point where they do not care to go any further. Other souls may choose dis-ease (lack of ease) to offer the opportunity to transcend genetic factors.

Copies of the Internet articles Daniel led me to shortly after he passed remained forgotten in my file cabinet so I had no idea that new energies were transforming our physical bodies. The higher vibrational frequency of our bodies is necessary for evolution. This change signifies new ways of being, which result in a deeper connection to God, as we step into the fifth dimension. Higher vibrational energies allow us to relate as more open, loving, expressive, and peaceful beings if we chose to do so. People not yet capable of using an advanced load of energy manifest dis-ease and have more difficulty focusing the new energy now coming through.

As part of the ascension process, people may find themselves in health situations that make it impossible to work their usual job. Some people may get laid off or be faced with other reasons why their "regular job" is no longer a match for them. Working a "regular job" becomes impossible when it's time to end old roles. Our soul's purposes and intentions now demand that we pay attention to the plan our soul chose to create, thereby learning that God is our support.

A wealth of information on ascension is available on the Internet and in books, audio tapes, and CDs. My favorite source at this time is a lightworker by the name of Karen Bishop.

My soul plan was ready to advance in 2005 but I was not listening to the Self within. I lived most of my adult life as *a workaholic, sometimes holding down two jobs at a time, while raising two children. It was time to come into balance, take a break, and then find work more suitable to a higher way of being. It was time to align with my Higher Self and remember my soul's planned contribution to humanity.*

I needed to reject the concept of illness, and substitute one of wholeness, realizing we are spiritual beings in human form. My soul's journey would escalate, as I trusted God to heal me of dis-ease. Soon, I would deny the genetic factors within my physical body to avoid the dis-ease so apparent within family and myself.

In the present moment, it's clear James is depressed after almost three months of pounding the pavement to find a job. The savings account normally used for family vacations and other luxuries is gone. Unemployment benefits are not enough to support us and it's time to cash in the life insurance policy. James and I drift further apart while I allow my fearful, threatened ego to avoid communication at all costs. Although we often sleep in separate bedrooms, we try to put up a united front for the family.

Limitation rules as I seek free medical care totally clueless that thoughts shape our world. A belief that it relieves the pressure on James as a breadwinner is strong. The God network works in my favor. Our usual doctor offers free medical care, provides free prescription drugs, and a form to fill out to get more. Michael, my acupuncturist friend, does cupping and scrapping without charge. His treatments make it possible to decrease the dosage of several medications. Isaiah, the psychic medium, also offers services without charge.

My mind continues to swirl into a spiral of negativity. Ignoring everything but publication deadlines causes the situation at home to deteriorate rapidly. The yelling that ensues upon leaving the sanity of my bedroom office serves to limit time in the rest of the house. This eventually works in my favor as I focus on myself.

God was looking out for me but I remained unaware of the divinity embraced in earlier years. I allowed fear to paralyze actions instead of using it to excite me, causing an adrenaline rush of courage to change life for the better. This led to a lack of strength and focus. Although I knew about the effects of diet and exercise, I remained unaware of the vital role of thoughts in good health. My actions did not always follow the good health routines learned throughout the years.

Crisis is a learning process in this schoolroom of illusion and the greater the dis-ease the greater amount of love and learning there is to gain from it. There are moments of great insecurity, during times of massive growth, in the soul's progression. As noted by Margaret Doner in her book Archangels Speak, to the archangels, dis-ease is the embodiment of fear, which blocks out God's light making it difficult to sense our connection. We need not hang on to dis-ease but can transcend it, by embracing more of our Source, helping us to recognize there is no need to punish ourselves.

:-)

Chapter Two

Party Time

The mental atmosphere that surrounds us is impressed not only with the thoughts and feelings we create, but the thoughts and feelings of those around us. James Van Praagh - Reaching to Heaven

The telephone continues to ring. I try to ignore it but pick up the receiver when the answering machine begins to record Rachel's voice. Abigail, my granddaughter, her mother Rachel, and Rachel's mother Joy spent the Christmas holidays out of state so I missed seeing them.

"I'm having a birthday party for Abigail in four days," notes Rachel excitedly. "There's going to be an animal farm. Can you tell the family for me?"

"Of course," I happily reply thinking of holding my beautiful granddaughter once again. "We'll come early to help you set things up."

James and I arrive at Rachel's front door on the appointed day two hours before the party. Spacious, finely manicured grounds reveal the results of the time James spends to help with weekly yard work. As Rachel opens the door, I quickly compliment her on the yard and sparkling clean house.

"I even stocked the pond with fish," she says with a wide smile looking at James holding a fly fishing rod.

The Fraser fir still stands beyond the living room pleasing my senses. For just an instant, I allow myself to enjoy the scent of fragrant pine needles, for we didn't buy a Christmas tree. Clearly, ego butts in; Rachel carefully planed the perfect party for three-year-old Abigail. Ego now compares abundance, which appears so real for Rachel, with the rest of my families increasing lack.

My plan to read the book changes when Rachel announces that Joy is trying to get Abigail to nap. It doesn't occur to me that Abigail might be tired, or that Rachel has things to do before the party begins. I listen closely filled with arrogance, instead of love, as Daniel guides me to leave the book in the car. My old ego-based self silently reacts with anger, resisting the aspirations of Higher Self, blocking the awareness that I'm part of something much bigger.

The book about Daniel's first three years of life sits waiting in the car. I hope to read it to Abigail and Rachel, thinking it will help them to cope with their new life, by knowing Daniel grew up largely without a dad. He was a happy boy who laughed, sang, and counted on his mom as they learned lessons together. Certainly, Rachel will understand, after seeing it, that I know what it's like to be without a husband in my only child's early years.

My plan to read the book changes when Rachel announces that Joy is trying to get Abigail to nap. It doesn't occur to me that Abigail might be tired, or that Rachel has things to do before the party begins. I listen closely filled with arrogance, instead of love, as Daniel guides me to leave the book in the car. My old ego-based self silently reacts with anger, resisting the aspirations of Higher Self, blocking the awareness that I'm part of something much bigger.

Ego continues to dwell in a sea of negativity, adding more fuel to the fire of separation, and marring the perception of everything I see. Fearful of losing more loved ones and lacking faith in God, I choose to continue the controlling behavior that rules my world. I want everyone to support my illusion and cling to Daniel's memory. The self-imposed prison within strengthens as I ignore the gifts our situation offers. Thoughts of my family's poverty, compared to the wealth Rachel and Joy appear to have, control me.

This physical arena is an exercise in soul growth, designed to help us grow spiritually. We are in something like a virtual reality game. It all seems so very real but it is not. Everything is just an illusion, a figment of imagination.

There is much more to life than any of us will ever know in the mind/body state.

Ego becomes strong in strife and thrives on conflict. It's happy anytime we react negatively. In time, I'll recognize ego's limiting ways, which prevent the realization that we're from the same source, a part of each other.

My soul chose this experience, to serve as a vehicle, to encourage me to let go and reconnect to God. It was time to be more, to question, to grow, to expand. But for now, not recognizing our unity, I continued to play the separation game, distancing myself from everyone else through thoughts and actions. Lost inside my fantasy world of separation, I refused to see the gifts that made it so much easier for me to wake-up from this dream called life. One of those gifts was the recognition that we need not live in limitation.

Daniel was born on the nineteenth of the month. In numerology, the number nineteen represents the beginning and the end, the alpha, and the omega. As souls, Daniel and I programmed many clues into our lives and those clues spurred me forward. The clues allowed me to unlock karmic information as I moved through emotionally difficult experiences and became more self-aware.

Humanity is an extension of God projected into physical reality so we can experience that which we are not. We are souls, having a spiritual experience, creating in human form. It is only in the illusionary human form that we have the opportunity to expand our awareness. We continue to play the game because illusions must be forgiven on the level experienced.

One of the biggest hurdles we face is amnesia for we forget that we are spiritual beings. The delusion is of our own making, designed with our thoughts. This state of forgetfulness helps us to be less homesick for our heavenly existence and allows us to start each life with a clean slate.

We create life based on the level of our consciousness before morphing into human form. Agreements before birth, *based on what our soul chooses to learn, determine souls that will serve as family, friends, and other key people. Some souls agree to play easy roles, while others choose challenging roles, which many humans may find distasteful. Yet, we all have played different roles to help one another in various lifetimes. There are no coincidences, for we plan both major and minor things that happen to us, in favor of soul growth.*

Reincarnation is the process that allows each soul to experience, every human condition, as the path to full spirituality and eventually back to the God Force. How we handle situations makes the difference of what happens next in our life. We may live in different dimensions simultaneously and have somewhat different lives based on our reactions to planned events. We stop reincarnating as a human and play somewhere else when the game on earth finally ends.

Although each life offers opportunity for soul growth, the goal, the end of the game, is the same for us all. We are here to help one another realize that limitation is only in our mind. We are here to recognize our unlimited potential of good. We are here to realize we are the same, each one of us a part of God. Eventually we learn to express our true nature through love, health and well-being, abundance, and creativity.

For the next two hours, I warm store-bought prepared snacks in the oven and arrange them on food trays. I'm glad to be busy and away from Joy, for even though my heart tells me to bring harmony to our relationship, I still dislike her greatly. It will soon become very clear that Joy is instrumental in helping me to recognize the parts of my little self that need to be let go, the parts I refuse to see.

The past ruins the present while thinking of many delicious foods made while working as a caterer. Ego judges this processed food as garbage, full of fat, preservatives, and empty calories. The wonderful feeling of connection to others, so strong when I worked as a baker, is gone. My only "real" friend is more than a thousand miles away and I feel totally alone.

By continuing to think negatively, and dwell on the past, I successfully separated from others and cheated my Higher Self of enjoying the moment. It was not clear then that I could improve life drastically just by changing my thoughts. Our thoughts are pure at birth as the mind thinks moment by moment. Those thoughts change as time passes and we learn to believe in the past, present, and future.

It's much easier, as a human, to rely on things outside ourselves until we increase our awareness of God. One of many valuable things Daniel's essence taught me, from the Otherside, is that we can change the way we think. Messages from Daniel (who soul planned to act as my Higher Self until I became more aware) came much more often, once my mind rid itself of negativity from the outside world. Messages increasingly came in a clear stream of thoughts, images, and ideas, based on my level of consciousness.

Rachel and James work together outside setting up party decorations and chairs. I hear them laughing and carrying on as if they're old friends and it makes me feel better. It's clear a new set of people now surround Rachel and Abigail as unknown guests began to arrive. For a few awkward minutes, I introduce myself as Daniel's mom. People seem embarrassed, and look confused, so I begin to introduce myself by first name adding, "I'm Abigail's other grandma."

I remain alone and lost within my own limited egotistical world trying to keep quiet. It seems important to avoid ill feelings, which often occur when I thoughtlessly blurt out whatever comes to mind. The idea serves to distance me from the new people in their life.

Abigail's party guests reflect her changing environment. None of the children from her new preschool comes to see the animal farm. There are seven kids at the party; three toddlers are new neighbors while the remaining four are older kids from her past. Abigail's godmother Eve pulls into the wide drive with Timothy (age 12) and Phebe (age 10).

Anger again overwhelms me, strengthening the invisible barrier between others and myself, when Rachel allows Timothy and Phebe to see if Abigail is awake. While I long to hold Abigail and whisper in her ear, once again, I let fear hold me back. A few minutes later, they escort her into the back yard to watch as the yard transforms into an animal wonderland.

It is a perfect day to be out in the huge, back yard. The light blue sky features puffy, white clouds amid a temperature in the lower 70's. Everyone stares with anticipation as a couple unloads large, red cages filled with animals from their truck. Excited parents and kids watch as animals spread across Rachel's yard. There are baby chicks, piglets, baby and adult ducks, roosters, rabbits, a goat, a calf, a lamb, and two ponies to ride.

Small colorful plastic chairs, placed around the cages, allow kids to sit and hold their favorite creature. Children and adults begin to take turns holding the small animals, and brushing the larger ones, but Abigail hangs back. I watch as she moves from her mother's arms to clinging to her mother's leg. Rachel promptly picks her up with a worried look. She brings Abigail to the redwood deck where I stand with my video camera and asks her if she is tired. Abigail just lays her head on her mother's shoulder.

"I'm going to put you," she says hesitating while looking tenderly into Abigail's eyes, "in your bed for a few minutes, okay?"

Abigail slowly shakes her head from side to side but stays silent. Looking both confused and excited, Rachel sets her down beside me and runs into the house for her camera.

"Oh, they're so cute," she exclaims about the animals over her shoulder.

I jump at the chance to hug Abigail.

"I love you so much Abigail," I say giving her a tight hug. "Nana and Daddy will always be in your heart."

I'm compelled to say the words without knowing why.

Abigail looks at me and for the first time pleasure registers on her small, heart-shaped face.

"There's a baby cow over there," she says excitedly pointing to the calf. "There's a pony coming! There's a pony."

We have the capacity to connect with the collective spirit of animals and must remember that their energy is essential to our future growth. Animals touch our lives, our hearts, and our souls. They teach us to let go of the past, to play, and live in the now. They love unconditionally, completely without judgment, and are an example of what humans need to evolve toward. Animals are totally without ego and they would teach us if we would listen. They always offer us unconditional love.

We are faced with abuse in certain lives. In others, animals help us to transcend that abuse through their use of unconditional love. It took me more than half a century to realize what both Rachel and Abigail intuitively recognized. Animals are a part of this God soup we seem to be in and they easily recognize human thoughts. Since they respond in kind, having the petting zoo was the perfect thing to do, for the warmth of the animals overshadowed the human dramas acted out during the event.

Timothy and Phebe run to us. They herd Abigail over to the small circle of colorful, plastic, kid chairs but she does not stay there for long. Abigail walks next to her mother, when she returns with a camera, and clings to one of her slender legs.

"She's acting shy," says James walking toward me.

"Could you please take some pictures of my granddaughter?" I reply handing him my digital camera while trying to get her on the videotape.

With great displeasure, I watch him walk over and snap a candid photo of the calf.

People keep standing in front of Abigail as I try to capture her image onto videotape. It's not intentional but I still resent them for it. Unwanted thoughts erupt. Maybe we're not meant to be close. Women in my family sense Abigail will never be a big part of our lives. Yes, maybe they're right and it's time to let her go.

"I guess it's time to give her up," I say out loud softly.

Ego silently counters as anger rages within, "Never, never."

It seems impossible to have any time alone with Abigail. I long to hold her in my arms but console myself videoing the scene before me because I don't want to chance another jealous outburst from Joy or Rachel. The memory of Daniel's last birthday party is too fresh. Ego leads me into the valley of fear even as I stand there planning to avoid negativity at any cost. As in the past, memories stop me from living in the present as I choose fear instead of love.

My fat legs rub together as I waddle into the yard to carefully step around the adults and animal cages. A woman stands in front of Abigail just as I focus my camera. She has her back to me and fails to know she blocks my way. Something again tells me that it is indeed time to let my granddaughter go. The Universe is telling me I have to let her go. Rachel lifts her and puts her on the pony as I retreat to my station on the redwood deck.

The goat walks up to me chewing while seeming to stare me down as I sit scowling in a wrought iron chair. I watch as James continues to take pictures of every animal on the lawn.

"You know what?" I call out angrily continuing to video the scene. "I really don't care if you get a picture of the animals dear."

White light whizzes past the goat's face as it watches

me. A band of multi-colored light appears at the bottom of the video screen, after minutes of what looks like changes in the vibrational field, in front of the camera. Does something from the Otherside direct the goat to stare at me swimming in a field of negativity?

The baby goat walks away to nibble on the checkbook sticking out of Rachel's back pocket as she stoops down. She jumps up quickly, and almost knocks over the red animal cage nearby, as adults roar with laughter. Papa James puts Abigail onto the pony with Phebe but when Phebe gets off, she wants off as well. Even his coaxing cannot keep her on it. Phebe stoops down beside Abigail to tickle a smile out of her.

The kids joyously coo over, and hold, bunnies and baby chicks as I hum along to background music. Despite the joy around her, Abigail needs constant reminding to smile.

"She's a night child," Joy notes repeatedly. "She'll come alive tonight."

I sense Daniel, still in "the middle," trying to take care of unfinished business. Intuition tells me he is very displeased with all of what he would call "dog and pony show tricks." Perhaps his daughter senses this as well and thinks these things are not to be treasured. As my feelings intensify, knowing he taught Abigail what is important, love and family, I again feel anger instead of love.

In my dream world, those who seem to die may stay in the astral dimension, a world of emotions, where they remain until their awareness increases. They may not realize they have left the physical body, or they may have died suddenly as Daniel did, and feel there is unfinished business. For whatever reason, their consciousness fails to move beyond the astral world and they are more able to connect with those left behind.

Daniel, I believe, needs assistance with relationships left behind for his sudden passing was unexpected. It's now my duty to help him wade through the astral plane and move on to higher fields of consciousness. I do not want him to be one of the entities who follow though with routines similar to the one left. Abigail continues to prompt Rachel, to fix her daddy a plate of food at dinnertime, so I know she feels his presence and that he feels hunger on the astral plane. It's time to help my spirit son resolve unfinished business so he can leave "the middle."

In his book, Walking in the Garden of Souls, George Anderson notes, although souls may regularly visit a loved one or location, they are not trapped in "the middle." Even though they may linger with us temporarily, they do not need our help to set them free or to progress to the Light.

Feelings told me otherwise. Our feelings are signals and always have purpose for nothing happens by accident. We are on our way to improving the world around us when we learn the purpose of feelings that fill us with negativity. By replacing negative attitudes with positive ones, we can discover the issue is with how we use, or are being used, by what we feel. It's a matter of changing our perception, our awareness of things, to form newer and more positive beliefs. Beliefs are imagination's fuel for the more we think of them the more they become a part of us.

Perception is a temporary attribute of the belief in space and time subject to either fear or love. It didn't exist until the separation from God introduced degrees, aspects, and intervals causing conflict. God has no levels. All conflict arises from the concept of levels but we find the peace within when we alter our perceptions. The time for me to find inner peace, to stop trying to fearfully control others or separate from them through comparisons, and instead foster love consistently, finally arrived.

Abigail's godmother Eve breaks though my self-imposed prison as I sit videotaping from my lofty perch.

"Do you know how to work Joy's new digital video camera?" she asks in exasperation. "It says 'tape full' but Joy just put a new empty tape in."

Each time my cameras malfunction I sense Daniel's essence is the source of the issue. Both my cameras refused to work while trying to video during a visit to Rachel's house a few weeks after his transition. The fully charged video battery was suddenly dead and my digital camera refused to take a picture of Abigail. It still acts erratically whenever I try to capture Daniel's presence at family events.

The thought of Eve calling me crazy, just like my family does when I speak of feeling Daniel around me, causes me to withhold the information.

"I could say something but I'm not going to," I reply calmly. "Sometimes you can video and sometimes you can't," I confide too softly for her to hear as she walks away shaking her head. "It all depends on what the spirits want you to do."

"Maybe Daniel doesn't want them to get any video," I think, not realizing the day would be much more enjoyable if I knew my thoughts shaped the world.

There comes a time when we all sense there is more to life on earth than we know. I believe every soul designs their earth life with clues to help them recognize their true nature. Hints from the Otherside are very subtle most of the time, and easy to miss, but constantly malfunctioning electronics are often a true clue that the energy around you is trying to communicate. Some people may ignore the subtle hints, planned as souls, while others may choose to investigate their feelings and experiences. I am grateful that, as souls, Daniel and I planned our lives carefully so I would continue to feel his presence as long as I needed to.

The rest of my family, cautious Rebecca, twelve-year-old Samuel, a negative appearing Terry, Ruth, and Momma, wearing the coral striped top, arrive right before the owners leave with their animal farm. Rebecca walks slowly up to Abigail and says hello as she clings to Rachel's leg. Abigail smiles broadly, gets up, and walks away to sit in a chair alone. I intuitively know Rebecca is remembering the negativity of Daniel's last birthday as she turns around and walks back toward the rest of the family. Abigail watches her, gets up from the chair, and quickly returns to sit on her mother's lap.

Victim mentality prevails while my family seems to join me in the game of avoiding conflict at all costs. Later, as Terry pushes Abigail's swing from the back and Ruth pushes it from the front, my heart swells with love upon hearing Abigail giggle.

"She's finally laughing," I tell Rebecca sensing everything is as it should be as karma balances. "Why don't you join them and spend some time with Abigail?"

Rebecca looks at me angrily.

"Don't tell me what to do," she says in a huff.

Fleetwood Mac sings, "You can go your own way…" on the radio, as I walk into the house ignoring the subtle message from Spirit.

"Life is suffering; it's a process; and it's okay," I remind myself as Rebecca joins the group at the swings.

It was time to bring love and compassion in to balance fear, and distrust, but I found this difficult to do. Harmony seemed impossible to imagine. As I chose fear over love, my demeanor reflected a lack of self-acceptance. It was time to overcome and learn from the difficult confrontations planned as a soul before my human birth. It was time to rectify my imperfections and allow the Light within to shine. I had to learn how to love everyone unconditionally, especially myself, just as I did Daniel and Rebecca. It was time to stop comparing, to stop judging others and myself, and to learn the ultimate lesson of love.

We possess the power to create joy amidst confusion, happiness in the mire of disappointment, and peace in a world of war. Van Praagh, in his book Reaching to Heaven notes, when we declare ourselves victims living in fear, anger, and resentment, we attract situations that create more of the same taking us further away from God.

Knowing that telepathy stretched much further than the communication shared with my children changed how I thought in later years. Thoughts increase when we give them away and they become stronger when more people believe in them. We send out thought-vibrations all the time and those thoughts go out into the ether to affect others. As "like attracts like" in the Thought World, we reap the results of our thoughts and attract things, circumstances, and people who think like us. Once we realize the Law of Attraction, the power of thought, we can rest safely and calmly, unaffected by the turmoil around us.

A Course In Miracles teaches that we can't possibly be a victim of this world because we invented it ourselves. We view the world as we wish to see it so all we need do is change the way we see the world. I refused to take responsibility and stop blaming others but remained full of resentment, remembering the past, and unable to enjoy the experience before me. Life would have been much easier if I'd realized it was all a game we chose to play, before we took on physical forms, and that by changing my perception the victim mentality segment would end. My world improved significantly, as I began to view the situations around me in a different way.

Emotions often point out the need for a change in perception. Staying lost in my own emotional drama made it easy to blame Rachel and Joy for my emotional well-being. In truth, Rachel and Joy provided me with opportunities to work out issues with traits such as intolerance and judgment. It was time to release them with love knowing there was no offense. We agreed to teach and learn lessons as part of our soul's contracts.

As humans, we recognize traits in others because we share them. The mannerisms I saw in Rachel and Joy were my own. I experienced loss, closed down, and then tried to manipulate others thinking they'd treat me better, the way I deserved. Fear held me away from reality as I allowed ego's emotions to rule. I failed to see that Rachel and Joy pointed out the fearful emotional behavior that caused me to try and manipulate people.

I also failed to recognize the negativity that was so prominent in me. Ignoring the purpose that others had in my life, I chose to form negative opinions that kept me in victim mentality and sent those thoughts out to everyone else. I had no idea of the damage I was doing to myself by choosing to *be negative. Yet, those feelings eventually served their purpose as I let go of the ego's negativity.*

A Course In Miracles notes, "Nothing the ego perceives is interpreted correctly." We must get rid of negativity in any form for it ceases to exist as soon as we stop feeding it our energy. By paying attention to our thoughts, feelings, words, and actions, we conserve the Universal Energy within us making it easy to manifest our perfection. Replacing negative thoughts with positive ones stops us from being used by the ego.

The truth is you have to maintain an upbeat attitude. Since all thoughts are vibrations that go out into your space, and beyond, it is vital to maintain positive thoughts. Think only those thoughts that you wish to come back to you for those are the nurturing thoughts. The thoughts in your daily life are distracting and can be let go as soon as they enter the mind. You need not hang onto these thoughts. You need not hang onto the thoughts of others day-to-day lives either. The nurturing thoughts are those that are of Love, of Peace, of Light. Those are the thoughts to maintain in the head. Those are the thoughts to send out in those vibrational waves that go beyond your space and out into the space of others.

All forms of negativity have no power except what we give them. Never doubt the capacity of the One Mind to bring the fruits of your divinity to you in any imaginable perfect form. The daily use of positive thoughts, feelings, words, and actions results in mastering our mind to the point where we no longer accept the negative qualities in the world. Knowing without a doubt that we are one with Divine Power, we eventually create a world where we are the master over all conditions.

As the air vibrates around the children, and candy pours out of the pony piñata, the video camera fades in and out even though the battery is fresh. Abigail and Phebe scoop up the last of the goodies under a setting sun. An unexplainable flash of light in the yard draws me outside but when I try to investigate Abigail calls me away.

She calls me to join her at the table where she and her mother sit as we eat. Each time she gets up to play with Phebe, I leave to sit near Momma. Our table's discussion turns to spirit orbs while viewing digital pictures. I know the see-through circular white spots are orbs because Daniel's essence led me to an Internet website of orb research shortly after he passed. Rebecca now regularly watches a television series on haunted houses.

"They say the orbs are spirit energy," Rebecca excitedly announces to the group.

"Tell James about it would you?" I ask with a nervous laugh. "He's going to commit me."

Phebe and Timothy take Abigail out to the swing set in the dark yard as Joy and Rachel prepare her cake. A ranch, with five, multicolored horses that stand grazing in a field near a blue pond amid a small, brown, wooden bridge, decorates the cake. Abigail comes back onto the porch frowning. She does not want to blow out the candles.

"It's your birthday Abigail," the kids chorus in unison. "You've got to blow out the candles."

Feeling the spirits around us, I silently hope they, and the children, will remain with Abigail. Pictures show orbs hovering in the air beyond Abigail and her cake.

A few minutes later, Phebe and Timothy sit on a wooden bench in the breakfast nook prepared to help Abigail open gifts.

"Which one do you want to open first?" Timothy excitedly asks reaching his hand out toward the pile of gifts.

I watch as a beautiful magenta-colored orb appears above Phebe and Abigail. It floats off toward the picture on the wall of Daniel on his last birthday as he holds his then two-year-old daughter.

"Just start with one and you'll get though them all," I find myself saying.

Abigail shakes her head and slouches down on Phebe's lap.

"She's just not herself today," Rachel muses sounding like a concerned mother.

Abigail's disinterest in birthday gifts continues until she holds Uncle Terry's gift with an envelope that reads "Pumpkin Butt." Her small, heart-shaped face breaks into a wide smile. Blue eyes sparkle as she grabs the orange envelope.

"Open it, open it," Phebe prompts her like a cheerleader.

Abigail gleefully drops the card onto the floor with a smile after opening it. My heart swells as I watch her beautiful smile. Playful Abigail is back to her usual self as she pulls the card out of Phebe's hands and drops it on to the floor again.

Orbs hover above Daniel's memorial poster sitting on the floor, to block the dogs from getting into the bedroom, as the kids help Abigail open many gifts.

"You have some old souls there," I tell their mother. "It shows."

Eve looks at me with a knowing smile and nods her head.

It gives me great comfort, as a human, to realize that Abigail chose the dear souls in her life just as carefully as the rest of us. These wonderful souls contracted to help her through what any child would consider difficult times.

Rachel begins to talk about her hectic holiday season as Uncle Terry gently places the smiley wind chimes I brought for Abigail on the kitchen table.

"This is the fourth time we've done this now," Rachel confides leaning back with a loud sigh in her wooden chair. "We had Christmas here, then Christmas and her birthday out of town, her birthday at school, and now this. Oh my God, I can't take anymore," she says with a panicky laugh.

My mind returns to the past, remembering the many friends, and family members, now gone from Rachel and Abigail's life. It seems unfair that Rachel and Abigail spend so much time celebrating without my family and me while we slip closer to bankruptcy.

A Course In Miracles reminds us, as humans, we either project or extend. Feeling distanced from everyone, the ego within me made sure to project my issues onto someone else. Projection, to the ego, is a means of getting rid of something it does not want. In truth, it is the fundamental law of sharing, by which we give what we value in order to keep it in our mind. The ego always tries to preserve conflict by projecting it from our mind to other minds. However, we cannot project conflict because it cannot be shared. Giving it away only insures that we keep it. The belief that by seeing it outside us, excludes it from within, is a complete distortion of the power of extension.

Anger and attack come from an attempt to project responsibility for our own errors. Projection means anger, anger fosters assault, and assault promotes fear. That is why those who project are vigilant for their own safety. They are afraid that their projections will return and hurt them. Believing they have blotted their projections from their own minds, they also believe their projections are trying to creep back in. Since the projections have not left their minds, they are now forced to engage in constant activity in order to recognize this.

The land of separation beckoned me once again. Instead of seeing how chaotic this first Christmas season was for Rachel without her husband, I thought only of the limitation my family seemed to be experiencing. Jealously, and anger, took the place of compassion and love, as my ego automatically switched again to victim mentality.

What we see in others is a reflection of our own consciousness. Projection is a way we use to cast our fears *and lay our shortcomings onto others. The more we project how we feel about ourselves onto others the longer it takes to help our soul advance. It was not clear to me at the time how the refuge of projection placed me in a prison apart from everyone else. I now see the pain others were dealing with that I in my own pain failed to see.*

The thought that we all choose our lives here is comforting. Judging any experience as unfair always leads to separation from others. At this time, my mind refused to recognize the abundance of opportunities to change the world around me. Victim mentality stopped me from creating my own experiences and filling my life with gratitude and joy. It never entered my mind that my experiences would change when my responses to what happened around me changed.

The time to align with new and higher ways of being, and living, arrived with Daniels transition and accelerated with each perceived loss, including the perceived loss of Abigail and Rachel. I had no clue it was all a part of my soul's plan to dismantle darker aspects of myself. It was time to change belief systems and perceptions. This opportunity presented itself as part of a complete dismantling of my life. The willingness to change inched closer with each perceived loss.

In time, I'd learn that the more we concentrate on positive thoughts such as unity, perfect health, love, peace, and Light the more we experience these things. As I began to choose love, over fear, my spiritual growth progressed with the use of clear thinking, meditation, and prayer treatments and I learned there is no loss.

The magenta-colored orb reappears after Abigail opens her last present. Her eyes look vacant as we sing happy birthday.

A few minutes later, back on the screened-in porch, Abigail asks Papa James, "Did you see the horses?"

"Did I see the horses?" James repeats with surprise. "Yes, I put you on the pony the first time. Don't you remember?"

Abigail shakes her blonde, pony-tailed head and answers, "No."

A review of the day's pictures at home fills me with immense joy. In one picture, there is a small orb between Samuel, with his shirt over his face, and me smiling as I hold the video camera trying to capture him. Other pictures show lots of orbs and energy strings, especially at dusk in Rachel's back yard. One of my favorite ones documents several orbs around Abigail as Phebe holds her up to the pony piñata. I wonder if Abigail felt the presence of her daddy when they appeared and fall asleep with a smile.

:-)

Chapter Three

Stuck in Fear

Only your mind can produce fear. It does so whenever it is conflicted in what it wants, producing inevitable strain because wanting and doing are discordant. This can be corrected by accepting a unified goal.
A Course In Miracles

Thoughts of lifestyle changes, confronting Rachel, disturb me days later. She seems so sad since Daniel's death. Her frame looks gaunt. Is she eating enough? Rachel now focuses efforts totally on raising Abigail alone. She prefers only the company of her mother. I find it hard to believe that she pushes everyone else away, and yet, it sounds hauntingly familiar.

Daniel's essence continues to comfort and guide. Blessings flow forth on most nights while standing in the hall. My hands rest on the wall under a collage of family pictures. I am reaching out to the other side, where the pantry is, because that's where the blackboard sits. It's the treasured blackboard of smiley faces that Abigail, Daniel, and I drew together the last day I saw him in human form. A wonderful feeling of loving energy always flows, into my palms, and wafts throughout my body.

That day stands out clearly in my mind's eye. Abigail was learning how to draw smiley faces on a small blackboard when Daniel arrived to pick her up. He happily joined in on the fun. We shared a special attraction to the sun and smiley faces reminded us of it.

The week now fills with work. Cash seems elusive so I dedicate more time, and effort, into making money by designing a sales brochure. The new brochure uploads easily to the Internet along with many published newsletters for subscribers. Intuitively led to change many things done in the past, I find the new ways of doing business much cheaper.

It's difficult to avoid television so I record world news to view later while working. "Democracy Now" headlines, for January 20, 2005, include articles on how Bush emphasized "freedom" in his Inauguration Speech. The 109th Republican Congress begins with a new progressive Senator, Barak Hussein Obama, who will be the 44th President of the United States three years later. It will be another four years before I more easily comprehend what an absolutely necessary and valuable service to humanity President Obama and President Bush provide.

We are in the process of a great shift moving quickly toward Christ Consciousness. The earth is moving to a higher vibrational state as it rids itself of humanity's negativity, through natural disasters such as earthquakes, volcanoes, hurricanes, floods, and fires. Catastrophic events pave the way for higher vibrating energies within individuals as well. Souls are here to help with that shift, to higher consciousness, by clearing negative energy from their physical, emotional, and mental body. This energy must first be recognized before it can be released.

Humans embody desired traits by experiencing the darker energies of things such as loss, dis-ease, and abuse. These conditions encourage us to search for something better. Tired of the old ways, we let go and create something new that is much more to our liking. We all have different paths and must trust that Universal Law prevails and all things lead back to the Source of utter perfection and reunion.

President Obama now fills the world with renewed hope and life as he offers us the necessary experiences to spur humanity forward. George W. Bush's soul also agreed to play one of the greatest roles in history. He also agreed to spur the willingness for change, by playing what some refer to as a "dark" role, so we could wake-up to the nature of our true being.

President Bush agreed, on a soul level, to assist us in raising our frequency by initiating the chaos that would lead us to the creation of a better world. We needed to recognize our mis-perceptions in order to purge their lower and more densely vibrating energies.

Both presidents motivated us, to think about what we really wanted, to look at things in another way, by showing us what we did not want. We are One and without the many changes they made humanity would have continued to separate instead of unify.

This is a world of duality. In Reality, darkness is illusion and Light is Truth; only Light exists. Many people who seemed hopelessly apathetic now search for something better because of the darkness souls agreed to create. We are moving quickly toward a world of unity, faith, trust, and unconditional love because both Obama and Bush provide us with the necessary interactions to support spiritual growth.

Over the next few years, many people will wake-up to a better way of living through a variety of experiences. Some will have a health crisis that spurs them, or their loved ones, closer to God. Intolerance and apathy will disappear as people experience loss or become involved in the care of loved ones.

Hell is a product of our passion to see judgment on earth. It took me nearly fifty-eight years to realize that I made my own version of hell, for most of my adult life, by thinking there was nothing more than what I believed. I know

now that souls come together to learn and grow. When a soul's contract concludes, if physical proximity no longer serves us, we can part and move on to another experience. It is something our souls agreed to experience, in this lifetime, as part of the Divine Plan.

The darker energies within are often released for those experiencing "a dark night of the soul." This knowledge doesn't make it any easier to bear when moving through experiences but have faith; things will eventually improve. I know this because my self-created hell of illness, loss, limitation, and losing everything dear spurred me to the heaven in which I now reside.

Days unfold perfectly when I begin them in conscious contact with Spirit. Based on reports from friends, and an increase in the number of emergency vehicles I seem to hear, the world is changing quickly. Emergency workers, I tell myself, are just testing sirens or moving traffic to get to dinner before it gets cold! In his book It's All God, Walter Starcke paraphrased the Twenty-Third Psalm to offer us a means for dealing with chaos. It is a powerful tool for those whose awareness has transcended the religious upbringing of our past. [1]

James talks loudly to his new kitten. Lost in a dream of limitation, I sense our shared loneliness. Prudence recently arrived on the back porch just like the first kittens that arrived last year. James notes she's more standoffish than other cats, yet, vies for his attention when ignored. "Perhaps the cat offers a way to connect," I think, while moving into the living room.

Prudence jumps straight up into the air as if trying to reach something. The hole in the back porch ceiling looms above her. Rather than view her actions as a way of getting attention, as James does, I see them much differently. The hole in our porch ceiling is a source of constant worry, for me, but seems insignificant to James. Our interaction ends, before it starts, as soon as I point out that she might be seeing something in the ceiling damaged the year before. We continue to drift apart in both mind and body as James retires quickly alone.

I just want to die and get out of my private hell but, instead of crying, I remember the heaven that Robert Monroe notes in his book *Journeys Out Of The Body*. I begin to read the book that Daniel's essence led me to buy.

"It is truly a state of being, very likely interpreted by the individual in many different ways."

Monroe describes a Perfect Environment where warmth is of, through, and all around. Ruby-red rays of light hold great meaning here and all colors of the spectrum come and go, constantly bringing a different soothing or restful happiness. This nirvana, a place where pure peace, yet exquisite emotion join, and nothing exists as a separate piece of matter, now beckons me.

"This is where you belong," Monroe reminds us. "This is Home."

The more I read, the more I relate to Monroe's words. Tears trickle down cheeks and my heart aches for Home while agreeing wholeheartedly. I want to again move slowly and effortlessly through a cloud, interlocked with others, flowing through soothing music and vibrating in harmony with *It*. Yes, it's the right place to be. But thoughts return to earth because there's work to do.

A long letter to friends and family consumes time. It's almost as long, and forlorn, as the one sent before Daniel passed, after Senator Robert Byrd discussed the end of democracy and the Constitution. A deep sense of loss prevails with the memory of watching the Twin Towers fall while sitting in my living room.

"The world will never be the same," I thought then.

As our family hastily drove home from an impromptu Tampa trip a month later, after seeing another plane go down on a special news report, I knew it was the beginning of something life changing for everyone.

As noted by Gary Renard in The Disappearance of the Universe, *the fall of the World Trade Center "symbolized the separation from God, the loss of Heaven, and the fall of man."*

There are groups of souls that return to earth to fulfill karmic ties on a global level creating advancement. At the time, I did not consider that the Twin Towers incident successfully woke souls choosing to experience loss through tragedy.

We react to things if they bring forth something within us that is a match in vibration. When we hear of somebody dying, or going through hardship, we may feel his or her pain and experience compassion. Or, we may feel pain and grief, as I did, forgetting our infinite and powerful spiritual nature and react negatively. The choice is always ours.

Rebecca responds to my letter by asking if there's anything she can do for me. She is the only one who notices the several times I write, "Not in my lifetime."

"You've still got some spit and fire left," she replies. "Don't even think of wigging out on us. Contrary to your beliefs, you are not always right. You have more to do here. Something good is going to happen to this family and you'll have some years of actually being able to have some fun!"

I wonder what she is talking about as I cry myself to sleep.

Now, exactly four years later, I am having fun in a heaven I never could have imagined then.

For the time being, I listen to Daniel's voice telling me to keep busy and get out of the house more often. My routine serves to ease the burden on family and helps to maintain a connection with the outside world. I work on business, pick Samuel up three days a week after school, and spend a few hours with Momma every two weeks. Remembering my promise to Daniel, months after he transitioned, I still telephone Rachel once a month. Happiness fills my heart when she lets me know Abigail enjoys receiving monthly cards with little gifts.

Rachel's telephone call of thanks, for letting James visit her and Abigail, is a pleasant surprise. It makes me happy to know the three of them enjoy their visits even though I'm still distraught about not being included. They have no idea their visits are part of my plan to get them together after my physical death.

Things seem to remain the same in February. My friend Mary continues to help with spiritual progress. She offers the second book by Dr. Brian Weiss, which prompts past-life regressions. Learning of the continuity of the soul serves me well as I remember many past lives with Daniel. It is now his turn to transition before me.

James continues to fish more than usual. Now he fishes two or three times a week, or more, if I count nightly trips to local canals. The reason for his frequent fishing, and infrequent visits at family gatherings, eludes me. Yet, his absence is a blessing in disguise. It allows me the freedom to do what I want without fear of intimidation or scorn.

On the day of a planned family event, James surprises me with a note. He's fishing with a friend this weekend at Fakahatchee Strand State Park.

"Really," he typed into my computer, "if someone has to rescue us, tell them they'll need to take a chain saw. The only way to get where we go is by canoe. If a boat has to get us, they will have to saw through a fallen tree. It's not as dramatic as it sounds, but if we need saving, they need to know that. I may be pretty late. If we get back early, I may stop at a club meeting. I'll leave a message on the answering machine if I can. Love ya... but not this computer. Me."

"What prompted the communication," I wonder. It's unlike James to leave a note, especially one that reveals feelings. My family, always very demonstrative, is totally different from his. Yet, we are attracted to one another because of our differences. The game of separation continues for I cannot recall when he ever said, "I love you." I ponder our differences before saving the message to my hard drive.

Like a character in Gregg Braden's book The Divine Matrix, James and I stay in the marriage long after we emotionally leave, fearful of uncertainty, and not finding anything better. We are in a holding pattern, building negativity, not happy, but rarely communicating to each other. Our true feelings are disguised as tension, hostility, or just being absent from the relationship.

Although irresponsible about my own nurturing, my heightened sense of responsibility often denies others the opportunity to be responsible. James possesses many traits not yet recognized in myself and ego tells me our union makes me complete.

My traits, and their opposites, come more into focus as my ability to help others changes after our marriage. Throughout the years, I slowly integrate many parts of myself hidden deep within. The crises of family loss, and ill health, fuel even more awareness helping me to realize I am, and always have been, complete.

Hours later, I'm happy to get Samuel from school to keep me company until Rebecca's workday ends. He plays his Gameboy as I watch world news on "Democracy Now." When Rebecca takes him home, I force myself to work on a new update for newsletter subscribers. It is one of many ways to avoid thinking about the upcoming birthday that would have been Daniel's thirty-eighth.

Rachel and Abigail telephone to wish me a happy Valentines Day. Rachel says Abigail still sees her daddy. She was frightened the last time, ran to Rachel, clung to her legs, and said Daddy was there. Rachel told her to go talk with him but Abigail insisted that Daddy wanted to talk to Rachel. So Rachel went into the spare room, sat down on the floor, and talked to him.

I thank her for telling me and admit; he lets me know he's still around.

"It's okay," I assure her. "You're not crazy."

In his book Destiny of Souls, Michael Newton notes souls use many methods and techniques to connect with us. Thought transmission is often successful, providing the living are receptive to messages. Souls may resort to using children as conduits, if it is difficult to reach the mind of an adult, because they are more receptive.

Daniel's presence fills the air as Rachel extends an invitation for James and me to visit. My excitement at the prospect of seeing Abigail outweighs the thought that James sees her every week. I gladly accept the invitation leaving it to Rachel to set the date.

:-)

Chapter Four

Communication

We are the mirror as well as the face in it.
Rumi

Daniel's soul continues to evolve as his essence guides. Crying jags lessen even though heart, and mind, still mourns over the loss of his physicality. He now prompts me to recall the wealth of Internet information found seven weeks, and five days, after his cremation.

A frantic search through file cabinets pays off when I hold the packet of papers. There are 142 pages of information. It's new but vaguely familiar information on a variety of subjects. Daniel leads me again as I shift through sheets of paper.

"No not that one," he says inside my head as I flip through several pages on spiritual growth.

Papers on karma, and powers of the mind, on laws of the universe, and forgiveness, fall quickly to the floor as Daniel guides me to an article on consciousness after death. It feels good to settle into the task chair to read parts previously highlighted by yellow marker.

"The Transition Known as Death," by Prophet Drew Ali, excites my mind. How comforting to know that guardian angels, and guides, are with us! And wondrous beings assist us into the realms of Light. But I plan on Daniel being there with a new Harley as I transition.

"Assure your loved ones who are nearing transition that your separation is only an illusion and you can reach across the realms via your loving energy and intent," Prophet Drew Ali reports.

Sorrow either allows us to release ties that no longer serve the soul, or becomes all consuming, leading to lack of discernment and increasing depression. Death is not something to be sad about because any tragedy is just a challenge to find the truth within the event. We are One so physical loss can never part us.

Daniel designed his passing to wake me up to the truth of our BEing, but at this point, I don't know the world is an illusion designed with thoughts. I still view myself as powerless, with no control over destiny. My selfish ego chooses to separate from God, feeling pain and grief over loss, instead of recognizing that Daniel and I remain eternally connected through our oneness with God. How much more joyful it would have been to understand this but in retrospect I see how my experience led me to help others toward the truth.

Daniel's essence leads to exactly what I need to comprehend. I now feel the joy that comes with an understanding of spiritual reality. Tears of joy flow while reading:

"Rejoice, and know that the enfranchised soul has found liberty, and, if you would but unfold the powers that the Creator has given you, you could share some of the new beauty and joy which is theirs."

Yes, Daniel's passing was a stepping-stone to the larger freedom of spirit realms. Of the seven levels of consciousness beyond this physical one, only the lower three are of importance to this plane and to the evolving soul. The level closest to the physical plane involves the astral, the emotions. This is the plane where many evolving souls get stuck.

At the time of physical death, Daniel's soul seemed in a state of intensified emotion, mirroring Rachel's, most of our families, and mine. It now makes sense that the key to resolving a fixation on this plane is a resolution of relationships.

With great excitement, I continue to read about consciousness and life after death. Yes, the key to moving up though the astral plane, and on to higher levels of consciousness, lies in controlling emotions.

Ego now changes my perception with thoughts of the past. The more I read, the more I understand why Daniel's presence remains so close to Abigail. In my mind, Rachel is totally preoccupied with her, demanding exclusive rights and as Daniel; Abigail is the center of Rachel's life, treated like a possession. Ego recalls family fights, fueled by jealousy over his attention towards them. Now it appears she possesses Abigail and treats her the same way.

I so love the drama and perceive Daniel's concern while reading; when the emotions are allowed to function in this manner people become nothing more than an object, a piece of property, a possession in the mind of someone filled with emotion. Isn't Rachel's relationship with Abigail ripe with emotion? Of course, I ignore the fact that my relationship with Abigail, and others, is highly emotional and possessive as well.

Possessiveness is an emotional imbalance. It does not benefit us to invest our life in someone else for it retards our growth; we need to feel worthy on our own. Daniel was the center of my life and although I'd shared him with others, I considered him my son and was hurt when he chose to do things with others seeming to exclude me. By holding on to someone, or something, we exclude the one life energy we share. Whenever we give, we release, and allow God to be all-inclusive.

During this period, I knew little about forgiveness or "shadow selves," which are the catalyst for initiating a new level of consciousness. Choosing to be a highly emotional being, this is what I often saw in others. All my so-called enemies seemed to display many of the traits I needed to change in myself. Now I know souls often agree to experience abusive, or painful, lifetimes with other souls deeply connected to them through love. Their strong connection allows the experience knowing that it results in greater unity.

At the time, it didn't occur to me that these perceived losses were another means to bring my mind in tune with the true nature of BEing, for all losses ultimately represent the illusionary separation from God, which we hold in our minds. As it says in <u>A Course In Miracles</u>, "Forgiveness is the great need of this world, but that is because it is a world of illusions. Those who forgive are thus releasing themselves from illusions."

Rachel was one of many who agreed to help my soul grow with a lesson about love and forgiveness. While I disliked the circumstances, I eventually learned to accept and forgive everyone, including myself. It still takes a bit of time to understand the aspect of myself that other people reflect but I know they are my mirror, reflecting an aspect of myself through their behavior. Yes, I am an active participant in a contract set up before birth. This is my constantly changing dream, my perception of life, my reality.

Intuition hints of a greater issue as I read that souls face the test of overcoming "bondage," which most people agree to experience on earth. Isaiah, the psychic medium, now helps me deal with many past-life memories of limitation and repression. Daniel and I share numerous past lives and it's time to break through the barrier of limitation to move on to higher levels of consciousness. Reading that problems associated with relationships must be resolved on the physical plane, and upon demise, verifies this. Undoubtedly, Daniel will show the way.

We continually release things that do not support the purest version of ourselves. Darkness is the fuel that ignites Light. In The Ascension Primer, Karen Bishop notes most Lightworkers chose (as souls) a life of abuse, to transmute lower vibrating energies. Experiencing darkness, through abuse, serves to spur us forward, by giving us the contrast needed to search for, and create something new. I now recognize my soul's perfect choice of parents for they created a strong desire for unity and something different.

Emotional karmic patterns begin to lose their appeal. Strong emotions seem to plague Daniel on the astral level. I'm ready and willing to remove limiting beliefs, to learn along with him so we can proceed to the mental plane. There's much work to do for emotions still control me. My choice of an untraditional marriage begins to make sense upon realizing that James must have succeeded in this effort. His physical plane relationships seem largely controlled.

Daniel's soul continues to find new ways to garner attention. The portable CD player started acting erratically months after his transition. I easily make the connection for music is a big part of our life. The player makes a beeping noise while skipping over songs. Within months, despite several cleanings, CD's often slide through songs like record player needles scratching across the surface of a record.

The portable CD player stops abruptly as I drive to Terry's house while listening to Daniel's memorial CD. I think it's time to replace the batteries and look at the player as Terry's drive comes into view. The player lays open on the passenger seat. Somehow, the essence of my last-born son opened the cover to the CD player.

Filled with wonder, I concentrate to hear the message. Daniel is delighted I am getting out of the house, taking

Momma to the park instead of to the doctor's office. He is happy to see copied pages from Deepak Chopra's book, *Peace is the Way*, for Terry.

I pick up the sheets of paper, walk into Terry's house, and tell him. He does not seem surprised that Daniel wants me to give him the pages. Terry nods his head slowly as I talk about the CD player opening up by itself. He's now accustomed to hearing strange tales.

"Two more days, two more days, and Daniel would have been thirty-eight," I remark while driving home.

He's still here just not in human form. His soul is a very good communicator and offers many, nice surprises on so many days, especially the bad days when I act like a human Mom and cry myself to sleep. Sometimes I wonder why I still cannot see Daniel. It is because either I am not yet ready to, or it's not part of my soul agreement. Obviously, my soul agreement differs from that of Gary Renard, and others, who see entities as if in physical form.

The music now changes while typing and listening to my new multiple discs CD player in the background. The singer's words seem to stutter. Daniel's essence is with me again. I smile realizing a communication is about to occur.

"I'm here with you Mother," I joyously hear. "You may type if you wish. I've never really left you. It is just that you've stopped sensing me. I hope you can understand that. Do you?"

I am excited but do not react with the usual emotion of sadness.

"I'm not sure," I reply as I stop the CD player.

Daniel's words flow without pause into my brain like a quickly moving river.

"I know you'll figure it out," I hear. "You are an old soul after all and coming Home soon, as soon as your work is done, and you know that work is increasing now and that's why you need to stop watching the world news. It will only

serve to dissuade you from the truth of who you are. It will only serve to stop you from doing what you came here to do. And what you came here to do is of the utmost importance for all of humanity.

"You are a Lightworker refined in the grace of God, knowing the Truth of your BEing. Do you understand that you need to concentrate on NOT worldly affairs? Do you comprehend the importance of this mission you have agreed to? I know you do and now you must finish what you have come to do. That is why I am with you, always, to prompt you to stop getting off of the track of Right life. Do not be dissuaded by what goes on around you for it will not affect you, ever. You, as all Lightworkers, are protected from on high and your missions will be fulfilled. That is what I've come now to tell you and it is what you wanted and needed to hear. Is it not?"

I am not a typist but my fingers fly over the keyboard as soon as the words come into my head. I type them while silently asking Daniel's essence to slow down.

"Yes, yes," I reply. "It is what I needed to hear. Please can you tell me what I need to prepare for now?"

"Your preparations are sure, and steady, and follow a path that is set. You do not need to further prepare for all is well in your world."

And then his presence is gone...

It is hard to concentrate on this book now. Yet, I know the sequence of events is vital for the reader to understand how my ascension takes place. Before I started working on the book today, I spent at least an extra hour on my other laptop computer reading the latest news and checking on a hurricane that might come our way. It was wasted time for it was time not spent on writing this second book. Now I write with increased fervor.

:-)

Chapter Five

Glimmers of Light in the Dark

The root of our "negative" experiences may be reduced to one of three universal fears (or a combination of them): abandonment, low-self worth, or lack of trust. Gregg Braden - The Divine Matrix

James visits Rachel and Abigail as emptiness surrounds me upon entering the quiet, depressing house. I again feel excluded but know all is well while lifting the red, computerized Furby out of a dark cabinet, just to see if James took the batteries out.

The Furby comes to life but does not babble nonsense like it does when James touches it. Electronic eyes blink as "I love you" fills the room. Furby makes a kissing sound, smacks it's tiny, yellow, so-called lips and repeats, "kiss me." It then repeats heard and unheard terms. When I place Furby back into the darkness of the hurricane box, it stays silent with its eyes wide open, as I close the closet doors. James always complains that it sings and keeps him up but the Furby does not do that with me.

Daniel's voice rings clearly through my brain. He tells me to keep singing. I do so love to sing while listening to the beautiful music on the *DIVAS Simply Singing CD*. Of course, when I sing "I Miss You," by Sandra Pires, tears still run uncontrollably down my face.

"I miss you. No one could take the place of you. No one could love me like you do."

The feeling of someone in the room is unmistakable. Yes, Daniel is again here in spirit form. Over the past several months, I have spent enough time searching the house for someone. There is no need to look further than my side. Crying slows as Daniel announces that it's ludicrous to miss him when he's right here. I smile glad to feel his essence so close.

"Keep singing the songs Mom, especially that one to desensitize yourself," he says softly.

"Maybe, maybe, just maybe," I think excitedly, "I'll see his energy soon instead of looking at his physical form in video's and pictures."

James, often silent about times spent with Rachel and Abigail, returns hours later. This time he shows pictures taken with his new camera. Pretty Abigail smiles in one, while standing inside a little club house talking with her daddy. Two pictures of Rachel and Abigail, at the local park, and one of them as Rachel makes dinner, show happy faces. There's even one of James with a surprising glow on his face. Abigail, probably under Daniel's influence, insisted on taking the picture.

James, I immediately suspect, is in love with Rachel. The recurring thought doesn't bother me at all. Figuring it will balance negative karma between Rachel and me, I've already mentally given him up. Who could be a better choice to raise Abigail and reap the profits of Daniel's hard work?

Feelings and behavior improve upon seeing the world differently. A lovely, new feeling makes it easier to get out of the way of Higher Self. Sometimes resentment, jealously, or other negative feelings seem to take a vacation. Our family celebrates what would have been Daniel's birthday by motoring along the waterways, in Ruth's boat, before a visit to his roadside sign. It seems silly to visit a roadside sign so I refuse to join them later and explain that no one dies.

"If you want to communicate with Daniel just think of him," I insistently announce. "There's no need to try and connect with him where the highway crew put a sign in his memory."

Family continues to call me crazy but stays close. While James fishes in the Everglades, we spend time in the local park. It often seems difficult to get everyone together for a little fun and exercise so I'm happy to finally play racquetball again. Beautiful March weather fills Florida's baby blue, clear skies. Temperature remains where the rest of the country envies us, in the lower 70's.

My video camera lies on the front seat as Samuel and I drive to the small neighborhood park. Scattered, long clouds begin to fill the air when we pull into the parking lot. My usually good memory seems a thing of the past. A note stapled to my shirt reminds me to ask family for books on metaphysical (beyond the physical) things loaned to them last year. In time, I'll understand that as we live in the present moment, memories of past events fade. It becomes a challenge to know what we did a minute ago.

Living in the present moment is vital because the thoughts we think have the power to create our world. Time and space are an illusion. "Now" and "Here" are the only valuable commodities because the present is before time was, and will be when time is no more. In it, are all things that are eternal, unseparated by an illusory past, and they are One.

Living in the "Now" affords us with a greater desire to make conscious choices, and take responsibility, rather than looking for others to blame. Like humans, every day is unique and filled with possibility. That makes it even more vital to live each day in the "Now" for it only happens once.

In coming months, I will display an unquenchable desire to learn, living in the "Now" and experiencing extreme feelings of bliss, love, and forgiveness. It will be a welcome change from self-imposed days of depression and limitation. As I learn that thought, just as everything else in this world, is energy, things manifest much quicker when I increase my focus, skill, and practice.

Life takes me on a journey where the vibration of my thought sets in motion a new way of living. It's glorious to learn that the focus of attention makes a difference in what shows up in my life. Mastery of Self, controlling thoughts, spoken words, and deeds, slowly becomes my goal. By the end of the year, I'll be more immersed in Self Mastery creating a world of wonder, and joy, that allows me to experience oneness once again.

Rebecca rests patiently on a silver bench basking in the sun. Samuel runs ahead towards his mother while I try without success to videotape him. My mind is in a constant state of motion limiting opportunities to hear God's voice. Humming fills the air while strolling along two small lakes. Samuel and Rebecca began to play racquetball as I noisily video the action commenting on their every move.

Ruth's old, black, Chevy van pulls into the lot. Never silent, I talk out loud, to myself, while videoing as she tries to find a parking space. The small, concrete lot looks uncommonly full so she pulls out of it to park on the lawn. Terry climbs out of the passenger seat. He gleefully pulls his pants down to moon me upon seeing the video camera. A fat, white butt peeks out of green, gym shorts, on one side, as he continues to walk backwards keeping up with Ruth. I notice that unlike me he continues to dye his hair auburn. My hair now looks unkempt, with dark roots almost three inches long, amid hairs of gray.

"What's that piece of paper on your shirt," Terry asks when we hug.

"You see how bad my memory is?" I reply, pointing to the note on my left shoulder. I then interrupt the conversation to take a picture of Rebecca.

"I look like my mother," she says with disgust when I show her the video screen.

"You're a much better version of your mother," I reply with dignity. "You're much more powerful."

"Ok Mom, I wasn't, didn't mean for you to start a metaphysical conversation," she retorts with a frown.

Naomi arrives. Samuel lies down on the concrete, feigning injury, as she walks toward the racquetball court.

"I guess Samuel can't play anymore," I remark with a sigh.

"Samuel's dead," Ruth replies. "We'll just have to throw him into the lake."

Samuel moves his head to let the small, blue, rubber ball under it roll aside. Rebecca walks toward him uncapping her water bottle. She trickles water from the bottle onto his neck and back.

"Oh, you are dead," Samuel, now head to head with his petite, five-foot mother, shouts while springing to life before chasing her around bushes and trees.

Envy erupts while watching them, upon remembering how little time young Daniel and I had to be friends. We concentrated on survival. Shared times were very limited until he ventured out on his own. Daniel and I never had the opportunity to play in a park for I worked constantly. Soul growth, increased by a life of struggle in Daniel's early years, never occurs to me. But it pleases me now to see the depth of my daughter's relationship with her son.

Two mini choppers drive by us later as we walk out of the park.

"They're so cute," I announce, instead of reacting with the usual sadness over Daniel's passing.

The parking lot is nearly empty as I scurry to say goodbye to Naomi before she pulls out of the lot. I gently open the door of her Explorer, exclaim, "love you," and give her a hug.

"Sure, sure," she says not knowing what else to do.

She's not accustomed to receiving affection, especially from me, because we have spent years as rivals for

Ruth's love. I'm now determined to demonstrate our identity as One.

"Drive careful," I advise gently closing the door before walking back to my car.

Samuel gets into his mother's little white car. I stand alone feeling empty again. My video camera is still on as I place racquets and balls back into the trunk. I turn it off and toss it onto the back seat before climbing into the driver's seat. The realization of Daniel's memorial CD in my portable CD player lifts my spirits. I turn the gadget on to sing along to the songs. I so love listening to Daniel's memorial CD and know all of the words. When a song named "Higher" comes on my singing gets louder.

"Can you take me higher to a place where blind men see?"

The music plays until the player pauses just as sunlight streaks through the car.

"Oh, come on now," I say feeling Daniel's presence. "That's not funny. You can cut that out now. Quit messing with me."

Playback of the video, which had somehow turned back on, shows magenta and purple colored orbs, amid green mist as sunlight enters the car.

The music starts playing normally again. I thank Daniel for the visit while joyfully singing and driving down city streets. It takes less than ten minutes to pull into my driveway.

"Oh, it's our song," I say out loud as "Nothing Else Matters" begins to play.

A short pause in the music reminds me Daniel's presence remains.

"Be nice," I announce out loud.

It is such a beautiful song, and I truly love singing along to the words, so I stay in the car to sing. The CD player continues to act erratically.

As I loudly sing, "open mind for a different view," it repeats "view, view, view, view."

"Come on," I remark loudly beginning to get irritated. "Never cared for what they do. Never cared for what they know but I know," I sing with gusto as the CD player continues with its cycle of pause and play.

I hear Daniel clearly.

"Mom there's only *One*. Don't you remember?"

I am enjoying myself, and although happy to feel him with me, I'm not pleased about him interrupting the music. Not caring if anyone hears me seeming to talk to myself, I plead with Daniel's spirit.

"Come on, I know there's no them, there's no us. Come on, I know there's just *One*."

The CD player starts working normally again until I get to "never cared for games they played."

It pauses again as Daniel's voice reminds me there is no separation.

"I know there's just *One*, stop!" I plead with him again.

The last line of the song plays as I happily sing loudly, seemingly alone, in my parked car.

"Forever trust in who we are and nothing else matters."

My heart is full of love. I am amazed that Daniel can still affect me so strongly even when out of his physical body.

I get out of the car and open the back door to lift my video camera off the back seat.

"Ahem, why is the camera on?" I ask as if talking to someone I can see. "How did you do that?"

A picture of Daniel's face with a wide grin comes to mind. Anxious to see what is on the video, I quickly enter the empty house to sit down on my big, brown, Lazy Boy. Rewinding and playing back the tape, I see that the camera appears to come on by itself as I drive singing the song "Higher."

:-)

Chapter Six

Dismantling the Dream

We are all one family in the consciousness of light whether we are talking with angels, masters, elves or a mosquito. To enter, the web of Christ Consciousness asks us to dismantle the hierarchical systems, which belong only to the limited three-D world. Dr. Christine Page - Spiritual Alchemy

Many unexpected changes occur within the U.S. in March 2005. National news focuses on an unprecedented intervention by Congress; led by Representative Tom DeLay, as the tragic situation of severely brain damaged Terri Schiavo becomes widely known. The event marks the first intervention for political gain into the most private of family matters by Congress. This event, and others, is part of the process of awakening to our true BEing.

Terri does not have a "Living Will." After fifteen years of maintaining her life with a feeding tube, family members choose to let God decide her fate. President Bush signs an emergency law to keep the feeding tube in place against their wishes. Many Americans, including myself, sign advanced healthcare directives or "Living Wills."

Despite reluctance, something compels me to continue the business. Things improve as more authors submit articles. Word of mouth increases newsletter subscribers. Business sales trickle in as I continue to sing day and night. Self-confidence boosts when neighbors praise my beautiful voice.

Daniel returns as I sing "I Miss You." He stands behind the task chair, tenderly touching my shoulders, while repeating, "Ludicrous." Daniel says it with a laugh because he's always in my heart and often lets me know in physical ways. I've lost count of the many times his vibration changes songs on the CD player, turns the motion detector light on in the always silent back den, or changes the television station. It's no longer odd but comforting to know that he, and other spirits, visit from time to time.

The number of email condolences, from people hardly known, amazes me. They seem to relate to the loss of a loved one knowing it's been almost a year since Daniel's transition. Several people share experiences of loss when I reply mentioning how I miss my son.

"One can only hope, and trust, and continue to learn," I tell them all.

Clearly, that's what really matters as spiritual growth continues. The rest of life's so-called issues appear as a grain of sand on a long, long, beach. Yet, a constant state of depression fills me while dealing with one illness after another. I fail to see dis-ease as the way each body expresses separation, the soul's confusion manifesting physically so that consciousness will see it.

James' visits to Rachel and Abigail continue but he rarely speaks of them.

"Oh did I tell you Rachel gave me these on Thursday?" he says, handing me pictures after a short visit.

The studio pictures disturb me because both Rachel and Abigail look odd, unlike themselves. I become ill after seeing the first two. It's difficult to work while having the flu so I rest much more than usual. A glitch in the vast system interrupts business email so there's no need to check for messages. The Web hosting company helps sort out the issue just when I feel well enough to work.

James, still out of work, appears full of anger. He spurts out a constant barrage of negative comments and seems to offer tasteless answers every time I speak. After years of matching moods, the effort no longer seems worthwhile. Two priorities fill increasing amounts of time, caring for myself and doing the right thing, the thing I'm here to do. But now I'm filled with frustration. A quick phone call to Rebecca, asking her to lure James away, helps me to restore the workroom's positive energy.

Suffering is an indication that we are out of harmony with our Self, with the law of our being. The sole use of suffering is to purify, to burn out all that is useless and impure. Change, a huge part of this life experience as I switched jobs, locations, relationships, and everything else many humans cling to, now seemed impossible. Yet, change is inevitable for spiritual growth.

It was time to expand the way I thought once again and rid myself of the anger that manifested dis-ease. In the book Archangels Speak, *Archangel Ariel notes we have the opportunity to take a scenario, or event, to a place of despair or great Light. It was time to follow my soul's plan and use the difficulty of "losing" a child, as a catalyst for spiritual growth, but I falter ignoring how that loss affects someone else.*

The need for surprises lessens but they sure are nice when I'm feeling down. Daniel's spirit visits often, especially when James goes to see Rachel and Abigail. Missing his presence, I decide Momma and I will shop at the 99 Cent store after getting Samuel from school.

The CD player skips over songs as I drive. It skips through parts of "Nothing Else Matters," the song I now refer to as Daniels and mine. Daniel messes with me laughingly from the Otherside as I start to sing. He stops the CD completely only to let it play again after I stop trying to sing.

We sing it through together as he clicks back to the song and plays it in full.

Tears flow later while listening to the car radio as Momma and I drive to get Samuel. A song that reminds me of the 'good ole days' begins to play.

"Change the station," Daniel says insistently inside my brain. "Change the station now Mom."

I change the station quickly before Daniel's voice fills my head again.

"You see Mom," he says softly, "it's that easy to control your emotions. You just change the station."

The loud disco music playing on the radio now reminds me of nights as a dancing cocktail waitress. I wipe the tears away and smile broadly singing along to the music, even after picking up Samuel. He and Momma do not seem to mind for they are happy to see me in a good mood. We leave the car and enter the 99 Cent store laughing, happy to buy whatever desired.

The car refuses to start when it's time to leave. It's the first time this car refused to start but I have lots of experience trying to pin point problems with other cars. The battery looks okay so I figure the starter needs repair. Our local auto club announces there could be a ninety-minute wait.

Momma lost her hearing aid again so it's very trying to be with her. Ruth offers to get Momma and Samuel after I telephone her. It's not fair to make them wait and seems impossible for me to continue to scream so Momma hears answers to questions already answered.

The auto club's tow truck appears within fifteen minutes to start the car. My hunch is correct. The car's starter is bad so I cannot turn the car off until I get to the repair shop. Ruth pulls into the parking lot, with Naomi quietly crocheting beside her in the passenger seat, just as I telephone to tell her the news.

"Come on," Ruth insists, "I'll follow you to the mechanic just in case the car stalls."

I'm pleased with the offer and thankful when we get to the repair shop, for Ruth reminds me, twice, to get forgotten things out of my car before driving us all home.

"You might have to pick up Samuel from school tomorrow if my car isn't ready," I announce as we drive.

"Why can't James get him?" Ruth inquires. "He's still out of work isn't he?"

"James will be visiting Rachel and Abigail," I admit sheepishly, "and he usually doesn't return until after midnight."

Answering Ruth's question as to why he visits them while I do not is even more awkward.

"I guess she's just not ready to see me," I reply cautiously.

"Sounds fishy to me," Ruth says with a quick glance at Naomi who grins and nods in agreement.

"He's paving the way for us, trying to help Rachel get the skidoos ready, for our family vacation," I tell them both knowing they too think he's having a fling.

A raging fire spreads within my bladder for I've been without bathroom access for more than three hours. I'm extremely grateful when Ruth drops me off first. We are so lucky to have each other, all of us spirits that travel from life, to life, to support one another. I kiss them all goodbye.

The portable CD player, with Daniel's memorial CD, sits in my lap after using the bathroom. I plug it into the computer to see if it acts erratically, as when driving. The bells and whistles begin as the player switches from song to song, for a minute or so, before playing through our song and switching to "Inside Us All." My voice fills the house as I sing along to the music.

"When I'm all alone, and no one else is here, waiting by the phone to remind me I'm still here. And shadows paint the scenes where small lights used to fall and I'm left wondering is it really worth it all."

Tears form but I smile and brush them away singing the best part of the song.

"There's a piece inside us all. Let it be your friend. It will help you carry on in the end."

I feel that piece, near the middle of my chest, and remain grateful that Daniel led me to the song. My eyes close as we dance in the Mozart era. Missing his human form, I remember his earlier advice but cannot stop the tears.

When they subside, I do what Daniel wants me to do; I disconnect the CD player and turn it off. The player stays on long enough to let me know he can power it himself. His spirit is happy I remember what he said about controlling emotions. It's now hard to think of anything else because I'm so full of pride and love. Yet, there's still earthly work to do and I must, this time, get it done.

:-)

Chapter Seven

Lessons of Forgiveness

All healing is a result of some kind of forgiveness, and all forgiveness leads to self-healing. Gary Renard - The Disappearance of the Universe

Dawn breaks on Easter morning as I focus on dying once again. Depression seems hard to control. The days of regular haircuts are gone as new brown roots merge with much longer than usual auburn dyed hair. It feels like I'm living in hell with thoughts of being kept alive, against my will. While celebrating at Rebecca's, I calmly ask Ruth to sign the renewed "Living Will" and "Do Not Resituate" orders, thinking James will not. We both remember Daniel signing my first one at age eleven.

Acting as my usual obnoxious self, I try to video everyone before dinner. James sits on the couch alone. He fleetingly averts his gaze from the football game to indulge me with a smile when I enter the room saying, "Smile for the camera."

"There's that smile I love," I announce moving on to bother Samuel.

"Excuse me," I say with authority upon entering Samuel's bedroom, "it's time to smile."

"Not for the camera," Samuel replies continuing to play his video game with his back towards me.

"If you don't smile and let me video you I will stand here in your room for the rest of the day."

His curious friend quickly looks up. Silence fills the air.

"While standing here, I will be giving a commentary to you and your friend," I state gleefully. "Do you know what commentary is? It means constant talking, talking forever and ever. Now today's subject is religion."

Samuel looks at the wall trying to hide his face from the camera.

"Until you two look at me and smile for the camera I will talk about religion."

Samuel considers any talk of spirituality as religious discussion and he dislikes hearing it.

"Okay," he says with resignation turning to smile.

The overbearing Nana with her big ego is happy to direct their position as she snaps a still on the video camera.

"Thank you very much," she says, pleased before walking away.

Continuing to be overbearing, and forgetful, I return to the living room to demand a smile from James.

"I already gave you a smile," James replies nonchalantly.

"No you didn't."

"Give me a reason to smile," James retorts frowning. "You're standing in my way in front of the television and aggravating me."

"Okay," I smirk while taking a still of his flustered face, "that's how your picture will be."

James returns his attention to sports as I walk happily away to bother Ruth.

No one wants pictures taken, not by me. Ruth talks of her job, delivering bread to grocery stores starting at three o'clock in the morning, as I try to take her picture. Work is more strenuous because she recently stepped down as manager.

"Aren't you going to smile?" I ask aiming my camera for the shot.

"No," she replies putting her middle finger next to her left cheek.

There will be a spirit orb in that picture.

Anxious to scan pictures for orbs after dinner, the car alarm goes off as I hurry towards it. Since Daniel's transition, my car alarm never fails to go off, either upon arriving for family gatherings or departing to go home. Pleasantly, surprised, I yell so family will hear from their stations on the screened in porch.

"Hey, guys, Daniel says hi."

"Get your head examined," Terry responds gleefully taking a slug of beer.

Four, of nine, photos show orbs when I review them at home. A picture of Samuel shows a small orb to his left. The one of Momma sitting on the love seat is my favorite for it shows a small orb hovering a few feet above her head. Another picture of Rebecca, sitting with the 'Daniel grin' on her face as we play pinochle, shows a white, round mist just below her right ear. It's a sign of Daniel's essence.

Days remain filled with activity, working on my failing business, caring for Samuel, or taking Momma out for lunch or to the doctor. Sunday family racquetball fills gaps and takes my mind off of Daniel, Abigail, Rachel, and James. Another time-intensive project, putting together a DVD of Daniel from old family videos, fills time by the end of March. A need to investigate every aspect of his life consumes my guilt-ridden head as I continually judge myself somehow responsible for his death.

In *The Disappearance of the Universe*, Renard notes, the ego secretly wants us to be guilty by thinking we are separate from God. It takes time to learn forgiveness and to get rid of the past. We either judge as an expression of fear, *seeing the physical, or forgive, as an expression of love, recognizing the spirit. Seeing Daniel and myself as bodies, I looked back to the past and judged myself as guilty of molding him to be the man he'd become, someone with a need for fast motorcycles.*

Walter Starcke in his book It's All God notes, "You will get rid of the past and release it once you realize that everything that has happened to you in the past has a divine purpose. Once you see how the past and all of its conditions were necessary to bring you around the circle to your spiritual fulfillment, the past ceases to exist except as a part of now."

Forgiveness is the only way to undo unconscious projections of guilt and to stop punishing ourselves. Only true forgiveness of relationships, and thus the healing of unconscious guilt in our mind, can really free us from compulsions or anything else. I was going through the motions, piling on guilt, while reviewing my life with Daniel. In time, I'll know that we dispel guilt with the realization that it has never been, for what we see is not true. We are indeed living in a dream of our own making.

April of 2005 brings a mass ascension that carries me further along my path.

"My milk expires on April 4, 2005; how's that for irony?" I write in my journal. "Can I trade it in for Daniel?"

I pour my heart out, writing about recent experience, while wishing for someone in physical form to talk with.

"I communicate better with Daniel, than I do with James, and it seems most other people as well. I was sick all last week and think my wish to be further away from earth was granted. After purging my popcorn dinner, it felt like I was dying for the next seven days with a slight fever.

"I slept a lot and dreamed a lot. I dreamed that I could go to the Otherside if I wanted to. All the members of my family on the Otherside told me I could. Aunt Deborah and

Uncle Wallace said they would be waiting for me when I finally decide to pass. People I forgot about like Helene, the drunk that Grandma Olive used to care for with the colonoscopy bag, were there too. I saw Uncle Freddie, Daddy, and Uncle Roger, and at one point, it seemed like they were all pulling strings out of me. They all yanked strings out of my sleeping body as I lay dreaming of whether to pass or not. In the end, as you can see, I decided to stay. I know I have not yet met my agreed upon destiny. It is not clear as to what I have to do to fully meet it."

The ability to move through time and space changes in dreams as consciousness joins the fourth dimensional state. Daniel and I often connected through dreams but emotions always kept us apart, for communication halted, as I lamented over his loss. Contact with other family members, on the Otherside, seemed easier to achieve during sleep, while contact with Daniel often occurred during waking hours when I was more able to control emotions.

A short while after this experience, there was a sense that I chose to push myself spiritually at a pace much faster than the path chosen for this life. I subconsciously took advantage of increased energy shifts on earth from the spiritual realm. It was my conscious decision to "jump" many lifetimes and achieve the end of karma. My mind soon opened to a new way of thinking, as I learned to clear, and clean, the so-called darkness of past lives through forgiveness, allowing my soul to move further along the path of spiritual growth.

Between naps, I force myself to do a second and third Daniel DVD. The third one is very hard to make because there's so much video to view with so little of Daniel in it. I splice videos together for more than six hours. As ego leads the way, I do it for me and anyone else who wants to see videos later, after I join Daniel.

After two bug-free days, I think my playful spirit son changed his ways because a palmetto does not appear after watching his plastic, trick bug on video. As I sit watching television, working on an article for the newsletter at the same time, a huge flying palmetto bug comes out of nowhere. It jumps, from the top of the television, to a picture frame on the wall by Daniel's face and drops to stand still on the floor.

I scream frantically for James who is outside on the back porch talking to cats.

"Catch the dam thing," I implore as James slowly enters the room.

As he captures the bug, I lament about how Daniel keeps sending the bugs.

"I think," James confides while looking into my eyes, "Daniel is trying to tell you something. You apparently have not gotten the message."

"Yeah, stop doing the DVD's if they upset me," I think.

Watching the DVD's comforts me to see him, to hear him, to know how well he turned out, even after everything we went through. Even after all the crap I put him through as a child, I hear him say, "Ah, come on now Mom, get over it." This life, I know, is just one tiny grain of sand on a very, long, beach but my family is getting tired of hearing it.

A picture of Daniel, laughing whole-heartedly, enters my mind as I squirm while James carries the bug outside. I hear Daniel say, "Okay, you will laugh about it later," and know he is right. He knows I have lived with roaches, rats, and mice but still I am upset for I thought we had a deal. I thought the palmetto bug visits were over as long as I put up with the ants crawling on me, and the mosquitoes buzzing around me, when Daniel thinks it's time for me to get up.

Later, in the wee hours of morning, blessings unfold while sitting on the dining room carpet, facing sliding glass doors. The porch beyond the glass is dimly visible but the backyard beyond is periodically lit by floodlights, from the nursing home, a short block away. Every night I feel the spirits of my family that are on the Otherside. Sometimes they give me golden balls of light to place into my heart or head.

I offer my human body, as a vessel, to the good spirits that travel with me throughout time, especially Daniel. It's to help them complete their unfinished business on earth. I fondly recall tasks Daniel led me to do. Things like sumo wrestle Samuel on our first Keys vacation without Daniel. There's no way I could have possibly had the energy, and strength, to get Samuel on the ground. Taking Terry on our first "field trip," to give Jeremiah and Judith Daniel's message for Thanksgiving 2004, and softly slapping Samuel "upside the head," like Daniel used to do, comes to mind.

The piece within us all, God, the Supreme Being, knows I will do whatever it takes without regard for what it costs this human body. This is but one life and I know there are only a few of us, relatively speaking, who have agreed to help bring all to the Light. Now I look forward to more unscheduled events and am humbled, pleased beyond comprehension, to be able to do these things.

Later in the year, I will hear that one of my tasks is to be humble but remain uncertain as to what that means. Pat Rodegast notes in Emmanuel's Book, humility means to be human and rest in a state of humanness consciously, openly, and willingly.

Perception begins to change but ego continues to get in the way of progress. The interaction of our illusionary egos alters them, as they were not made by, or with, that of which God is. God is Unalterable. A Course In Miracles informs us, "Humility is a lesson for the ego, not for the spirit. Spirit is beyond humility, because it recognizes its radiance and gladly sheds its light everywhere. The meek shall inherit the earth because their egos are humble, and this gives them truer perception."

Samuel is on spring vacation. James is still jobless so he watches over him when Ruth and Naomi cannot. Dread of the unknown fills me with gloom. Perhaps that's why I've been sick. After remaining home for a week, Daniel asks me to get into the car in the early afternoon. He quickly guides me to the post office to get mail. Intuition prompts thoughts of Rachel and Abigail.

Daniel switches songs on the CD player. "Open Arms" begins to play as we motor down tree-lined streets. He asks me to telephone Rachel, even though I've left two messages for her in the past month. Concern for Abigail and worry about Rachel's state of mind fills my brain while checking the company mailbox before heading home to make the call.

Time eludes me. It's much later in the evening when I finally call. I dial her number and leave another message when the answering machine asks for one. She returns my call minutes later. As we speak, I understand Daniel's concern. It sounds like Rachel is playing what I refer to as the "opposite game" where everything you say is really about yourself and not the person who you say it is.

The fine art of projection rules as I apologize for not recognizing how special Daniel was, for taking advantage of him, and overburdening him. I announce it was not my intention to hurt Rachel's feelings when she confides that I have done so in the past. Rachel is adamant that Daniel's family did not appreciate how very special he was. The audacity of her mind is quite astounding, while she explains how we are the ones with the guilt, the ones that treated him badly and asked too much of him.

I listen as Rachel notes how our family wronged Daniel, abandoned her, and know she must have said these things to James. But he hasn't told me. They are in their own category; I silently note, still listening to Rachel's rage as ego strengthens the bonds of separation.

This is my dream and I must take responsibility for it. A Course In Miracles reminds us, "When you are willing to accept sole responsibility for the ego's existence you will have laid aside all anger and all attack, because they come from an attempt to project responsibility for your own errors."

"As you condemn only yourself, so do you forgive only yourself."

We recognize traits in others that we possess. The situations we face are the ones we create in our own mind. Sometimes our grief and pain seems more manageable when we blame, and lash out, attempting to make others hurt as much as we do. Finding fault with someone else hides the fact that we believe mis-thoughts to be ours.

The ego always tries to continue conflict by projecting it from our mind, to other minds, in an attempt to persuade us that we have gotten rid of the problem. However, we cannot project conflict because it cannot be shared. We cannot make someone responsible for our errors but must accept responsibility for ourselves. Giving conflict away only insures that we keep it. It is a complete distortion of the power of extension to believe that seeing it outside of us excludes it from being within us.

It's important to trust that what we feel in our heart is Truth and to take responsibility for our thoughts and actions. We give our power away by allowing someone to hurt our feelings, for in doing so we decide to believe what they think, rather than give validity to our own thoughts. Once our perception changes and we recognize perfection in ourselves, we are less apt to give our power away to others. Ultimately, we are here to recognize that we are a unique part of God, unerring and perfect.

This is a dream world where we project hate for ourselves onto others but judge and forgive only our self.

People are symbols of what is in our mind and forgiving releases us from the illusion.

Gary Renard spells it out in his book <u>The Disappearance of the Universe</u>. "Forgiveness recognizes what you thought your brother did to you has not occurred. It does not pardon sins and make them real. It sees there was no sin. And in that view are all your sins forgiven." Each time we use our free will to forgive, recognizing there is no separation, the ego loosens its grip on our reality.

A few days ago, I experienced another opportunity for forgiveness when I went to drive Samuel home from school. Rebecca picked him up and forgot to tell me she was doing so. I considered a subtle message that she would do so days before and, in fact, hoped she would, but failed to call and confirm what intuition told me.

"You should call his mother," said the teacher with a knowing look as I sat in the line of cars waiting for him, "for she should have called you."

I took his advice immediately. Rebecca was apologetic, over forgetting to call, but I realized she was an illusion in my dream as we talked. If anyone was to blame it was I for not calling her to confirm the subtle message, received days before.

Thoughts now include the concept of living in a dream world. I often wished, for the benefit of a doubt, and now realize that it's not helpful to disregard another person's perspective or to cast my expectations onto others. Of course, in order to do this I had to open, and examine, my "wounds" carefully. After grasping the idea that we come from the same Source, and are here to help one another through lessons, becoming more aware of our true being, I became more able to free myself of ego-based fear.

The long road to the land of forgiveness shortens as I begin to forgive others, and myself, for mis-thought. Lessons of loss and limitation come less frequently as I love more fully. (A smiley face – :-) – mysteriously appears on the page before my eyes, to confirm my words are true, as I type into the computer.)

After nearly an hour on the phone, and offering several times to visit with whoever else Rachel wants to spend the night, exactly one year after Daniel's transition, she agrees to a family stay.

Three-year-old Abigail takes the telephone from her mother's hands after she asks Abigail if she wants us there.

"Yes Mother," she replies quietly while trying to talk to me.

I silently hope the speakerphone is not on.

"Abigail," I softly say, "I'll sing to you with Daddy tonight when you dream. What song do you want me to sing?"

Abigail listens as Rachel continues to talk to her in the background.

"Yes, Mother," Abigail quietly repeats.

"Do you want me to sing, 'You are my Sunshine' or 'Don't Sit Under the Apple Tree'?" I ask cautiously.

"Apple tree," Abigail says before handing Rachel the telephone receiver.

"Abigail looks very tired," Rachel confides. "It's funny that she called me Mother because she doesn't call me that, ever."

Daniel sometimes tells me I cannot sing to Abigail, in mind, so I sense it's unstable at Rachel's house. Now I'm happy to know it is okay.

"Tonight after I say my blessings," I think, as Rachel continues to talk, "I'll meet with Daniel. He will allow me to sing to Abigail and Abigail will know it is real."

We have our dreams, some of them at least. I will mention in my blessings that it go okay. We all need to help Abigail. Life is a lesson and I am still learning.

Daniel wants me to take another step to wake-up Rachel. The light of the soul, that piece in each of us that holds us together by love and an undying desire to help one another, glimmers just enough for me to recognize it's there. When Rachel ends our call, I wonder how to help her see that we are One. Yet, I'm surprised not to have attacked her out loud.

"At least there is progress," I think smugly before saying nightly blessings. "My next lives will not be ones of abuse, or servitude, and hopefully, will not involve having to deal with people who speak against things that they know nothing about. And now, it's time for a shower and a rest and my blessings."

I thought I was learning my soul's lessons but ego remained intact to foster separation. Forgiveness was a subconscious priority for there were many conflicts to deal with in every aspect of life. It was important to learn how to place myself along with those I thought were different, knowing we are One. I needed to practice unconditional love for every living thing. This was difficult to achieve for I had no idea that there is no darkness, no evil, for all is evolution as we learn to choose the Highest Wisdom.

One of the most important lessons I learned, using my new perspective, is that everyone sees things differently, all according to how their ego operates. It took a while more to learn that we deny our unlimited power as creator, and give it to others, when we are unable to forgive the wrongs we believe others have done.

We may often carry emotional hurt causing us to harbor ill will toward the person we believe is responsible. This encourages and feeds negative thoughts and feelings. The sense of hurt permeates our space and draws to us similar elements of equal negativity. Illness often results from negativity, but healing is the end result of forgiveness, and all forgiveness leads to self-healing. I'll soon learn to automatically forgive, rather than react through judging, because this is all just a dream and no one exists separately from God.

We let the pain go and move on after allowing ourselves to go through the feelings of anger and frustration. And when we give it up to God, we hear there is no separation. Once we look through another's eyes, knowing we are all parts of God, forgiving becomes a natural thing to do and feelings of misery, pain, and anger disappear. Forgiveness puts us in a "state of grace," ecstatically happy knowing we are on the right path. Grace is a level beyond concepts (beliefs), an anointed state of consciousness.

It was time to educate myself and learn about unconditional love, a state of acceptance of self and others, knowing that in essence it's all God. The task seemed impossible as resentment, disappointment, anger, and hurt took precedence while trying to meet basic survival needs. I was lost in a sea of 'victim mentality' adamantly working to convince others that I'd "been wronged" but that perception would change.

:-)

Chapter Eight

A Surprising Spring

*Every time I close the door on reality, it comes
in through the windows. Jennifer Yane*

The next milestone as a bereaved parent comes exactly a
year after the last time I saw Daniel. Abigail and I enjoyed an
unusually long surprise visit that day while Daniel went to
the acupuncturist with Rebecca. It was the day she learned
how to draw a smiley face.

Daniel and I joked and laughed our way to his SUV
when it was time for them to leave. The memory of that
goodbye is still intense for I remember how we kissed, and
hugged, three times instead of the usual once. We seemed
reluctant to let go of each other. I often wonder if Daniel
sensed it would be our last time together as he and Abigail
drove away.

The day now fills with television, work, and music. Later in
the evening, I move back out to the living room for more
mindless television. Habits include a variety of shows,
without commercials, but something prompts me to switch to
a movie channel with frequent ads. A motorcycle movie
begins to show. Deciding to watch my favorite show instead,
I switch the channel and set the television receiver on the
table.

The channel on the TV promptly changes back to the
Biker Boyz movie. Daniel's presence permeates the room so I
decide he wants to watch it. The thought of him being with
me overpowers the distress of watching a movie where

young men ride motorcycles way too fast. Daniel always told us he would meet his fate on a motorcycle so no one was surprised when he died that way.

Joy erupts with memories of many motorcycle movies seen with Daniel since watching *Easy Rider* at age eighteen. At one point, actors talk about how fast they drive. One of them notes it would be instant death for anyone if they had an accident while driving over 125 miles per hour (mph).

"I was going 140 Mom," Daniel says softly inside my head.

Yes! Daniel's essence guided me to see the movie so I would know he had not suffered during his transition. The rest of the show unfolds as I sit joyfully feeling his energy. Daniel's essence seems to leave as credits row across the screen. I'm still in seventh heaven, filled with love, while documenting the event moments later.

"It's nearly one o'clock in the morning on March 20, 2005 and I'm thrilled that Daniel is still living through me. It feels good even knowing that it is exactly one year since I last saw his beautiful, heart-shaped face, hugged him, and told him I loved him. I am thrilled to feel him here with me, pushing me to watch a biker movie, and to remember those good old days. The days when working hard, living hard, and partying hard was all there was to life. He watches the movie through me and is glad to be able to experience the sensation again and so am I.

"I allow my spirit guides to relive life through me, to do things they lacked the time for when in human form. It is all a lesson that I hope will end one day. I expect it will be later than I want but that is life. I love my group of spirits. They hold me up and keep me going. They let me dream of them and I greet them all with warmth I never knew existed. We are one."

Happy, but tired, I put the journal away. The day's work is set aside as nightly blessings flow from head to lips.

As souls, Daniel and I planned many such events where I would experience living in the fourth dimension with him. It would make it much easier for me to become aware of my Higher Self's purpose and to progress spiritually. Journals, and other ways of documenting life, would become more valuable with the realization that I am here to help others, through the maze of human awareness, by writing. The feeling of joy as I discover my true self, and help change the world, is unmatched by any other emotion on earth.

More surprises come to break the monopoly of work and watching Samuel. The passing of Pope John Paul II is prominent in world news. Italian scientists report creating their second cloned horse and I now wonder if humans will be next on the cloning list. Three days before the anniversary of Daniel's transition, on April Fool's Day, I check my email to find a message from Rachel.

"I think I just want to spend the weekend alone with Abigail on Sunday," it notes. "Next weekend would be better for a visit."

Tears of disappointment fill my eyes until I read, "Please get together with everyone and see if next weekend could be better, for the family, and maybe Abigail and I can come down there or something. You will all be in my prayers."

I'm grateful Rachel seems to connect to God but pour my disappointment into text. Writing offers a way to get thoughts on paper and lessens the despair. It feels great to rip up and discard the communication when done.

James arrives back from job hunting insistent on cashing in my only retirement account although he has several accounts in his name.

"It's time for you to support the family," he tells me angrily.

I offer my disability documentation for review but he refuses to look at it.

"If you don't care to learn the truth about my health, stop trying to get me to support you," I tell him matching his anger.

Yet, I do not argue about cashing in my individual retirement account (IRA). After all, how long could I retire on $14,000?

I'm finally aware of the wonderful choice made when I married James. He refused to buy into my illusion and, therefore, propelled me to end it. As souls we agreed to go through the process of dismantling the life I thought was mine so I'd fully wake up to the truth of our BEing.

It's a good thing that I'm in charge of the checkbook, and all the banking, for many times my Visa card pays for grocery store trips with family. I am generous to a fault, preferring to spend rather than save money for the future like James. To me, money is just something to keep a roof over your head and food in your belly. Intuition tells me I will not live long enough to receive retirement funds or Social Security payments. My needs are relatively small. I have never needed or wanted the glamorous extras many friends enjoy but admit that vacations, and conferences, are enjoyable. Now, I think it would be nice to travel more and go back to Las Vegas.

Money for incidentals is tucked away upon returning from the bank after cashing in my tax-deferred IRA. Email consumes time as I pour over political issues with increasing dread. There seems to be a general unrest. The world is going mad, again. This time, I sense, things happen as they should.

Family members visit Daniel's memorial sign on the first anniversary of his passing. I continue to work, knowing it's easy to connect with him. Emails from colleagues alert me to issues that are more important. The American Dietetic Association (ADA) is thinking about dropping the credential of DTR (Dietetic Technician, Registered). It is my only credential. I no longer support the ADA and do not need their approval to do what I do. It feels good to continue to blaze my own path.

Despite the bodies increasing dis-ease, it's business as usual. I take naps between pecking at the computer to edit articles or surf the Internet. People who offer article information now receive free newsletter subscriptions. It helps subscribers learn where to send their hiv-positive clients and boosts newsletter distribution rates. Authors and editors get plenty of time to refine articles for I plan issues well ahead of publication dates.

This contribution to humanity brings a great feeling of pride even though money remains an issue. To-do lists, reminders, and schedules fill the computer desk keeping me busy. Constant feedback, from the outside world, reassures me of the need for information on nutrition and hiv so I disregard negative comments from family.

Just when I think my computer is working well it begins to act erratically when conducting business. On some days, I cannot get past the dreaded blue error screen. It works flawlessly, while designing and setting up a memorial website for Daniel, but takes much, more, time than expected, making it a struggle to get business work done. It again seems like invisible barriers are popping up to stop me from working. My email box overfills with junk but there's no personal email. The Internet Service Provider responds to my email for help by noting I need to contact them through their online support form.

My vibration level was changing; making me no longer suited for the work I grew to love. The ascension process continued to unfold as my usual job became increasingly impossible. It was clearly time to end the old role and pay attention to my soul's purposes and intentions.

We have to rid ourselves of the old and make some room to incorporate new circumstances into our life. It is the way of this dualistic world. My soul chose to embody desired traits at this time, by experiencing the darker energies of loss, and illness, so I would be encouraged to search for something better. Tired of depression, sickness, and negativity, I would soon let go to create something much more to my liking. Over the next few years, I would fully awaken to the true nature of our BEing.

Terry, Rebecca, and Samuel come to our house to meet Rachel and Abigail days later. They talk with me, as I work in my bedroom office, until Rachel arrives with Abigail and Joy. It is a pleasure to give Abigail the talking bunny from K-Mart since I missed seeing her on Easter. The adults allow me time to interact with the children alone when they go out to smoke, and talk, on the back screened-in porch.

Abigail is such an amazing child, full of energy and love. It's hard to believe she has experienced so many losses already. I can only guess how hard it was to lose Daniel, then Bruiser the pit bull, Sassy their oldest dog, and the fish. The little dog she got for Christmas kept peeing on the floor so now she has two Siamese kittens instead.

Samuel seems happy to see his cousin as I watch them play together. A thin horizontal mass of energy flies above their heads as they try to hide from my video camera. They quickly run from the room to play hide and seek. As Abigail searches for Samuel, under the futon in my home office, an orb hovers above her head. I sense Daniel but do not see the orb until I play back the video. Rachel announces it's time to go moments after the orb appears.

James settles down to tie flies for more fishing after the rest of the family leaves. I load digital pictures onto the computer to check for orbs. A picture of Samuel crawling on his knees, with a big smile on his face, has two orbs in it. One orb is on him while the other floats above his head.

Daniel's memorial CD plays in the background as I look through photos. When the telephone rings, odd noises come through the answering machine; no one is on the other line. It's now a common occurrence so I smile knowing Daniel called me again. "I Speed at Night" begins to play and stops abruptly.

"Mom it's time to change the songs," Daniel says inside my brain. "That's not how I want to be remembered."

Daniel's time in "the middle" served to further soul growth and now he no longer wants anything remotely negative on the CD. We work together, for the next hour, replacing songs of feelings when the accident occurred to how he feels now. I'm pleased with the result and plan to play the CD when family watches the sun set in the Keys.

Daniel delivers another message, this one unwanted, before his essence leaves. I am to destroy all the CDs with negative music. It disappoints me to stop listening to the now loved music but I trust his judgment and break them all in half.

The next week family meets at Ruth and Naomi's house while James fishes in the Everglades. I take a picture of Ruth, usually in a sour mood, with a huge smile on her face. She sits on the couch, with closed eyes looking very happy, as if feeling something delightful. It's an awesome sight to see for twelve orbs are scattered nearby. One sits on the left side of her chin.

Several other pictures reveal spirit activity. How delightful to know that spirits join in our celebrations! Many orbs hover near Terry and Rebecca. At least nineteen orbs float around Samuel, after I thoughtlessly forget how much it hurts and demonstrate family's method to tease each other as children, with titty twisters. He lies on the living room carpet crying. He's growing quickly and it's difficult to convince him he is too big to rough house with us.

I look at pictures again after arriving home. A combination of awe, over seeing the orbs, and disgust, at seeing the results of my impulsive actions, fills me. I print an 8 x 10 inch picture of Samuel crying and promptly tape it to my file cabinet. It's my daily reminder to think rather than act impulsively.

Business as usual is now a thing of the past. James continues to fish often and monopolizes the telephone when home. Connecting to the Internet becomes an impossible chore. I fill the house with music whenever he leaves. It seems to change the feel of the house and boosts my mood. His weekend fishing trip with the fly-fishing club offers an opportunity to fill the house with my favorite music. I happily clean, throughout the weekend, thanking God and Celebrex.

Weight seems to hang on me like a plague for I'm still morbidly obese. On the first day in May, I step out of the shower, weigh myself, and happily realize a few more pounds disappeared. I have lost twelve pounds since the first of the year. Perhaps it's due to Daniel's advice. For the first time in my adult life, I sit quietly, instead of work, while eating.

Ego fights to keep me locked in limitation. Hair lies past my shoulders for it's too much effort to leave the house for a haircut. Cash seems hard to get for I don't want to deplete the small hidden stash of IRA funds. Rebecca has my car because her car broke down and she needs to get to work. Rachel doesn't answer the phone so I leave a message to keep our connection strong.

Ruth and Naomi sense my despair and host more family events. Rebecca transports me there for dinner and a game of cards. Terry arrives later, with Momma, who he says is digging at her face. Raw wounds beneath small, brown eyes shock me.

"Is she taking her medication?" I ask shaking my head.

Terry and I remain in a constant power struggle as he ignores doctor's orders. He now ignores me.

The consequences of Momma's conditions incessantly plague me. It seems that Terry does not care if she forgets medications, eats forbidden foods, or does any forbidden things. Distress consumes me upon knowing she fails to follow her prescribed diet or abide by the many restrictions doctors place upon her. It's clear that we are in a fight for power, the energy many humans feed upon.

"Is she taking her medication for the schizophrenia," I ask again.

"I don't know," Terry defiantly replies, "for I'm not her babysitter. Why don't you live with her and make sure she does?" he sneers.

Everyone knows Momma prefers to live with Terry and her Social Security checks help him pay the rent. I back down and sheepishly hang my head not knowing how to reply without feeding his ego. Yet, I allow my own free reign.

"Schizophrenics are known to pick at themselves when they don't take their medication," I finally say angrily while walking away. At least Medicare pays for her prescriptions, I think, as ego leads me into the land of separation.

Rebecca drives me home. I now remember it's time to fill out the hardship form, for the urologist to sign, so a drug company will consider giving me free drugs. We cannot afford the $400 a month medication without insurance. Thoughts of limitation and sorrow prompt tears as we sit at the last traffic light before my house.

I turn my head so Rebecca will not see them. My eyes catch a familiar sign in big, black, bold letters, "Religious Science Fort Lauderdale."

"You need to go in there Mom," Daniel says.

"Not today," I answer silently, promising to go online and check the place out. Once home, I log onto the Internet, visit the website, and admit it looks inviting. Sleep claims me after emailing a request for more information.

Something about karma and Momma fills my mind upon waking. I still feel bad thinking she's not as cared for as

I would like her to be. After a trip to the bathroom, I pull out the papers on karma from the file cabinet.

"You can't interfere with someone else's karma," I read with growing interest. "Every experience, even suffering, is fair in this school of illusion."

I cannot help but wonder how to avoid any more karma if Momma suffers due to my recent unvoiced decision to let Terry take over her medical care. It seems like a real dilemma to make sure she is cared for without getting into the, all too familiar, power struggle for energy. The decision to remove myself from the drama of Terry and Momma's life feels comfortable but I do not exactly understand why.

It was not my role to judge the adequacy of anyone to do anything. We all chose our life, as souls before birth, based on past life experiences. I had no right to interfere with any of Momma or Terry's soul lessons. Karma is the law of cause and effect, the compassionate dynamic through which we learn to create responsibly. It is neither good nor bad and when we choose the cause that choice includes our choice of an effect. Now I choose to show compassion, practicing restraint, when my interfering ego decides to act on another's behalf.

A funny noise fills the air as I sit in front of my desktop computer. James enters my workroom minutes later holding a new cell phone, which he got from his sister.

"Rachel is on the phone," he quietly tells me holding his hand over the receiver. "She's really upset because there's something wrong with Bear."

"Well, you'll just have to go and help her," I calmly reply thinking Bear is Daniel's only surviving dog.

I quickly turn back to my work. James pulls out of the driveway minutes later. When the sound of his van disappears, I take the time to pray that Bear will be okay. I know another loss is unthinkable for Abigail and Rachel.

The day passes quickly. It's almost midnight and James is still not home. A ringing telephone startles me before I pick up the receiver.

We just got back from the vet's," James says with a weary voice.

"Is Bear okay?" I quickly ask.

"We don't know if," his voice pauses and lowers, "if he's going to make it. He just had surgery."

My heart becomes heavy thinking of many losses experienced by Rachel and Abigail.

"I'm really bushed," James continues.

"Just spend the night," I quickly reply thinking he and Rachel will become closer.

James returns home early the next afternoon. I can tell something is not right. It seems like he has a rain cloud above his head and negativity fills the air. When I ask him, "What's wrong?" he tells me everyone is crazy. He then asks what it will cost him to divorce me. I calmly reply, "Half of what you have," and return to my workroom when he answers it is never going to happen. Experience tells me that our conversation will disappear like a strong gust of wind before the rain.

On Saturday, the day before Mother's Day, Rebecca, Momma, Terry, and I drive to Lydia and Joseph's house for a combination baby shower and Mother's Day celebration. Terry's hair is now orange and cropped quite short, making him appear younger, while mine makes me look older. Rebecca's friends' house is always a fun place to visit with a pool table, and slot machines, where most people keep dining room furniture. We arrive early so Rebecca can help with the party preparations. I plan to hide behind my video camera and enter the house filming 'before' scenes.

Lydia's pregnancy is a big deal to everyone. This is the first time she has carried a fetus to full term after several attempts. When I see Hannah, Lydia's mother, I think she should be the party's focus. It's clear she is nearing her time to transition. Her words slur as she talks and she seems weaker than the last time we saw one another. I notice she has lost more weight and the brain cancer treatments have caused her hair, and eyebrows, to disappear. The day quickly becomes more about Lydia, and the children that mill about, than the mothers who had them.

A female bartender is ready to take our drink order but I do not need her services. My usual drink, a huge container with four shots of Myer's rum mixed with Diet Coke, sits nearby.

"When you're a human you've got to have a good time," I say adamantly taking a gulp out of the cup.

Within the hour, I feel the liquor's effects. I don't tell anyone the number of medications I'm taking but make sure to point out my family's errors in judgment. The disc jockey sets up outside on the patio as I sample the delicious food everyone brings. I'm disappointed that she has no spiritual songs for me to sing for now I listen to Christian radio stations.

Lydia's best friend, Officer Lou, arrives during the first game of pool. I find her shortly after arrival sitting alone as I roam the grounds taking pictures. The digital picture shows a small orb on her left leg. It seems like she's looking directly at another small orb to her right. Officer Lou later wins the contest of drinking beer, from a baby bottle, and eventually calls someone for a ride home. She will soon play a significant role in helping to wake-up the world through her well-publicized transition.

It feels good to be in a family atmosphere with a lot of friends, even if they are not mine. Spirit orbs from the sun fill the back porch later as I video the action. The white, green, and magenta colored orbs are absolutely beautiful. I enjoy singing along to tunes played by the DJ without taking the mike. Rebecca and her friends sing their usual "I Will Survive" as I watch and sing from a distance. Drunk by now, I stop singing to note, repeatedly, how bad they sound.

Rebecca drives Samuel and I home a while later. We discuss Samuel's issues at school on the way. I decide to see if there are schools for kids with ADHD (attention-deficit-hyperactivity disorder). Samuel stays with me as Rebecca returns to the party. He falls asleep so I scan my digital pictures for orbs. Numerous pictures delight me, particularly one of Rebecca, Lydia, and others in the game room surrounded by orbs. A pinkish colored orb appears prominently in a still picture of Hannah with family members. After putting the camera away, I fall asleep quickly, forgetting it's now Mother's Day.

Growing up in a big family, as I did, has many advantages for soul growth. One of them is recognition of our own mis-thoughts by finding them in family. We act as each other's mirrors. The means to recognize our own ego increases as the egos of our family struggle to be recognized. Family member actions, that we react to, are things we need to change in ourselves.

I remained unaware of a better way to live. It's appalling now to see ego in control, while watching the video, as I degrade my family with words. My constant chatter ruins the video for I continually enter into other people's conversations, making sure people are filmed whether they want to be or not.

As humans, we may use different methods to get past the pain we cause ourselves. We may try to hide from life by using things such as alcohol, or drugs, making it more difficult to connect with Source. Alcohol slows down the vibration of the body and makes it more difficult to get in touch with higher frequency dimensions. It's a mystery to me what I would have done if I'd known that by choosing silence, instead of alcohol, I could go within and connect to my Higher Self.

:-)

Chapter Nine

Loving Energy

Beneath the reflection from the mirror of life, there is unlimited love and infinite truth. In each one of you there is God. Pat Rodegast - Emmanuel's Book II: The Choice for Love

Sleep became erratic months after Daniel's transition. Before the drastic change, I repeatedly woke crying upon remembering him in dreams. His dream visits only served to further a constant emotional state of loss. I suspect the change occurred as a remedy to help me change my way of thinking. Fifteen-minute periods of sleep now fill nights as I wake again, and again, and again. It is the second Mother's Day without my human son as I wake for what seems to be the hundredth time. Depression increases as James prepares to take Samuel home to Rebecca. James peeks into my workroom.

"Are you sure you don't want to come? Rebecca said she'll fix dinner."

"I went out yesterday," I announce, still thinking about our short divorce discussion.

Daniel's essence fills the room minutes later.

"Mom, it's time to go to the Religious Science Center (Center). You'll really like it there."

"I'll just take a short nap," I reply, while laying on the uncomfortable futon.

The service is almost over when I get up an hour later. My workday begins after deciding to visit the Center on

Wednesday evening. When it's too difficult to concentrate, I sit in the comfy, brown Lazy Boy, in the living room, ready to watch television.

Many cards from Daniel sit next to the chair, up against the wall and behind the magazine rack, so no one else can see them. I have not allowed myself to grieve much this year and now begin to savor each gift. Tears well, upon reading the card and letter Daniel wrote when living with his first love in another state. They flow in a steady stream upon seeing a single piece of paper stuck underneath the Lazy Boy. Daniel's name, in red typewritten letters, stands out.

"I want to say something about my nephew, to pay homage to the child who gave me so much joy and happiness, to the man I respected, cherished, and loved," it reads below his name.

Curiosity gets the best of me, as I settle back in the chair, not knowing where the paper came from.

"I sit here thinking of something I could tell you about him that most of his family and friends in this room don't already know."

My lips quiver with the realization that this is my son's eulogy. I avoided his funeral and had no idea someone took the time to share his or her thoughts.

"He was a generous man, a kind man. Daniel would take the time to find out what it was you wanted, or needed, and he would go out of his way to make sure you got it. He gave his time and skill to anyone who asked something of him. There is not a family member or friend that Daniel did not give aid to."

I quickly flip over the page to see some sign of who wrote such meaningful words. Tears continue upon seeing Ruth's signature. She helped me raise him since birth.

How difficult it must have been for her. How difficult to write, to stand up in front of a room full of people, and mourn over the loss of her beloved nephew. I turn the page over to continue reading.

"If he knew you needed help he would be there. He gave of his-self unselfishly but most of you already know this. What you may not know is Daniel had a very rough and bumpy start to life."

I cringe wondering what she said next.

"For the most part of his early years, he was brought up and taken care of by his mother and my-self. Daniel was not given a lot of monetary things while growing up. He was born to a poor and uneducated family; there was no silver spoon in that boy's mouth. He was given all the love we had to give, taught right from wrong, and how to respect others."

Her words prompt memories of Daniel's heroin addicted father.

"Daniel was a very good baby, a quiet, passive baby. As he got older he became a fun-loving, passive man who felt the need for speed."

I wipe the tears from my face with the back of my hand and wonder if she listened to the first memorial CD his spirit prompted me to make. The song "I Speed at Night" is one of my favorites.

"I can say I have never seen, or heard of, Daniel ever hitting or hurting anyone. He was our peacemaker. If he knew you were mad at him he would just disappear until he knew you were over it."

The paper slips from my hands as I cover my face remembering how early in life he took on the role of peacemaker. Those days are long gone and I thought forgotten. Yet, the memory of them reminds me how far we have come in our journey of life. I retrieve the paper and wonder how Ruth felt as she repeated the words to follow.

"He was a hard working man who worked for everything he had. Nothing was ever just given to him. He loved the outdoors, camping, fishing, boating, and of course his motorcycle and ATV. As a child he raced bicycles, as a man ATV's.

"Daniel loved working with his hands, taking things apart and putting them back together again. As a child, he would take things apart but could not quite get them back together. Many times Aunt Ruth would get home from work and find a pile of parts that used to be the lawn mower."

I wonder if her words made the crowd smile, as I now do, and read on.

"As a child he was taught God, family, and friends were the most important thing in life and, as a man, he loved and held close those things. He stayed close to his mother and family and always made time to spend quality time with his friends. He was a loving son, a good, supportive brother, a dedicated and loving husband and father."

I nod remembering many years of family fun. A feeling of love envelops and strengthens me to continue reading.

"I will always remember the different stages of Daniel's life but most of all I will miss the laughs, the quiet times we spent together, and the free spirit which was in him. Daniel was the center of his mother's life and the anchor, which held our family together, our peacemaker. As I say goodbye to him today I also celebrate his new life, the one he began on Sunday, April 4, 2004. God Bless and hold you in his arms Daniel."

The sobs start again as I finish reading.

"Sincerely, your loving Aunt Ruth."

It's clear she wrote the eulogy as a message to Daniel and presented it at his funeral with love. I let the paper drop to the floor knowing something led me to read it so I'll understand; I am not the only one who feels a loss.

Making my way into the bedroom, I pick up the big, furry, stuffed, brown bear Daniel gave me when ill and ninety-nine pounds. A picture of his smiling face flashes through my mind along with an image of the upper part of his body as he wags his right finger.

"Ah, ah, ah, Momma," he says moving his finger back and forth, "you don't need to cry. I'm right here."

The love he sends envelopes, comforts, and strengthens me in a way I never knew existed. I get up with a smile to finish laundry and work on the computer while listening to the new memorial CD. It plays through twice as I joyfully sing along before listening to the *Divas Simply Singing* CD. I sing to that one too.

By the time my work is done it's nearly 11:00 PM. My eyes fall on Abigail's Mother's Day card sitting on the desk. I wonder what she was thinking when drawing it. There's a circle, made with a green marker, in the middle of white paper. It has an arched doorway inside, with a doorknob on the left, but she scribbled all over the door. I decide to telephone Rachel and wish her a Happy Mother's Day.

It sounds like Rachel has been sleeping and is now worried that something might be wrong. I tell her everything is okay and ask how she is.

"Bear has one-hundred and fifty stitches and his chance of survival is about twenty-five percent," she reports.

"Wow, James didn't tell me that!"

"His stomach turned upside down and that was why he needed the surgery," she confides. "I expect him to live so we're not going to join the family on vacation. I just can't leave him."

"That's understandable," I reply knowing I would do the same.

When our telephone call ends, I sense it's time to say goodbye to Bear. It seems prudent to comfort Abigail and offer her hope for the future. James is still not home so I leave a message for him on his cell phone in case he tried to call me. Then I call Rebecca to see if he's still there.

"Yes, we're watching a movie but it almost over," she informs me.

Working on the laptop computer as we talk, I check to see if I turned the screensaver back on after defragging the hard drive. The screensaver is not on. Something prompts me to click on the Scrolling Marquee instead of my usual screensaver. Pink colored words, in capital letters amid a blue background, scroll across the screen from left to right, as I scream.

"ABIGAIL LOVES NANA VERY MUCH!!!!!!!!!!!!"

"What's wrong?" Rebecca quickly asks with concern.

"I can't believe what I see," I reply. "Could you ask James if he messed around with my laptop screensaver?"

Seconds later, Rebecca informs me James has not touched my computer.

"Well then, ask Samuel if he has," I tell her insistently thinking of Daniel's last Mother's Day message from the Otherside, left on my desktop computer.

"Mom, what's going on?" Rebecca asks now sounding a bit perturbed.

"I may be looking at another Mother's Day message from Daniel."

"Are you sure no one else used your computer? Samuel said you won't let him touch it."

"No. I'm the only one who has the access code."

I smile with a spark of recognition knowing that Daniel typed the words before he passed away. His surprise message from the Otherside came just like one last Mother's Day. How astonishing to know he typed words of love into both computers and led me to find those words on the first two Mother's Days after his transition! Even after passing into another plane, Daniel still manages to make my heart full. Now I wait with anticipation to see what else he hid, for me to see, at just the right time.

Rebecca still has my car. I hope she gets her car fixed soon so I can see Isaiah, the psychic medium, to learn what else may be worth knowing.

James soon returns home but stays in his den to make fishing flies. I leave my workroom to speak with him.

"Are you going to see Rachel and Abigail as usual on Thursday?" I inquire.

"I'm not sure," he replies without looking at me. "I might go out there on Tuesday."

"Would you ask Rachel if I can come with you when she calls to finalize your plans?"

"I'll think about it," he says as I head back to my work.

The next night, before his bedtime, James asks what time I will need to be up if we leave for Rachel's by 10:00 AM. He knows I retire in the wee hours of the morning.

Upon rising this morning, February 17, 2009, I'm reminded to call DIRECTV to disconnect their service.

"The promised movie package never materialized," I say to the lady with a cold.

"I'm sorry," she replies offering me three months of free movies.

I am adamant about letting her know I no longer watch television. She tells me I signed a two-year contract and will be charged $320 for breaking it. My original plan was to be in this house for a year and I do not recall signing a two-year contract.

"I won't pay," I tell her.

Later, while reading A Course In Miracles, it occurs to me that disconnecting the service brings me one-step closer to Source. Television is part of the illusion of our so-called separation from God.

I turn my old laptop on, ready to work on the book, but the screen begins to flash just as I open the file. I ask to hear the message. Daniel's words come quickly. He tells me once again that he never was and never will be.

"Don't you remember Mom?" he asks. "I am a part of you that came to remind you of your unlimited potential. Everything is a part of you. That's the nature of God, unlimited in all that is good. The more you create, the greater God becomes, so create more and more. Don't limit your thought of creation for there is so much more you can be and do. Let it come and stay in the flow of God's wisdom. Let it guide you and continue to protect you as we all grow nearer to God's bosom."

The computer screen continues to flash as I type his words. I just keep typing knowing typing errors can be corrected later. Daniel's essence leaves when my emotion begin to peak. The computer screen goes black as I wonder what to do next.

It appears that global economic collapse lies in our future. I am trying to decide what to do with my cash so it will not decrease in value. The thought that I could buy a new car came before waking. Daniel then told me to envision exactly what I wanted. My only requirement is that the car be the light green color I like. The Universe will present me with the perfect new car when the time is right.

My attention turns to the new laptop used to go on the Internet. Several emails merit attention. I happily respond to a new Lightworker group before joining another group recommended by a friend. A message from Michael, my acupuncturist friend, relates news of the car industry's demise. It shows numerous pictures with hundreds of unsold new cars. I thank him for the email smiling at the thought of owning my first brand new car. A quote from _A Course In Miracles_ comes to mind.

"How you perceive at any given time determines what you do, and actions must occur in time. Knowledge is

timeless, because certainty is not questionable. You know when you have ceased to ask questions."

I am not 'there,' yet, for my mind still asks questions…

On May 10, 2005, the Tuesday before vacation week, I rise filled with excitement to soon see my granddaughter. What could be raw energy appears before me as I sit on the toilet. At first, I think it might be dust particles floating in the air, spotlighted by the sun. Then I remember the television show seen a short while ago about energy.

What I see seems hard to explain even to myself. Extremely tiny, round, golden sparkles float in the air. There are so many that I cannot count them all. The round forms change into very short lines, golden in color, which vibrate in the air. The lines began to break apart and form many different shapes, including rectangles and circles that turn around, some to the left, and some to the right.

Another odd-shaped form, like the number eight on its side, appears below two golden spiral shapes moving in opposite directions. The mass of energy changes and now it looks like two hurricanes next to each other with an oblong shape below them. They are all moving in different directions. I cannot believe my eyes but sit there watching the ever-changing paths of energy for at least ten minutes.

My mind is in shock while watching shapes, knowing, it's a privilege to see something most human beings never see, pure energy. Perhaps it is the pure energy of my last-born son, still in the middle plane, where I hope to be as soon as possible. I now decide "the middle" is where we help more humans evolve than we can while in human form.

James announces we will leave after he takes his shower. I decide to draw a picture of the energy while waiting. My crude drawing does not do justice to what I saw. Each tiny energy form held perhaps a hundred short lines, each much less than a centimeter long. There were about twenty, or more, lines making up each short segment of the form. The shapes changed into another pattern as soon as I recognized a pattern.

There's no one to share the experience. Several family members already think I'm crazy and have talked to one another about committing me for mental health treatment. How can I make them understand something I do not fully understand myself? People feel threatened by things they do not understand and try to rid themselves of them. Perhaps they may find a way to rid themselves of me. Writing in my journal, as James showers, seems like the best way to document this grand demonstration.

Maybe my earth time is almost complete. More than 6,000 people still visit the business website each month so perhaps that is my major contribution to humanity. I have helped many individuals with their spiritual growth, especially Samuel and Rebecca, and I have taught James all he is ready to learn. A number of people in my family closed their minds so they will not grow spiritually but that is not my concern. I am here to be, to help when called upon, and to learn when an opportunity presents itself.

We all have different paths to follow and I think my path is now the same as Daniels before he passed. I am grateful for lessons learned and the people who have come into my life. I am thankful for the misery, the pain, the small spurts of joy, and mainly for the soul group that my spirit soars with throughout eternity. Our maker and my soul group help me to stay centered and on task through difficult times. I hear Daniel reminding me to enjoy my time in this life form.

"Are you ready to go?" James asks as he stands in the doorway.

I turn away from the computer full of love and follow him out to the van.

The power of Love surrounds us in many ways and we need only open ourselves to its many possibilities to experience them. Pat Rodegast, author of Emmanuel's Book II The Choice for Love tells us:

"Just be aware of your loving. Do that and watch the change. See the faces light up. Notice your cities becoming safe. Feel the kindness of your world. You need not say or do a thing. The power of your love will transform every corner."

The turnpike drive flashes quickly by, while I read the unexpected magazine from Religious Science that arrived in the mail. Its theme is letting go as they bid farewell to Rev. Jim Lockard who is moving to California. I read his short blurb on "Letting Go."

"Sometimes letting go is painful. Sometimes it is easy. Always it is part of the process of becoming… The snake sheds its skin to allow for new growth. You shed old beliefs to allow for greater inner awareness, let go of relationships that keep you bound to allow your continued evolution…"

I have been searching for a group of people who think as I do and am pleased to think I've found them. As I near the end of the thirty plus pages, I know I must give the magazine to Rachel. We arrive at the electronic gate. James uses his cell phone to tell Rachel the gate is stuck while I finish reading. She flips a switch to open the gate within minutes. By the time we get out of the van, Rachel is standing in the front doorway with an excited Abigail in her arms.

"She won't take her nap," Rachel says. "She's just too excited."

As Abigail leads me around the house showing me her things, Rachel and James discuss yard work. Abigail's bookshelf is now overflowing. I am surprised when she shows me a book with a voice recorder.

"Here Nana," she tells me, "talk into it."

I record a cheerful "hello" and "I love you" then hand it back. Her energy amazes me as she moves quickly from one thing to the next. She is forcing herself to stay awake so I sing a few songs to try and get her to sleep. Abigail is still too excited and asks me to sing her favorite songs a few more times before she pulls me into the living room.

It's a beautiful day, with perfect temperature and a baby blue sky, clear of clouds. Abigail and I play outside while Rachel and James work on the lawn. Her sandbox is wet and moldy, with green weeds, so Rachel tells us to shovel it all out. The energy that radiates from Abigail amazes me as we shovel sand onto the ground.

It feels marvelous to be outside getting some exercise. I sense it is now important to be more active, especially if I am to enjoy snorkeling in the Keys during our upcoming vacation. Abigail looks at me with an impish grin. She shovels the sand out of the sandbox but some of it lands on me.

"No sand on the Nana," I say with a laugh.

Delighted, she giggles as more grains of sand land in my lap.

I look down into the sandbox still laughing and see what looks like a nest of caterpillars so I slowly shovel them over to Abigail's shovel. She gently puts them onto a pile of sand outside the box. I tell her teamwork is good and we are working as a team, just like Papa and Mommy.

After a few hours of play, Rachel wants Abigail to take a nap since they both missed a lot of sleep during Bear's emergency vet saga.

"James and I are going to the store to get food for dinner," she tells me.

"Good," I answer brightly, "his mind is closed to me but maybe you can teach him what he needs to know."

Rachel looks reflective.

"Can you try to get Abigail to sleep?" she asks, while moving into the other room.

I hear James ask if he can use her computer for a minute. They talk together, for the next twenty minutes, in her home office as I try to listen.

It sounds like Rachel is playing with the two kittens while James checks email. It occurs to me they are "two of a kind." James and I have never been friends but he and Rachel always seem to enjoy each other's company. They tease one another seeming not to realize what they are doing. I sense things are as they should be.

Rachel leaves the room to ask if I need anything as James continues checking email.

"Is it too hot in here for you?" she asks concerned.

"No, no, it's fine," I reply feeling sweat on my back as Abigail and I sit in her daddy's big, green, leather lounge chair.

I am hot but do not want to complain because for the first time in a long, long, time I hold Abigail in my arms.

"Do you want me to change the television channel from Abigail's show to one you'd like?" Rachel inquires.

I shake my head no overwhelmed by her attention. Abigail is beginning to get drowsy and I do not want to excite her. The sweat is beginning to show on my forehead as Rachel turns the air conditioning down. She then switches to a channel I like and moves the chair around, with us in it, so I can see the television. It seems as if she reads my mind or gets instructions from Daniel. There's an assured calmness about her, for the first time, and that makes me very happy.

James announces he is ready to go and they head out the door for the store.

"You know," says Abigail sweetly, opening her eyes to look up at me, "Mommy doesn't like you."

Her voice says the words as if they are a matter of fact. I am shocked.

"People don't have to like everyone," I reply softly. "Sometimes even though people may not like someone they might still love them."

Abigail looks at me quietly, as if registering the words for future use, and hands me a book from the table beside her.

"Read this, okay Nana?" she asks.

I read the book and begin to sing softly when done. Abigail promptly falls asleep in my arms as we melt into her daddy's chair. I feel Daniel with us, happy that we are finally together again. Abigail feels hot. I touch her forehead, a few times, but my 'Nana Meter' does not detect a temperature so I fall asleep too.

I am aware that Rachel and James are back from the store when one of them snaps a picture of Abigail and me with my camera. Abigail sleeps soundly as I slide out of the chair to help Rachel. As she puts the groceries away, I slice the squash for James to grill with chicken and sausage. It is nearly 9:00 PM.

Rachel wakes up Abigail and senses she has a fever as we eat. She goes into her bathroom for a thermometer, takes Abigail's temperature, and then calmly gives her children's Tylenol when the thermometer reads nearly 101 degrees.

"The doctor said Abigail is one of those kids whose temperature shoots up quickly so it's good to give her the medicine early on," she confides.

What a pleasure to see Rachel so calm and knowing for it is quite a change from the past! She seems to have grown a lot since Abigail's January party. I did not detect the change weeks earlier because she stayed on the back porch most of the time. It's now wonderful not to be on guard against attack. The day turns out to be an unexpected pleasure for Abigail, and I, and it seems for Rachel and James too.

James and I drive home in silence shortly after dinner as I happily think about our visit. It appears that the worst is over. Good changes are occurring. Maybe Rachel's run of bad luck is ending. Yet, I think the losses affect Abigail much more and perhaps Rachel is past her grief enough to see that too.

When we get home, I put the four pictures from my camera onto the computer. The two of Abigail are beautiful. The one of Abigail and I sleeping is nice too but the best one is the one Abigail took of me. It shows the ceiling where Daniel's spirit floats near the picture of him and Abigail, taken around Christmas 2002. I wonder if Abigail saw the white orb and knew it was Daddy's essence. Still longing to be with him, I decide to be happy wherever needed the most. Things are looking up.

:-)

Chapter Ten

Break Time

Ingrained habits may be difficult to break, but not impossible. Pat Rodegast - Emmanuel's Book II: The Choice for Love

Thoughts of commitment wake me. Daniel and Rachel married nine years ago today. Although Rachel did not mention it, I think her gift to Daniel was to let me visit with Abigail. Daniel again prompts me toward the Center.

"I'll take a little nap first," I reply.

Again, the service is over when I wake. An image of Daniel, shaking his head from side to side and looking perplexed, flashes through my mind.

"Remember Mom, I never was and never will be," Daniel says softly.

"I still don't know what that means," I reply, while heading to the bathroom.

A fly appears, out of nowhere, to drop into the empty, blue bathtub as I sit. My physic friend's talk of auras comes to mind. A white light surrounds and follows the bug. Sometimes the light glows brighter. The bug stops, after moving laboriously, as light slowly follows behind and then surrounds it. And then, the light fades away. The fly lies motionless when I get up to flush the toilet. Its aura is gone.

All the while, I hear Daniel talking. What strange happenings! I'm either nuts or spiritually progressing. Only time will tell. "It's okay," I tell Daniel, "if it's time for either Bear or me to die. If it is I, the rest of the family will learn from Rebecca and Samuel. James and Rachel will learn from each other."

The week passes quickly and soon we're on our way to vacation at Bahia Honda State Park. I'm sure of one thing while we drive down the turnpike; nothing stays the same, except my constant chatter. James remains silent. I'm counting on my new mantra of "Peace, Harmony, Love, Laughter, and Light" to get through the next eight days. Our once active sex life slowed down considerably, before Daniel died, and now it's nearly nonexistent. It's unlikely to change while hugging opposite sides of a smaller bed.

An orb appears inside the cabin while I video the next morning. It's a magenta colored, misty, oblong blob that hovers between the west and north windows. I thank it for appearing and ask for it to follow me outside for a video commentary on everyone's activities.

James works vigorously, cleaning the grill, as Ruth sets up fishing rods. Playback of the video shows blue, pink, and green colored lights, coming out of nowhere to sit on a dirty, straw chair nearby. Ruth leans down to set up the fourth fishing rod. Orbs move into her small head while I talk, oblivious of their presence.

Unwilling to sit in a boat without bathrooms, I opt to set up the camcorder and CD player on our open, wooden porch. James, Ruth, and our Michigan friend Sara soon leave. Spirit friends accompany me while singing along to old Carole King songs.

"I won't be happy until I see you alone again," I sing to Daniel. "Till I'm Home again and feeling right."

Between songs, I talk to my earth family, thinking that someday they will watch the video without me. It will be a while before I can go Home but they need to know that I'll see them again, after physical death.

"And I just want you all to know; you can be alone and still be happy," I announce to the wind with assurance.

"We'll all go Home one day and be together again. There's power in music, in song, so sing."

It feels wonderful to be in the Florida Keys, once again, looking out at the beauty of nature. My singing pays tribute to the glory all around. I love to sing, especially when music goes up to high notes, and then down to lower ones. While videoing the landscape hoping to catch orbs, I bask in the blue sky with its puffy, white clouds, above a dark blue bay. Several birds entertain me as I repeatedly scan the sky. The camera records orbs, amid triangular dirty spots covering the inside of the lens.

James, Ruth, and Sara return several hours later with amberjack for dinner. It's not as good as the usual snapper but fresh and a welcome relief from meat. No one places demands on me after dinner so I remain lost in my own little world narrating the video. They all appear respectful, of my so-called loss of Daniel, giving me space to heal.

As the sun sets in the west, a bright, white orb, within the usual pink diamonds appears. They stream forth from the sun. Daniel's essence fills the area as a beautiful mass, of light green, floats below the orb.

"Shouldn't you be helping someone?" I inquire.

"What," James asks coming out of the cabin, "are you getting? You're videoing directly into the sun."

The others see only the reflection of the sun on my dirty inside lens when I show them a still picture. Daniel's presence is gone and now there are not as many pink diamonds. The bit of bright, white light is gone as well.

"I'm glad you took my advice," I say out loud to Daniel. "You've got to go where you're needed."

The glorious sun continues to set as the others discuss fishing schedules. Hues of pink and gray fill the sky. Viewing them fills me with wonder. There will be no more schedules for me.

The next morning, James leaves to fish with two buddies from his fly-fishing club, who happen to be renting the park's only efficiency cabin. Ruth and Sara decide to shop but I stay behind preferring to video the bird show from the cabin porch. As the seagulls fly, I sense Daniel once again and know, he's happy to be free of physicality.

Another beautiful day in paradise unfolds as I watch the tarpon roll out in the bay but my sinuses seem clogged. Ruth and Sara removed their cabin's air filter and I now remember hearing them complain of stuffy noses as well.

Huge tarpon roll out in the bay as another beautiful day in paradise unfolds. A small rainbow shimmers above clouds to amaze me. The fantastic blend of blue and green, where water meets sky and shore, seems almost too pretty to be real. My right arm begins to numb while videoing the magnificent view. Fingers on my right hand tingle, as if falling asleep. Thinking the camera might drop, I plop it onto a chair to prepare coffee and take my morning Celebrex.

A gargantuan, pale brown turtle, which hangs out in the bay, soon graces me with its presence. I'm now sensing the value of nature, finding beauty in videoing the landscape, rather than people filled scenes. Today is a new beginning as I take more time to be in nature.

The sun is beginning to set when I open the heavy, wooden, cabin door, realizing I've slept for nearly three hours. Ruth and Sara continue to nap so I decide to walk down to the new bridge. It's been a long time since I went anywhere alone and it surprises me to remember how good it feels to walk amid fresh air.

There are unseen forces all around even though I feel alone. I smile remembering many pictures with orbs. Something within me recognizes the white circles in digital photos as spirit energy. I now scan photos for them after snapping the shot. Thoughts of a new orb website discovered before vacation comes to mind. If only I'd taken the time to read the lengthy article explaining orb meanings and colors!

Most orbs, I believe, signify Daniel's spirit. In pictures with Samuel, it's his soul group, surrounding him with love and protection from negative energy. Spirits seem to be with Samuel the most but I know Daniel continues to watch over, and protect, Abigail. I am certain of this, even though I rarely see her or a picture of her.

Both eyes focus on the mangroves to my right while walking toward the bridge. Several pink orbs accompany me. There are at least six of them. I walk up the tar-paved road looking at them, instead of ahead, and notice they keep up with my rather slow pace. Their presence radiates happiness into my heart and fills me with love. Instinct tells me the orbs represent members of my soul group. Both Daniel and Uncle Freddie are among them and, I sense, other members of my soul group are with those humans who need their presence. The pink orbs remain until I get to the second opening, in the mangroves, where one sees the shoreline, on the bay side of the Atlantic Ocean. A delicious feeling of loving peace makes me feel confident about venturing out on my own.

A couple with bikes stops to look at the beautiful sunset when I reach the curve in the road. An older couple fishes off the side of the road up ahead. I immediately start a conversation with the Puerto Rican woman while her Cuban husband reels in an amberjack. They are retired and fish to eat but do not understand why people fish for tarpon, and other game fish, if they cannot eat them. I agree watching as she points to a small fishing boat near the bridge. James is in the boat fishing for tarpon with two buddies.

Talk of spiritual experiences, and unbelieving family members who think we're crazy, fills time as I tape the sunset. An unexplainable feeling of familiarity overwhelms me. She shares experiences with ghosts after I discuss Daniel. My family, I announce, will walk up the old Bahia Honda Bridge, Saturday at sunset, to toss a few things into the ocean for Daniel. She says she and her husband will join us.

Ruth drives up in her gray, pick-up truck to worriedly ask what I'm doing. She and Sara have been searching for me.

"Sorry," I say sincerely. "I'll head back to the cabin in a few minutes."

I sense James will eat dinner with his buddies and do not feel urged to end my companionship with a kindred soul.

Ruth drives away shaking her little head. Her short, brown hair moves from side to side. After the sun fully sets, and the woman's husband leaves and returns for her twice, I tell her I really must return to my family.

We both have so much more to say and do not want to part. Intuition announces that there's something left to relate. Sensing she will experience a passing in her family, I report that we don't really die; we just pass into another form of energy. Some of us, like Daniel and like I will, chose to, and get to, stay in a middle plane where we are between earth and a higher plane. That is where we help humans to grow spiritually and take care of unfinished business. It's where we choose to stay rather than be born again. I think we only get to stay there, for longer periods, if we learn enough lessons or have unfinished business on earth.

We never lose the ones we love, I tell my new friend, but always hold them in our heart. She seems to understand and again says she, and her husband, will see me Saturday night for Daniel's "memorial." After we part, I walk quickly back to the cabin.

Minutes later, Ruth notes James called to let us know he's eating with buddies. We eat with Sara and settle down for a game of pinochle.

James arrives later as I read. He goes directly to bed. I stay up for my usual 3:00 AM blessings to thank the force within us all, for my new friend, and to connect with Daniel. It still seems the best time for us to interact because everyone else in the family is asleep. I'm anxious to see if the usual golden balls of light appear. Although I sense Daniel, there are no gifts of light to receive.

The next morning we snorkel around the small island near Bahia Honda at slack tide. It feels wonderful to immerse myself in saltwater, swimming effortlessly. We know Rebecca will be jealous when she arrives later that evening. She's jobless again and has two job interviews before she can bring Samuel to join us.

I continue to video and talk of limitations upon returning from the water, never giving a thought to the possibility of ending them. James and I are cordial but something is missing. Things have changed between us, since Daniel's death. I'm surprised to see him with a drink in his hands throughout the day.

Rebecca arrives with Samuel giving me new subjects to focus on. Samuel now dislikes my video habit and tries to hit me with his pillow. I immediately inform him of the pinched nerve in my neck and talk about how my body aches from snorkeling around the island.

While videoing the sunset that night, alone once again, I decide sunsets are better when shared. The pinkish orbs that accompanied me the last time I walked are nowhere in sight. I walk along the road toward the sun hoping Rebecca will join me as the camera focuses far ahead.

"Maybe that's my Puerto Rican lady friend," I note out loud spotting someone.

Rebecca pulls up in her car, before I reach the bridge, and asks if I want a ride back to the cabins. She is not interested in seeing the sunset and heads toward the cabin to unload groceries. I continue to walk talking to myself.

"Finally, I am focused on myself," I say loudly to the wind. "At fifty-four years old it's about time."

A Spanish couple, drinking beer, argues near the end of the bridge so I stay away from them to watch the sun set in all its glory. The blaring music from the couple's portable radio reminds me of myself many years ago. It makes me smile. The sky is much prettier than previous nights and filled with pink and gold. Changing hues of pink, gold, gray, and blue are spectacular but my right side is beginning to fall asleep again while holding the camera.

My new friend stands on the other side of the arguing couple. I walk over to congratulate them when they catch a large fish.

"Look," she says as her husband holds up a large amberjack, "it's my friend." She turns back to greet me warmly and touches my arm while asking, "How are you today?"

We again talk of spiritual matters as the sun continues to set. She shows me the nice snapper she caught before I say goodnight. While I walk back toward the cabins, she again tells me she and her husband will see us on Saturday at sunset.

I decide it's time for a drink when the cabin comes into view. Rebecca unloads groceries while James sits in the cabin reading. The drink, a Myer's rum and Coke, mixes in my brain as the sun sinks below the horizon.

"Who could fault an old lady with a poor memory?" I announce sneaking up the stairs of the last cabin, number six. "What, you mean this isn't cabin four?"

The birds' sweet song fills my ears. As the sun sinks even further, I try to recall a poem written at age thirteen when I remained immersed in Southern Baptist religion.

"The earth has many wonders but I only know a few.
There's lovely Indian summer with its radiant sky of
blue.
There's winter in the valley when the ground is
hushed with snow.
And Spring when all the lovers pay heed to Cupid's
bow.
There's Summer in the meadow…"

I forget the rest of the line but recall the last part of a childhood poem created when my mind sought the God within.

"But there's one thing, oh, so perfect, not a single soul can see.
He's the Lily of the Valley and as radiant as can be."

The same wonder, felt then, fills me now realizing, as Shirley MacLaine notes in her book *Dancing in the Light*, "Nature is a manifestation of the state of simple beingness." There is no judgment or morality attached to BEingness; it just is, in its purest sense, perfect balance.

Suddenly, I realize it's not a very pretty sunset but I'm in awe, just BEing. In a flash, gray clouds fill the sky to move quickly with the wind. I climb down stairs grateful not to have disturbed the guests in cabin five, which shares the porch of cabin six. The car for cabin six pulls up as I reach our stairs. My drink waits at the top.

Joining James, Rebecca, and Samuel inside the cabin, I focus my video hoping to document Daniel's essence as Rebecca talks about her last job interview. After they are asleep, I say my blessings out on the cabin porch. My words seem garbled while thanking unseen forces for helping us. It is becoming ordinary for me to confuse words or say something I have no intention of saying. Now I think about a check-up for brain tumors.

The next night we feast on the day's catch of mangrove snapper, yellowtail, moonfish, and mackerel. James prepares the fish while I video the action between sips of rum and Coke. It's unusual for him to help in the kitchen. A small orb sits on his neck that lets me know Daniel is influencing him somehow. I'm surprised at how good his dish of cerviche tastes after he dares me to try it.

Ego comes out of hiding more, and more, with each sip of alcohol. Within the hour, it's in high gear, as my mouth moves constantly with senseless chatter. The video camera zooms in on the ceiling as a carpenter ant convention gives ego the excuse it needs to drink more.

"Well, I guess I could just get really drunk and forget that I saw them," I announce to the room. "I think that might be the best course of action."

Despite increasing spirituality, I fit right into the family's vibration when drunk. As everyone tries to get Samuel to sleep I calmly announce, "I've got ten pages left to read in this book. If you are not asleep when I finish, I am going to hit you in the head with the book. And I know violence begets violence but he knows I don't mean it."

It's an idle threat, a habit of days past, an error that still needs correction.

The next day I safely snorkel, once again with my soul family, while my earth family takes in the underwater show at Looe Key. Everyone is surprised when I'm the last one to board the boat for our hour trip back to the cabin.

Later in the day, for the first time in all our years of Keys vacations, there is a pod of dolphins just outside the bay. James offers to take us out to be near them.

The pale, blue sky holds puffy, white clouds as we pile into the boat. We head quickly out into turquoise colored waters, headed west, keeping a look out for fins sticking out of water. James spots the pod with binoculars after several minutes of scanning the now deeper green water.

We watch the large pod in awe for several magical minutes as they swim toward our fishing boat. One glides quickly out of the water, and back in, as hearts fill with joy. We hear them breathe through blowholes as they glide in and out of the water a few feet away.

Samuel reaches his hand into the ocean and asks a nearby dolphin, "Will you let me pet you?"

He sucks in his breath as we move closer to watch them.

Their beauty takes my breath away. I feel Daniel around us once again. Another boat begins to approach the area at a very fast speed. They have no idea they are about to hit a pod of dolphins. My right arm holds the video camera as I hold up my left hand, like a traffic cop, to get their attention. In less than thirty seconds, they stop on a dime as their engine cuts off. The five passengers all clamor to get to the front of their boat for a better look. We leave them and head back toward the cabin feeling invigorated.

Emmanuel's Book notes, *"A dolphin has seen great Light and feels great love and now wishes to reach out to share such love." Love is a gift, which we must give, and the consciousness of love within seeks a place to express itself. Dolphins help us to experience love more fully communicating through vibrations, sonar and synchronized movement, acoustic images, feelings, sounds and group-energy fields. They are one with nature emitting the pure energy of unconditional love without judgment.*

Dolphins dwell within the realms of water (emotions/soul) and air (intelligence/mind) accessing multiple dimensions. They have active intelligence, stemming from a large brain, with a frontal lobe covering a greater area than the human brain. Dolphins teach us we are more than our physical bodies and can communicate telepathically. They possess an innate healing ability often displayed by sound vibrations. Many individuals strive to experience 'dolphin therapy' by immersing the body in dolphin-filled waters. People experiencing this type of therapy note dolphins display intrinsic tenderness, compassion, and a heightened sense of spirituality.

The last full day of vacation comes too quickly. I gather things for Daniel's memorial, as everyone else gets ready to see the sun set on Old Bahia Honda Bridge. It's our second Keys bon voyage to Daniel and we plan to toss several things into the Atlantic in his honor. I place all the things that made Daniel who he was inside an empty water bottle. Stones, dirt, wood and other building materials, pain pills, beer can tops, cigarette butts, Tums, and flowers fill the bottle that holds his picture. Ruth's coveted piece of wrecked motorcycle is too big to fit in so I leave it on the table.

I plan to wrap the bottle and motorcycle part in one of my favorite Hard Rock tank shirts because it holds special meaning for us. It's from the first suite hotel I took the kids to on a business trip. Memories of the plush resort that turned out to be another way for me to open their small world to greater possibilities prompt wide smiles. After scooping up the treasures, I head outside to watch tropical fish swim in the bay while waiting for everyone to get ready.

My new portable CD player is ready to play Daniel's latest memorial CD as we all pile into Ruth and Naomi's pickup truck for the ride to the bridge. I turn it on remembering how Daniel and Rebecca loved riding in the back of their aunts' pickup truck as small children. Ruth drives as she did when the kids were small, swerving from one side of the road to the other, like a drunk driver. Rebecca, Samuel, James, and I laugh as we watch Ruth, Naomi, and Sara in the truck's cab.

"Get the moon Nana," Samuel commands as I video the action.

We cannot hear the sound of the CD so I hand the video camera to Rebecca. It is barely audible, even upon turning the volume all the way up, so I know Daniel is with us. He will turn it up when he wants to.

The almost full moon is clearly visible, along with the setting sun, as we pull into the parking lot. A lone motorcycle stands parked near the water as we climb out of the truck. I'm not out of breath as usual when exercising. Rebecca walks behind us videoing our uphill ascent along the dirt path. She comments on how well I am walking.

"She's always the last one, talking about her limitations, and look at her now she's in the lead," Rebecca reports with surprise.

"She has physical forces with her now helping," Sara answers matter of factly, "mind over matter."

Physical limitations, and talk of the many prescription drugs taken to control them, keep me in the center of attention during vacation. The thought that I am reinforcing an illusion of limitation does not enter my dream world. We are our own creators working within the cosmic laws of Source. As Ernest Holmes wrote so long ago, "Life is a mirror and will reflect back to the thinker what he thinks into it." Thoughts do manifest into conditions.

The lower part of the sky is hot pink as I start up the concrete path. In thirty minutes, the magnificent sun will sink below the horizon. Other park visitors soon join us to take pictures. I set the CD player down at my feet when we reach the end of the bridge. Only those near the player can hear it.

Hues of pink climb up the sky as small, gray clouds float slowly past. James sets the video camera up on the ledge and I know that, despite the wind, it will be okay. We watch as Ruth ties the bottle and motorcycle part securely up with the Hard Rock shirt.

"Bye Daniel, see you later," Aunt Sara says loudly as Samuel and I toss it together into the ocean.

James retrieves the video camera from its perch to film the tank shirt as it slowly sinks into the sea. Jon Bon Jovi's voice is clearly heard singing, "Hey, man, I'm alive. I'm taking each day and night at a time."

"Turn your radio up honey," James says softly as we stand together.

"Daniel won't let it go any louder," I reply calmly watching the sinking shirt. "This is it. The volume has been at full blast ever since we got into the pickup truck. He just now chose to turn it up so we can hear it."

The rest of the family watches schools of tarpon, and permit, glide through the water as I sing along to "Dust in the Wind."

"Don't hold on. Nothing lasts forever but the immense sky," I sing mournfully.

In a move of gentleness that amazes me, James sits the camera back up on the railing and has us all pose in front of it.

"This is us guys. Come on lets get the whole family in here," he says directing Ruth, Naomi, and Sara into the fold just like Daniel would have done.

It is the first, and last, time I hear him include himself in "the family."

Ruth turns and bares her bottom.

"This is Daniel's farewell, he would like that," she says.

And the moment is over.

"He Knew," by Kansas, plays loudly as we walk back down the path toward the truck. As I listen to Samuel's chatter, two dashes of bright, white lines of light come down from the sky to the left of the camera. They quickly disappear within a foot of my face. Samuel begins to run up ahead to avoid the bugs. James now walks by my side.

"Here," I say handing him the CD player as I continue to video our descent, "do you want to hold this?"

We walk silently and as I strain, to hear the music, it suddenly gets louder again.

"I only feel it needs explaining. And though I said it, said it, said it."

The CD skips.

"Ah, ha," James inquires, "you've got a scratch on the CD?"

"No," I tell him adamantly. "It's a new CD. He's just messing with me."

"So turn around, turn around, it's on the other side," the music blares even louder as we continue to walk down the small hill.

"You should end the video on the moon," Rebecca suggests as we climb into the back of the pickup truck.

The moon appears full. It's just clearing a big, gray cloud when I train the video on it. Our fifty-minute memorial event is over. I sense my new friend lost a loved one after the last time I saw her for she did not come to the bridge.

Two magenta-colored diamonds appear before me when I leave the cabin in the morning. One is brighter and both fade quickly, from magenta to blue, before they disappear. I video as the others pack up to leave but now my video camera seems to malfunction. Static replaces the picture but the sound still tapes clearly.

I sense it's time to tape the tranquility of the bay before the tape ends. A brown pigeon lands next to the black and gray ones, to eat our extra bread. It's time to venture inward but ego remains in control. Although my subconscious knows tranquility is needed, I talk most of the time while taping the serene scene.

We soon decide to take one last boat ride before leaving the park. Another pod of dolphins, to marvel over, miraculously rewards us. Still not ready to end vacation, we stop off at a local restaurant for lunch before heading home in three vehicles. I get into Rebecca's car and let Samuel drive with James.

My perspective on life is changing rapidly. The future remains uncertain. For now, I just want to sing along to loud rock music in Rebecca's car. The camera films a spiral stream of gold, green, pink, and magenta coming from the sun as we near her house. Another picture shows a streak of white light with a circle of golden light in the middle. It's the second streak of spirit energy that I recall catching on camera.

Vacation pictures reveal a few more surprises. Many photos hold spirit orbs. Orbs fill the living room as Samuel begins his pillow fight. The photo of James playing with a game, as Samuel watches, is my favorite. A small, white orb sits between two birds in the Lagoon picture on the wall. The final picture, taken as Rebecca drives the last block to her home, shows a multicolored orb that I know was from Daniel.

:-)

Chapter Eleven

Surprising Times

The universally connected hologram of consciousness promises that the instant we create our good wishes and prayers, they are already received at their destination. Gregg Braden - The Divine Matrix

James calls on Rachel and Abigail while I work on the business newsletter. Daniel prompts me to visit the Center shortly before sunset. Again, I nap until the service ends. Pangs of guilt, upon waking, spur an online visit to read more about the place Daniel feels so strongly about.

A wealth of information on spirituality soon lies before me. Links to "Religious Science International" lead to a message titled "Faith and the Law." My right-brained approach to life takes a back seat while intrigued by phrases such as the "Law of Cause and Effect" and the "Law of Mind." Fear, born of ignorance and doubt, still rules my world as I ponder my current situation while reading the article's last paragraph.

"Dr. Holmes teaches us that fear is the negative use of faith. If we are in this state of consciousness, we will be defensive and seek to protect what we have for fear of losing it. Fear of loss inevitably results in loss."

I'm fearful of just about everything and have had enough of loss. Yes! The Center is where I need to go.

James returns with hopeful news later in the evening. Rachel wants the family to visit on Saturday. He shows me a picture of Bear, looking lethargic and thinner than usual, lying in a comfy dog bed while looking at the floor. Then he places a picture of Abigail, holding one of her white kittens up under its front paws, into my hands. Upon sensing Bear will soon join Daniel, I decide to see the psychic medium again.

Isaiah welcomes me to his home with a hug. I've seen him several times this year, without charge. Each time I learn something new about myself. A credentialed Hypnotherapist, specializing in past life regression, verified a past life last year, after I'd accessed the information upon reading a book by Dr. Brian Weiss. It's now important to assure that the work I do on my own remains fruitful.

"I want to investigate past lives," I inform Isaiah eagerly.

"Sure," he replies with a twinkle in his eye, "we can do that."

We arrange our chairs to face one another. Isaiah takes both my hands into his while we slowly drift into another level of consciousness. The image of a freckle-faced, five-year-old, Irish girl in a castle fills my brain. I quickly realize this is the past life verified by the expensive Hypnotherapist.

"Everyone dies in the fire except me," I solemnly tell Isaiah. "Now, I have to save them all."

The gentle squeeze on my hands is welcome when I report seeing myself at ten years old running through a green meadow. Two older boys run behind me and quickly knock me down to the ground. The scene that unfolds is not agreeable so Isaiah brings my consciousness back to the room.

He smiles, looks into my eyes, and softly asks for permission to go back to a shared past life. The request takes me by surprise but I readily agree.

"Don't be afraid," Isaiah whispers softly. "I'll guide you and if you feel the least bit uncomfortable we'll stop."

Images unfold behind closed eyes. A young, very skinny, black girl rides in the back of a carriage through a yellow field of wheat. The open, wooden carriage bounces, up and down, as it weaves through the field. She's a slave of about ten years in age and sits on the floor clinging to the side of the large cargo area.

A large-boned, middle-aged, white woman sits in the front of the buggy staring ahead, as if in a trance. There's a very big and stern looking white man next to her. He holds the reins of two horses pulling us forward. The man's straw colored hair sticks out of a big, black, pilgrim's hat. We're all dressed in black but he wears a white collar.

As Isaiah softly asks what I see, I realize this past life is one recalled on my own several months before. I see more now.

"Do you see how skinny I am?" I ask in disbelief.

"What else do you see?" he asks softly.

When I answer, he asks if I see beyond the fields of wheat. Since I have not mentioned the wheat fields, I know he sees the same scene as I.

Isaiah now describes things I do not see. Again, he stops to ask what else I see. The images abruptly end while sensing the stern looking man was not a kind master. Isaiah stops the regression when I voice discomfort. A feeling of compassion overwhelms me as we look into one another's eyes.

"Thanks," I say sincerely, "you've helped me to understand that one of my tasks for this life is to end any thought of bondage. I sense a pattern of abuse in many lives, including my current one, and now I know without a doubt it's time to let the thought of them go."

Isaiah looks at me compassionately and hugs me like a father.

"You are much more powerful than you'll ever know," he says softly.

I begin to cry feeling as if I'm finally releasing a secret bottled up inside for many lives.

"It's never necessary," Isaiah confides as he reaches for a tissue, "to live in limitation."

After squeezing my folded hands softly, he gets up and goes to a table in the corner of the room. He returns to my side quickly and places a plastic CD in my hands.

"This meditation CD will help you connect to the higher consciousness you seek," he announces. "It's a healing CD."

In her book Beyond the Indigo Children, P.M.H. Atwater notes, meditation nurtures and enhances the prefrontal lobes, the part of our brain responsible for higher modes of functioning. Enhanced prefrontal lobes structure and process information differently and are common in children known as Indigos or Crystals. Violence virtually destroys the prefrontals stemming the incidence of higher states of intuitive knowing. Meditation is effective at any age, and brings more oxygen to the brain, cleans out body toxins, and aids in concentration and calming.

A heavy weight lifts off of my shoulders. Isaiah walks me to the car, yards away, instead of leaving me at the door as usual.

"If you're one of those who abused me in the past, I forgive you," I say starting to reach for the door handle of my car.

Isaiah bows his head, thanks me, and then quickly holds the car door open while I get in.

"I'll give you a call for another session after I think about all this," I remark before driving away.

Dr. Christine Page, author of Spiritual Alchemy reports that, "Whenever you are joined to an energy line that has absorbed humiliation, defeat or scorn, you know shame somewhere in your cells." There is a possibility of shame that greatly limits self-expression when we hold secrets. Many of us chose the path, which leads to freedom, clearing age-old patterns of suppression and hence raising consciousness to new levels of compassion and tolerance. Divine love is elusive until we are willing to embrace the darkest facet of shame, and love that part of ourselves. When we do, a source of tremendous power is liberated.

Life seems to change. Journal entries lessen while experiencing unexplainable things. There's no way to describe them adequately and I'm not sure they are meant to be shared. Two weeks later my friend Mary sends an email to announce that Isaiah and his wife Priscilla moved to northern Florida. Although stunned by the news, it's clear that our time together was preordained and is over. They lived in many places, both in and out of the U.S., and I sense they travel for a reason. Maybe their mission is to search for people from previous lives to make things right.

Life really improves when I start meditating, creating a reference point for a higher state of being. Isaiah's CD helps me to discover whom I really chose to be in this life. Body changes lift me to another plane of consciousness each time I listen to the guided meditations. Dis-ease slowly fades as I allow the Light within to expand, to purify and cleanse everything in my consciousness and beyond.

:-)

Chapter Twelve

Many Perceptions

The greatest revolution of our generation is the discovery that human beings, by changing the inner attitudes of their minds, can change the outer aspects of their lives. William James

Earth is indeed a strange and mysterious place to learn. It's May 28, 2005 and what I see and experience continues to amaze me. Although now used to abnormal experiences, it's still odd to sense spirits communicating upon sitting in the bathroom. I understand that is when, besides sleeping, I am least likely to have pressing thoughts. This is a time when I'm more open to communication from these generally unheard of sources. Still, it's peculiar to communicate with spirits and see things most people do not.

Family meets at Terry's house, the day before James' forty-ninth birthday, to visit Rachel and Abigail. A hard habit to break, the struggle for valuable energy seems ingrained. My complaints of illness match those of Momma's when she and Terry get into the van.

James begins to fish in the pond as soon as we arrive. Rebecca pulls her car into the gravel drive and Samuel, after letting Aunt Ruth out, joins Terry, Abigail, and Rachel on the small dock to watch. Momma and I move into the large house leaving the camcorder outside for others to use.

The comfort of the air-conditioned house feels great for it's hot outside. Memorial posters remain, scattered between pictures of Daniel, Rachel, Abigail, and Jesus. As I sit trying to talk with Momma, it seems clear that I'm dying. It's time for the family to get used to my absence.

It never occurs to me that constant complaining bothers anyone, especially not James. I'm too preoccupied with my own dream drama. Many souls create dramatic emotional environments as they work through karma from other lifetimes. I carried the burden of unconscious guilt, from many lifetimes, believing myself unworthy to accept good health or wealth. It's time to release guilt by forgiving others, and myself, with the realization that we are spiritual beings, here to learn and grow from experiences. I'm not yet ready, at this point in time, to do that.

James videotapes Rachel as she sets up Abigail's small plastic pool on the green grass. The hurricanes of 2004 damaged both Rachel's above ground swimming pool and her roof. Rachel replaced the roof and bought the small pool to use until she got the larger one repaired. Video documents the telltale static of spirit when Rachel stands next to James as he videos the kids playing.

James looks comfortably at home later in the afternoon while watching television on Rachel's bedroom floor with the kids. They toss towels over one another's heads and both kids pile on top of him laughing. I see something out of the corner of my eye while videotaping but fail to capture the glob of transparent energy.

"Let's see what I get by putting the camera right here," I note, placing it in the den.

A transparent energy field passes in front of the camera as soon as the words leave my mouth.

Rebecca remains unemployed but seems hopeful her last job interview will be fruitful. She brings food for lunch, to make our visit easier on Rachel, and now takes the time to grill meat. James watches Samuel play with Daniel's game system later, while Rebecca follows Abigail into her bedroom. Familiar static fills the video as Rebecca reads to her. It's gone when I return to the den as Rachel displays the cake she bought to celebrate James' birthday.

Rebecca reports a short while later that Abigail is finally asleep. We decide to wait until she wakes before showing James his birthday cake. Rachel has a brand new copy of *White Noise* so I ask to open the package.

"I don't know why I bought that movie," Rachel confides. "I don't even know what it's about."

It's a movie I've wanted to see about spirit communication," I reply, ripping plastic off the case.

"Can you check out the new ATV for me James?" Rachel says, heading for the garage. James and Samuel follow her outside. We hear the roar of two ATV's on the country road minutes later. The rest of us sit and watch the movie as Terry videos the living room.

Terry and Ruth voice concern as I watch the movie and talk of spirit orbs. They admit thinking about committing me to a mental institution.

"Just because you're not as educated in these things does not mean they're not possible," I tell them all adamantly.

Playback of the video later shows the living room before the scene changes back to the den. There's no sound at first, and then, it's just static until Ruth's boss unexpectedly calls her to work.

Ruth looks at Rebecca with an anxious grin and notes she has to work.

"I'll meet you outside," she says getting up to head out the door.

"You're going to miss the birthday cake," I announce.

"Mom, I don't understand why Rachel and Abigail got a cake for James," Rebecca says anxiously. "It's not like we've all been that close."

It's impossible to explain. I've encouraged James to visit them often but have not told my family when he does. In my mind, I've given James to Rachel through words and actions. I'm ready to join my son on the Otherside. But I cannot tell her that.

Rebecca is not happy as we argue. Static fills the video making it impossible to hear us.

"I didn't," says Rebecca adamantly, "I didn't say you were crazy."

"I'm not crazy," I reply loudly. "I'm just a little more educated in the Light. I know some day you'll be just as educated, even more educated than I in such things."

Rebecca voice rises to match my own.

"You haven't shut up since the movie started."

"That's because you've been ignoring me."

"It's time to go home," she says to Momma, Terry, and Samuel while walking away.

As I put this book together, on February 20, 2009, it's clear, once again, that an unseen force guides me. There are no coincidences for everything happens as the result of our soul's plan. How we react to these things makes the difference in our lives. This morning before I got out of bed, I got another "God message" and spent some time considering whether to put it into this book. Here it is, as received. (I'm reading The Divine Matrix, by Gregg Braden, but did not read it the day before this message.)

"We are brothers and sisters of soul in the Light ever strengthening the Matrix in which we live. And that Matrix grows as we grow. And that Matrix strengthens as we strengthen. And that Matrix is never-ending. We are part of that fine Matrix, that substance of life that sustains us, and we feed that Matrix with our thoughts. Just as in the book you read, thoughts, beliefs, make the physical manifestations in your life.

"Carefully chosen thoughts, those are the thoughts to be nurtured. Those are the thoughts that will make the best life. You must tell your brothers and sisters this. You must let them know that these thoughts go into that ever-flowing Matrix and become their life, eventually, whether in this so-called life or the next. There is only one Matrix and the beings that form it and the beings that hold it together are one. Go forth and spread the word of the Matrix. You have been heard. What you seek is already found."

I would love to write only of messages, such as these. Yet, I realize there's a reason to write as I do. Some people may not be ready to receive the messages but it's important to know that anyone can get them. Understand, all humans get messages from God. It's just a matter of being ready, and open, to receive them.

*Since Daniel's transition, I have actively purified and cleansed the body and mind in which my soul lives. The chaos is gone and I've learned to be open and receptive to the Voice of God, Spirit, **All That Is**, whatever term you wish to use for the Vital Life Force within us. We are all the same, having come from the same Source, and we will all return to that Source. My task, as other Lightworkers and wayshowers, is to make that return happen as soon as possible. So, bear with me as I relate how the process unfolds within me.*

Rachel and James are still riding on the ATV's. No one knows where they are. I stay alone in Daniel's favorite green, Lazy Boy chair watching the movie about a man trying to reach his dead wife.

"No, no," an expert tells the leading man, "you are misreading everything. It is one thing to contact the dead. It is another thing to meddle and you, you are meddling."

I don't recognize the subtle sign spirit offers as Abigail and Joy enter from outside the house.

"Did you have a nice nap?" I ask Abigail.

"Well she slept for a little bit," Joy replies looking fondly at Abigail, "but James and Rachel went for a ride on the ATV's and she woke up as soon as she heard the engines roar."

"They were meant to be together," I say with my eyes still glued to the television screen.

"Who was meant to be together?" asks Joy in surprise.

"James and Rachel," I reply.

"No, no they weren't, please. Ha, ha, please," she answers with a half-hearted laugh. "He's not my daughter's type."

My attention focuses on Abigail as a small boy appears on the television screen.

"He looks like he's your age doesn't he Abigail?" I ask.

Abigail seems concerned because it has started to rain.

"Don't worry," I tell her in a soothing voice, "don't worry Abigail. It will be okay. Nana knows."

Abigail jumps as the sound on the television increases during a scary part of the movie. I don't even consider how inappropriate it is to watch the movie with her there. Smart Abigail decides to leave the room to get the birthday cake she chose for James.

"Oh, I'll get it," Joy says happy to leave the room as she quickly follows Abigail into the kitchen. "It's too heavy for you."

They look for the cats after the cake is safely on the kitchen table.

Rachel and James return barely wet minutes later. They seem quite happy.

"Hi," James says softly as he walks up from behind my chair. I continue to watch the movie pretending not to hear. He sits down on the couch as the surround sound system fills the room.

We stand around the cake minutes later. It's clear, to me, that Abigail got help in choosing the cake. The beautiful, four-layer, chocolate cake has a wide circle of thick, yellow frosting above green stems, sprouting from a smiling sunflower.

The closeness between James, Rachel, and Abigail is undeniable. So are the orbs that often cover James' face in pictures. A magenta colored orb appears in front of the video camera as he begins to blow out candles. Color variations, and faces, stand out later upon placing the pictures on my computer.

It dawns on me now that my own drama overrode words and actions. Rebecca did not understand my actions because I was not open with her. James certainly didn't understand, for our marriage changed dramatically after Daniel's passing, when I stopped all communication. We lived in perfect bliss for several years. Our vastly different habits and ideas on family life didn't matter. I found my soul mate and knew he felt the same. I was happy to make him happy, happy to do what he wanted to do, and oh so happy to stop giving so much of myself to others, except him.

I have never liked routines but the routine nature of our marriage became very comfortable. Things changed when my body began to take on medical conditions. It became necessary to spend more time caring for myself rather than catering to the needs of a husband. Wrapped up in the perceived loss of Daniel, I now had even less time for James. My perception of life and our marriage changed drastically but James may have wondered what happened.

We built our marriage on the altar of a shared body. Promises to protect each other from sunburn, alert one another of obesity, or lumps, shifted responsibilities. James and I based our marriage on everything staying the same, and yet, in my world, nothing remains the same. Perhaps, in his mind, I abandoned him.

My plan to avoid another divorce was set. I was ready to tie up the loose ends of previous lives to be with my beloved son. Sensing I had taken Rachel's mate in another life, I planned to give her mine. The thought of Abigail having a daddy, who knew and seemed to love her, was a bonus.

James and I meet the family at Ruth and Naomi's house the next day. We plan to celebrate Memorial Day and James' birthday with a coconut cake purchased during our Keys vacation. James and Momma watch television as the rest of us play cards. Ruth and Naomi's house is active with orb activity, as usual. Orbs fill the pictures I take between hands. Everyone remains leery of the unknown as I share pictures. They all tell me to get my camera fixed.

I begin to design Daniel's memorial website upon arriving home. In a short while, a car pulls into the drive and someone knocks on the door. Rachel's voice wafts through the house. She and Abigail are on their way home after visiting a friend. I'm pleased to think we may all become close again. When they leave, Daniel's website occupies me until the wee hours of the morning, long after James retires.

:-)

Chapter Thirteen

Highway to Change

They are makers of themselves by virtue of the thoughts which they choose and encourage; that mind is the master-weaver, both of the inner garment of character and the outer garment of circumstances, and that, as they may have hitherto woven in ignorance and pain, they may now weave in enlightenment and happiness. James Allen - As a Man Thinketh

June brings increased traffic as representatives of the thirty-four nation "Organization of American States" gather. I'm glad to have my car back from Rebecca while avoiding the convention center. Traffic remains considerably increased many miles away. News reports focus on media credibility. The issue no longer concerns for I already limit television and do not read newspapers. A great deal of time will pass before I consciously watch only uplifting movies or reconsider my choice of companions.

The Universe announces, in various ways, that it's time to let go of the past. My largest regular source of income, writing articles for journals, ends. Rumors speak of a bankrupt journal company that owes many people back pay but they pay me in full. The desktop computer and year old laptop malfunction constantly so I jump, between computers, while finishing Daniel's memorial website and DVD's. Daniel prompts me to rest. An unseen force keeps removing costly software programs, when online, so I reformat, and reload, the desktop hard drive. Daily backups onto external hard drives limit data loss but are very time consuming.

Daniel's friends email to let me know they're pleased about his website. Some mention deceased relatives who hang around to make them feel protected. I switch while online between canceling professional memberships, due to lack of funds, to reading links of world news from "Democracy Now." Reports of voter fraud capture attention. Democrats continue to protest election results, eight months after the vote. Email seems an easy way to get files from the desktop to my laptop so I email them to myself. The laptop computer refuses to work. Now, I must ship it back to Gateway for repairs.

Memories of Daniel's last two Mother's Day messages, from the Otherside, warm my heart but the reformatting process deleted the first one from the desktop computer. Concerns of losing the laptop's screensaver message rise while shipping it in for repair. Gateway reassures me days later. They have the laptop and will return it soon, depending on part availability.

The desktop computer operates normally as I begin to weed through email. It usually takes hours to go through hundreds of messages, sorting out junk mail. Today is different for there's much less email to view. In shock, I realize that the email addressed to myself is not there. Determining the source of the issue takes time, but eventually, I learn it's due to my Internet Service Provider.

Family changes warrant attention. Rebecca remains unemployed as Ruth schedules surgery before a lay off. Our house is no longer a haven or a place for celebration. It seems full of clutter and empty of good energy that took years to create. Grief, anger, and sadness over Daniel's death fill it. The distance between James and I widens as projection replaces communication. Our sex life is non-existent. It comforts me to know that at least James and I have assets to cash in while he continues to seek employment.

Daniel's essence appears more often and I try to capture it on film. Several pictures reveal orbs amid increasing amounts of green and magenta colored substance.

"Life is a lesson," I write to a friend. "I guess I ain't through learning yet. I tend to sleep more now and hope I do not wake. Ah, the drama queen forevermore. Don't fret, I'll feel better after my nap."

An email from Gateway, noting the laptop is on its way back, cheers me upon waking. Increasing amounts of time serve to boost spiritual awareness. Time spent surfing the Internet pays off when I find Beliefnet. After wandering upon a cornucopia of information on Buddhism and Hinduism, I join both groups. Many others are in the water as I dive into this new world. Messages intrigue me.

"Hatred is created when people start to think who's right and who's wrong. When they neglect the essence of their religion and start following rituals 'blindly'."

How many years have I wasted on that effort? Daniel's voice reminds me that tomorrow is Sunday. It's time to try a different way of being. I ignore the message while following links to various websites, message boards, and meditations. The computer malfunctions so I retire for the night much earlier than usual.

Life improves on the first Sunday in June upon visiting Religious Science Fort Lauderdale. Family beliefs no longer serve and I'm eager to readjust my way of thinking. Daniel's essence permeates the air as I walk to the front door. A smiling greeter, in blue jeans and a colored shirt, welcomes me with a hug instantly making me feel at home. Imagine that, a perfect stranger hugged me!

"See, I told you Mom," Daniel announces.

I silently thank him before scolding myself for waiting so long to visit a center just two blocks from the house I've lived in for eighteen years. My heart sings. These are my peoples. I have found my peoples. They dress in blue jeans, and wear t-shirts, and talk of one Spirit as I do. I am so pleased with myself for finally coming here!

In these early days of self-discovery, I cannot attend the Center enough and would set up a cot in their back room if they would let me. Many people appear to feel the same way. Some even cry with joy upon walking into the building. How comforting to hear God referred to by names such as the Living Spirit Almighty, Creative Mind, Universal Spirit, or One Spirit! Their "Declaration of Principles" blows my mind. A number of sentences catch my eye.

"We believe in the eternality, the immortality and the continuity of the individual soul, forever and ever expanding."

"We believe the ultimate goal of life to be a complete emancipation from all discord of every nature, and that this goal is sure to be attained by all."

"We believe in the unity of all life, and that the highest God and the innermost God is one God."

These things seem oddly familiar as the truth of my being flickers ever so slightly. Yes, I can learn to believe "in the healing of the sick through the power of this Mind."

The electronic update seems directed specifically to me as I read the Quote of the Week:

"Illness is a result of sending signals to (the) Law of Mind that we do not really love or respect ourselves. Self-love is the great healing signal. We may not have been loved appropriately by Mom and Dad at certain times in our life, but we can't blame them. We have to accept that we are the ones who have the responsibility for our health, success, wealth and everything else that we want to demonstrate. No matter what has happened before, we have to make the choice to love our Self and to put that choice into action. By Dr. Tom Johnson."

It's the beginning of a new life but for now I'm stuck in the old one. Celebrex seems more necessary during the rainy season to soothe joints. While checking for business mail I still shuffle my way slowly as the body's osteoarthritis calls out for attention. Feeling low again, I'm ready to "cash in my chips," while preparing to nap, after tossing unopened mail on the desk.

Daniel's voice rings softly inside my head.

"Open the company mail Mom."

My arm reaches out to grab the mail as I lift myself up from the futon. A check, for a newsletter order, sits on top of the usual token check for co-authoring a book. I decide to ready the order for shipping. *DIVAS Simply Singing CD* plays while I work. My heart soars while singing along to "I Miss You." But soon I begin to cry. Even though I sense Daniel is not able to be with me, as much as before, I have not cried since Mother's Day. Tears pour down my small, heart-shaped face.

Sensing a presence, I turn around expecting James. Daniel's loving essence surrounds me. His hand strokes my hair before softly resting on my left shoulder.

"It's ludicrous to sing this song," Daniel whispers in my ear, "because I am with you always. I am you, you are me, we are one in Spirit."

A feeling of complete wholeness consumes me. I smile and wipe away tears.

"Keep singing the song Mom to desensitize yourself," Daniel says softly. "When you can get through it without crying, your goal will be met."

After I agree to work on controlling my emotions, Daniel asks me to make a few more copies of the last memorial CD. I'm to deliver one to Jeremiah and Judith with the same Daniel message for everyone else.

"It's the one I want them to keep and remember me by," Daniel confides.

He wants us all to forget about the 2004 CD because, as with many of the things he and I have done together, it was a transition. After making more than ten CDs together,

Daniel now has me down to the one he wants us all to hear, keep, and believe in.

Thoughts of Rebecca's thirty-first birthday surface so I phone to ask how she wants to celebrate on Thursday. As we talk, James walks into the room. He's talking to Rachel and Abigail on his cell phone. He hands me the phone so I try to get Abigail and Aunt Rebecca to communicate from phone to phone.

Abigail says hello but keeps repeating "Nana." Rebecca ends our call so I can talk to my granddaughter. She sounds excited to speak with me and joyously breaks out into song. It's an odd song, for a three year old, but the words make sense and are very meaningful. Through my haze, I catch the words, "we will always be together; that's a promise. You and me will always be together."

Abigail continues to sing and I also hear Rachel in the background sounding completely amazed.

"Where did you hear that song?" Rachel asks her darling daughter when the song ends.

"Daddy said it," Abigail confidently replies.

"No," Rachel tells her.

Abigail speaks again, breaking the silence on the other end of the phone.

"Daddy sang it when I was a weenie-tiny baby," she now tells her mother.

I know Daniel put the words into Abigail's head as a way of reaching out to me. Rachel takes the telephone receiver from Abigail. We speak for a few minutes until Abigail again takes the receiver. She is back to her usual self, singing about poo-poo and nipples, for she just discovered that Bear has nipples.

"It's time to say goodbye," I hear Rachel tell her.

"Talk to me on the telephone and not in my dreams," Abigail quietly tells me.

Utter astonishment overwhelms me upon her acknowledgement of mind trips to see her late at night. Right before I give the phone back to James, Abigail tells me she will see me in her dreams, in her and in her mommy's dreams. I remain astounded at how we spirits cross planes to the Otherside when love overflows from our hearts. "I know my path and am on it," I tell myself silently as James leaves the room to continue his conversation with Rachel. "That is the best I can do."

The next evening, at the Wednesday mid-week service, I learn of a workshop scheduled for the following night. It has been a very, long, time since my last class but I'm sure this one will make a difference. I smile, upon recalling community college courses that spurred me to break the mold after thirty years of limitation. Although it was tough raising two children alone, while attending school as an older adult, it was also very liberating and gratifying.

Recollections of Dr. Vendettuoli's classes on religion rise to surround me with unexplainable warmth. It seems unlikely the memory of his classes would cause such a reaction because I hated him, over a period of several months, for turning my world upside down. In 1980, it was shocking to learn that God did not write the *Bible*. Thoughts that the book might contain anecdotes, which may or may not be true, contradicted a strict Southern Baptist upbringing.

A vague, uneasy feeling of a loss of spirit plagued me at thirty years old, even without knowing exactly what it meant. It seemed necessary to live against moral beliefs to survive. Life after two divorces, with two children and no child support, wasn't easy. In order to support us, and improve life, it became necessary to apply for welfare and a Pell Grant to attend community college. It seemed the only way to secure a job with medical insurance and other benefits.

Government funding wasn't nearly enough so I worked an unreported, after school, part-time job to make ends meet. Daniel took on the responsibilities of caring for his three-year-old sister while I worked nights. Placing this burden on him, my new lifestyle, and failing to report the meager job income, made me feel further from God, creating restlessness and a need to live based on new beliefs and values.

I always believed the *Bible* to be the true word of God. My state of consciousness quickly changed upon learning that there's only one Spirit moving through all life. God is in the depth of our hearts, Dr. Vendettuoli kindly assured me, making it possible to expand consciousness. It didn't matter what religion I practiced, or even if I practiced any religion, for if I allowed him to, God lived through me.

Now, the Religious Science workshop beckons me like an infant to its mother's breast. I do not want to attend this new class alone, especially since the four-week series starts on Rebecca's birthday. She recently earned a certificate in accounting but remains unemployed. I quickly decide to ask her to join me.

Rebecca readily agrees to attend when I telephone her.

"I'll do anything to get you out of the house," she says brightly.

Minutes later, I email Rev. Jim to see if I can get a discount rate. The cost will go onto my trusty Visa card.

"Living Your Authentic Life" does not sound that spiritual but it clearly is as Rebecca and I sit in class. Rev. Jim says many things that I've already told my darling daughter. It surprises us both. Together we learn of practices for self-discovery and self-expression over a four-week period.

The "Spiritual Practice To Do List" looks dauntingly lengthy. Yet, my practices of community service, analyzing dreams, meditation, journal writing, praying for others, and thanking God for blessings received are all on the list. I now look forward to completing the list and learning what spiritual principles are.

Rev. Jim talks of a new way to pray that amazes me. I have always asked for things sometimes bargaining, and pleading, with God to get them during prayer. Now we learn that prayers directed to a God apart from ourselves are objectively oriented. They serve to detach us from our Creator. This new way of praying, described as treatment, is totally different. It calls for recognition, and unification of the Absolute Love within, before affirming what we want is already ours. It's a real stretch of the imagination for me to consider that this type of prayer works. Rebecca is even more leery of changing her habits than I.

As noted in Life and Teaching of The Masters of the Far East by Baird T. Spalding, the Supreme Intelligence lies within.

"When you are looking at your body you are looking at the complete and perfect God temple."

We will find every answer and be ever-permanent, stable, and all-knowing when we recognize we are God.

Ernest Holmes relates, "The secret of prayer and its power in the outward life depends upon an unconditioned faith in, and reliance upon this inner Presence. Prayer has power by belief and acceptance."

In her book Beyond the Indigo Children, P.M.H. Atwater notes many benefits of daily prayer. It instills the importance of faith, and gratitude, and deeply affects brain patterning that initiates coherent waveforms that can produce physical effects. Affirmative prayer empowers people and is the most effective.

Class work introduces us to the works of Ernest Holmes, Barbara Marx Hubbard, and Joseph Campbell. There's so much information over the four-week course that I began to feel overwhelmed. I fill out the "Personal Spiritual Practices Survey" and am surprised to see how I feel about spirituality. On a scale of one to ten, I rate my primary relationship, in terms of spirituality, at the lowest point possible but my time alone rates a nine. Clearly, my marriage to James needs a makeover.

Although happy to begin increasing the quality of my spiritual practices through the power of affirmations, now I need to determine priorities. Attention focuses on a piece of purple paper containing a quote by Ken Keyes.

"The purpose of our lives is to be free of all addictive traps, and thus become one with the Ocean of Living Love."

There's no doubt that it's going to take a lot of work to be my authentic self while viewing "The Twelve Pathways." Questions rule. Can I really be "tuned in" and act freely without being emotionally upset when things don't go my way? Can I receive the wisdom that flows from love and expanded consciousness? What is consciousness anyway? What are the Seven Centers of Consciousness and how can I open them?

Rev. Jim explains consciousness, the chakras, and answers many questions without a raise of the hand. I happily thank him when the last class ends and wish him the best of luck as he moves toward a new life in California.

Now I regularly attend mid-week services and skip the usual Sunday mornings most people like. Smaller meetings help me feel more at ease, with less people around, and I like the idea of different speakers. Everyone is friendly and seems to think as I do, for their heads nod right along with mine, as we relish each talk. Rev. Donna Conley, Rev. Steve Hooks, and Rev. Heidi Peck quickly become my favorite speakers.

It's time to get together with positive, supportive people and study the laws of the universe. Yet, there are hurtles to cross before I more fully recognize the emotional blocks that stunt spiritual growth. Internal conflicts continue to hold me back from fully embracing life but Science of Mind opens the door to a better way of living. In time, I'll learn to close off the outside world of rationalization, and judgment, and stop judging others and myself. Tuning into the world of consciousness, which Isaiah introduced me to with his CD, suddenly becomes much easier.

Even though they do not approve of where I'm going, the whole family rejoices for I've found something that lures me out of the house on a regular basis. Their concern is well founded. I still spend most time on the computer. The only difference is that now I spend less time on the business of hiv nutrition. Email increases as daily messages from spiritual groups arrive making it harder to get anything done. I often follow links, disregarding the day's work. Everything seems to change, even my body. Naps become routine as I sleep sporadically throughout the night.

Life took on a whole new meaning the first time I read, "thoughts are things" in The Science of Mind *textbook by Ernest Holmes. The idea that what I thought shaped the circumstances around me captured my interest and inspired me to read everything I could find on the subject.*

My entire life changed upon learning that my reactions controlled what happened in my world. Limitless thinking gave way to greater perception and I soon realized that all things are possible. I now know we can master every condition by changing our perception of how we see it.

Yes, just by using our thoughts we can change the circumstances around us. The moment we stop thinking of a difficult issue it begins to disappear. Although some issues take longer than others to master, I've found that this is true. Universal Energy belongs to and works with everybody. We are a part of this indestructible energy that many people call Spirit. Once we realize the divinity within we set that energy free to show us we are unlimited in all that is good.

The more we train our mind the simpler it is to connect to our Higher Self. But first, we must remember that it can *occur. Tuning in to higher thoughts is much easier when our mind is clear of clutter from negative thoughts, things, and people. My quest towards positive thought started by changing the kind of music I listened to and accelerated as I refused to read the newspaper or watch the usual television. With practice, it becomes effortless to tap into that consciousness in which we live, and move, and have all BEing. It is a learned behavior, like anything else, but this learned behavior is much more rewarding because it frees us from limitation.*

:-)

Chapter Fourteen

Changing Reality

One person must choose a new way of being and live that difference in the presence of others so that it can be witnessed and sealed into the pattern. In doing so, we upgrade our programs of belief and send consciousness the blueprint for a new reality. Gregg Braden - The Divine Matrix

Tropical Storm Arlene gathers strength as Terry's last minute request via telephone spurs a grocery store visit. His car is broken down again. Power struggles between Terry and Momma make me feel very uncomfortable upon arriving to ferry them to the market. Information from the *Celestine Prophecy* fills my head while remembering we live in a universe of dynamic energy.

Terry continues to steal energy by the way he speaks to Momma and now to me. He has cut himself off from the energy of Source. The resulting weakness and insecurity leads him to seek attention constantly. Palpable energy pours from Momma to him, as he successfully manipulates her, while we drive.
It's time to admit that I no longer chose to play the families energy stealing game. We share the same energy stealing methods so it's now my task to remind him of unconscious actions. Learning of our own control drama (intimidation, interrogation, aloofness, or poor me) frees us to become conscious of our actions. If we are aware, we can find a

higher meaning for our lives. Gray clouds fill the sky as I explain the way humans get power from one another. Terry turns his head away upon hearing that he uses the "poor me" and "intimidation" power plays.

"There's a fifth way to get power," I calmly note. "It's the one I now employ at three o'clock in the morning while connecting with the Force within us all."

He seems to take it well.

Rain flows from the skies as I charge groceries to my trusty Visa card before heading out to get the car. Daniel's voice fills my brain when I pull the car up to the store entrance to pick up Terry and Momma. Daniel does not think Terry is wet enough. He jokingly tells me to lock Terry out of the car after he loads groceries in the trunk. Memories of many fun-filled times prompt a wide smile.

Ignoring Daniel's request, I tell Terry about it as he enters the car.

"That's okay," Terry says abruptly. "Daniel has been messing with me for the past couple days by turning on my stereo at 7:30 AM and playing some kind of rock music. It plays for a minute or so and then turns off."

Thoughts of limitation go by the wayside while driving away from Terry and Momma. "Life is suffering; it's a process and it's okay," I tell myself, remembering Daniel's treasured words with a smile.

"Life is good. The world is good. Enjoy yourself."

I'm hanging in there just as I tell everyone else to do, counting blessings and knowing it could be much worse than it is.

After a shower in the wee hours of the morning, Daniel guides me outside to say nightly blessings on the back porch. It's dirty and cluttered with James' stuff but the rug looks freshly vacuumed. Several coolers and containers catch rain as it seeps through the porch roof.

I place a big, clean rag upon the rocking chair before sitting. Scents of jasmine fill the night air. It feels good to sit silently staring at the dark water fountain. A kitten comes onto the porch through the cat door. Wiley does not notice me at first but soon begins to sniff at my left foot and toes. She looks up and sits there on her haunches as our eyes meet. The usually wary kitten remains motionless as blessings quietly fill the air.

A firefly sort of glow appears in the wet grass beyond the screened-in porch. Whispered thanks and blessings continue while watching the reddish spark. The spark changes to remind me of pure energy, seen in the bathroom. It doesn't turn into the spiral shapes of short strings but constantly changes form.

What a privilege it is to see what my son has evolved into, a form of pure energy! This is the next evolution humans will make once we reach a certain point in our growth. I am delighted and full of love to know that Daniel chose to show me this and that our Creator allowed him to do it.

Wiley scampers around the large room after my blessings end. We then begin to play. She jumps high, when I move my toes, but runs away upon seeing my body in the chair attached to what she thinks is her new play toy. As she dashes to the opening in the screen, I bounce a ball nearby and announce that it's her toy. Daniel says it's bedtime before the reddish sparks disappear.

The ringing doorbell wakes me with a start hours later. After rising several times during the wee hours, to urinate and take medication, I'm still tired. Samuel sits in the living room on my rocking Lazy Boy looking dejected.

"Where's Papa?" I ask.

He averts his eyes from the television to point towards the den and then voices dismay because Mom took his Gameboy away.

"We can do something together," I say while heading towards the coffeemaker.

"Can we play Poke' Man Monopoly?" he asks excitedly.

As we play, Samuel again voices dismay over not being able to say goodbye to Uncle Daniel.

"I don't know what Aunt Joy said but when I tried to go and say goodbye to Daniel at his birthday party, Mommy told me I couldn't," he quietly tells me.

I think about how long he's kept this bit of information to himself and, for the first time, ponder how to react.

"I think Uncle Daniel is always around you," I finally say tenderly, "but perhaps you just can't feel him. Do you want to hear about my new theory of evolution?"

"Be quick about it," Samuel blurts out impatiently.

I ask if he knows about evolution. His previous knowledge makes it easier to explain what I have to say.

"Our next evolution," I announce excitedly, "is to be pure energy. Protons and neutrons that look something like the sparks from a sparkler. All living things emit photons (light) that communicate information."

Samuel looks at me carefully as I continue with my new theory.

"Some of us can see the people that have passed into this form," I tell him excitedly, "and I have seen Uncle Daniel in this way."

Samuel does not seem surprised, or upset, so I begin to point out orb pictures on the wall of family photos.

"These white orbs are also Daniel's spirit," I inform him, pointing to white circles.

Samuel views photos quietly but becomes adamant about not seeing the two pictures of him with orbs. The seed is firmly planted and now he asks me to be quiet. Silence fills the air. We continue the board game while I ponder the things Daniel does to get my attention. Daniel now flushes the toilet in my bathroom.

Ruth and Naomi, who is now unemployed, host a birthday party for Rebecca days later. My video camera captures Daniel's essence. There's only the sound of static for several minutes. I sense him and move the video around the room to see if anything shows up. After eleven minutes, we hear the sound of our voices but the static returns. It goes away after thirteen minutes but returns less than four minutes later when I sense he is gone.

We sit at the table outside while eating to discuss the lawsuit initiated on our father's behalf. The wrongful death suit is moving ahead with Aaron, who continues to live in Michigan, now taking the lead. Conversation quickly turns to a Busch Gardens trip but I only talk of limitations.

"I have limited use of my right side and on Thursday you'll learn that I don't even get disability for it," I tell them with assurance as we play cards. "They will say I can work a job with my left hand."

"Why don't you go for a mental disability," Ruth cheerfully asks.

Guffaws of laughter fill the air.

"Yeah," James agrees, "that would be a lot easier."

I concur, noting that mental agony is part of my three incurable conditions.

"We can come," they all say looking at one another, "and witness your craziness."

The back patio fills again with guffaws of laughter

Rebecca drives me downtown to see the Social Security judge three days later. I'm afraid to drive because my right arm falls asleep while holding the steering wheel. Pecking at the computer is now my way to document life's trials because I cannot grasp a pen to write. The surgeon's report sits among other papers on my lap. His advice from our last visit remains undocumented. Without spinal surgery, I'll be paralyzed in two years.

Fortunately, I was on my way to adopting higher ways of being. Dis-ease seems to worsen as fears surface along with an increase in body aches and pains. Health emergencies can impact us, and the people around us, in many ways. They last until we adopt new ways of being, until we align ourselves. A health crisis forces us to let go of the usual ego-based ways of control, which opens the way for a greater connection to Source.

We have the power to transform our environment but need to seek the quietness necessary to go within and restore inner peace and centeredness. Illness often forces us to take the time we need. The healing of the body in the ascension process requires letting go of all things, even the thoughts we consider our own. Non-attachment to this illusion helps us to overcome it. Fear and doubt disappear as Divine Love flows through us.

A Course In Miracles teaches that healing occurs as we recognize we are parts of the One. Our external universe, internal physiology, and perception directly control the activity of our genes. We can control our genes by challenging thought patterns. Our bodies are learning devices for our minds. They change as we transmute the denser energies of fear, dis-ease, and limitation allowing more room for God to enter.

Although the body makes its own illness, sometimes the illness has a sufficiently strong hold over the mind to render a person temporarily inaccessible to undoing it. Bodywork, using methods such as acupuncture, toning (sound and vibration), and Eye Movement Desensitization and Reprocessing (opening of the crown charka), all work to release physically held fears from the past. The Law of Attraction works in our favor as we raise our vibration. Lower vibrational energies clear away from us for they are no longer comfortable being around us.

Tears fill my eyes as I leave the private courtroom in search of a bathroom. There will be no disability benefits for me because I cannot prove I was unable to work in 1997, the last year I qualified for them. We contemplate options as Rebecca drives me back home. I have successfully decreased the dosage on several medications. Now, I take only eight of thirteen prescribed medications and believe it's due to Michael's treatments. Perhaps the treatments can make this better too. [2]

Health is our natural state of being. Illness and disease are the result of beliefs and the resulting fears that block emotional flow. The soul attracts what it secretly harbors, loves, and fears, but body is the servant of the mind. Our thoughts make the difference between health and disease. People who live in fear of disease are the ones who get it for anxiety quickly demoralizes the body. Cheerful, strong, pure, and happy thoughts build up the body and dissipate ills.

The energy required to repress feelings causes a strain in the body and in the spirit but there's no conflict if you release your feelings. Resistance creates conflict, and causes the energy flow to turn back on itself, but where there's no resistance there's no harm. The original fear we carry deep within is the fear that we are separated from God and are ultimately alone. Understanding that our fears are illusions, and not reality, frees us from the original cause of illness and dis-ease.

We are individualized reflections of the Source, a part of God. If we are unwell, there is always something to forgive. Forgiveness, remembering the truth of who we are, always leads to health and well-being.

:-)

Chapter Fifteen

Love Comes In Many Forms

Love is the law of God. You live that you may learn to love. You love that you may learn to live. No other lesson is required of man. Mikhail Naimy - The Book of Mirdad

Some days I surrender to my "old self," pouring my heart out to fill journals with notes.

"Well I guess I'll just get drunk," I write one night as James attends a fly-fishing club meeting. "It does not seem like I can get any work done, even after taking a Celebrex, for the bad weather still affects me. It's hard to move, even to be, but I manage to say my blessings."

Life worsens for James too as he moves through various trials. I sense it's his time to wakeup but he does not recognize these signs.

"Okay Ma," Daniel reports, "the cat trial is over. I'm taking them now."

One cat repeatedly uses areas where rain leaks onto the floor as a porch litter box. Another disappears after a midnight raccoon raid. The other two leave as well. James is accustomed to confiding in them but covers the cat door to keep them off the screened-in porch. I trust Daniel led them to a good home.

"Someone," I assure myself confidently, "will take them to the vet, watch over, and love them, as we all deserve to be loved."

No one listens to me for they all think I'm crazy. Projection serves as a regular way of communication while I continue to pray for deliverance. I want to get to the Otherside as soon as I am more useful to those who are there instead of here. There does not seem to be an escape route while pondering my current life of anger, frustration, and confusion. Daniel's encouraging words boost spirits.

"I'm so proud of you Mom," he says cheerfully.

Strange things happen once again as I drive to the mid-week church service. The CD player changes songs quickly as selected words from various songs play from his 2005 memorial CD. A motorcycle passes when "I Speed at Night" plays and, as tears well, the song switches. "Remember who we are" fills my brain as the volume rises. The CD player continues to change songs until I move out of the car in the church's parking lot.

"Rough times are ahead," Daniel announces.

He's proud of me for sticking it out and trying to make some sense of it all by attending the Center.

Today's service is unusual for the speaker is unable to attend. One of the newer reverends takes charge to make it a question and answer session. Upon speaking more than others, I'm consoled to know that their pictures also show orbs, and yes, others believe it's spirit communication.

Daniel's essence appears later in the evening after James goes to bed.

"Turn the television off and sit down with me for a bit," he announces softly. "Don't worry Mom. You're going to get a new laptop but things are going to get worse for the family. It would be good if you called Ruth and Rachel to encourage them and offer love and support. Let James be for you've already told him that he has choices and is not stuck taking care of anyone."

Before our time ends, he lets me know that taking Rebecca to the classes at the Center is the best thing I could have done.

"When the time comes," Daniel discloses softly as I sense his arms around me, "she will carry on and help the children."

Things seem to escalate negatively, as James and I fight more, and news of my stolen laptop becomes known. Someone stole it from the shipper after Gateway repaired it. The woman I speak to says they have no idea how it could have disappeared for it's not common for laptops to disappear at DHL.

I regress to use the familiar "poor me" power play while emailing Gateway.

"Please help," I implore. "I'm extremely upset about this for my laptop was being used to make DVD's of my son who passed away so his three-year-old daughter will have memories of him."

Gateway responds with apologies and initiates an investigation, which soon leads to the delivery of a brand new laptop. I'm still a fanatic about backing up personal work to external hard drives but devastated over the loss of Daniel's screensaver. His voice fills my head.

"Consider it a gift Mom."

There's little time to dwell on the imagined loss for it's time to celebrate Terry and Joel's birthday. Joel, Terry's son, will be twenty years old and now lives with him and Momma. Joel is on his way to becoming a professional wrestler. We all fondly remember the Detroit wrestling matches Grandfather took us to as children.

Uncle Daniel, Joel confides while we sit alone at Ruth and Naomi's house, guides him from the Otherside. He smiles upon hearing that Abigail still sees her daddy. The rest of the family continues to voice doubts about my sanity. Everyone tries their best to avoid turmoil when we're together but no one wants to be the subject of pictures. They do not want to hear talk of orbs. As usual, orbs are clear in many pictures and most prominent when someone jokes or laughs.

"This ain't no dog and pony show," Daniel says when I try to capture him on film.

Days later, while taping a PBS special about nuclear war, the den motion detector light turns on and off repeatedly. I've noticed the abnormality before and have taken time to talk with Daniel when it happens. This time I don't because Daniel wants me to turn the television off.

The concept of adding energy to negative events, just by thinking of them, never occurs to me. Even as I write this, I still find myself unconsciously adding energy to news headlines viewed on the Internet. Whatever I focus on and think about becomes my reality. It's only now that I begin to catch myself after, or while doing it, and laugh at my foolishness.

I know changing this illusionary world by what we think is possible for I've done it. However, the more I let go of old habits the fewer friends of like-mind I seem to have. But being around new friends is like heaven, for we think and focus on the same things, making the creation of those things much faster.

Samuel and I play Poke' Man Monopoly a few days later while James works on the broken clothes dryer. It's time for my treatment with Michael before the game ends but I haven't seen him in at least a month so I hurry out the door. My CD player again changes haphazardly from song to song all the way to Michael's office. Daniel lets me know how happy he is that I have the courage to take care of myself now.

A few meaningful words play before the CD player switches to a different song to make up the rest of a sentence. It's oddly comforting, but somewhat frustrating, when I start to sing a song only to have the song change. I feel like such a lucky woman, this time around, and am grateful to sense when Daniel's spirit leaves to visit someone else.

- 162 -

"You know," Michael says, upon learning of my visit with the judge, "I can unblock those channels. Just remember, sometimes it gets worse before it gets better."

Years of Michael's articles on Oriental Medicine increased the trust between us so now I'm confident that he will make a difference. Sick of the "system," I decide to give him a chance.

His treatment uses a combination of Gua Sha (scraping method) and Ba Guan (empty cupping method) now commonly known as Ba Gua Fa. The neurological and vascular decompression technique affects acupuncture points, channels/meridians, and organs. I switch between wincing and smiling as loving hands begin their work. My body soon feels rejuvenated and more alive. There's no doubt that his loving care will help me to become whole again.

:-)

LightworkersLog.com

Chapter Sixteen

Messages to Deliver

*Lives of great men all remind us we can make
our lives sublime, and, departing, leave
behind us footprints on the sands of time.
Henry Wadsworth Longfellow - A Psalm of
Life*

Sometimes I say and do things without knowing why. Daniel
now asks me to call an old friend who distanced himself
before Daniel's transition. Our conversation fills with love
and hope. Today, his friend reports, is a day of celebration,
his tenth year sober from crack. Just like my brother Amos,
Daniel's friend lost much because of addiction, including a
close friendship with Daniel.

"Daniel and I are very proud of you," I sincerely
announce, now knowing it's why Daniel asked me to contact
him. It makes me very happy to repeat other things Daniel
wants to say. What a blessing to know that, from time to
time, I'm helping the spirit known as my last-born son to tie
up loose ends!

One more task warrants attention before bedtime. I
log onto Daniel's new electronic news list to send a heartfelt
message.

"I just want to thank you all for being a part of
Daniel's life," I write, with a huge smile. "He learned a lot in
his life and taught a lot too. He taught me to believe in
myself. It was a hard lesson for us both. He taught me that
fear is just a stopgap for people who do not want to learn.

And he taught me that eternal love overcomes all. Peace, Love, Harmony, Blessings."

Soul group members surround me while blessings flow forth at three o'clock in the morning. There's no sparkle light so I figure Daniel is doing good elsewhere. As usual, I rise frequently to use the bathroom and take medication. Now I sleep only on my back, with a pillow under my thighs and a comforter rolled up under lower legs. Any other position causes the right side of my body to go numb.

James wakes me at 9:00 AM as he loudly packs things for a weekend outing with the fishing club. Two uninterrupted hours of sleep follow his departure ninety minutes later. The day unfolds as I tape world news programs while reading local newspapers. Hints of upcoming chaos make it important to save news items for grandchildren to review after my physical death. They'll be wondering what happened to this earth and how it all came about.

The desktop computer makes it difficult to work. Several expensive, trusted, software programs magically disappear. *Norton System Works 2005*, "Common Client Program" accesses the Internet, and then removes them as I view email online. Another computer error tells me to reinstall visual basic. Telephone answering software is gone and it's hard to reinstall *Jaws PDF Maker*. The computer shuts down when I try to reinstall it using the registered license number. Thoughts of reformatting hard drives fill me with the fear of losing data.

Constant error messages increase anxiety. The body's right side numbs when I type too long making my right arm useless. I mentally plan more visits with Michael to release blockages by using Eastern medicine instead of surgery. The need for a nap is strong, after struggling with the computer for hours. But I must beg a pesky mosquito, three times, to leave before it finally goes.

Daniel words wake me.

"No one else can understand the way I am, and be with you."

"Not even Abigail," I think, opening both eyes and wiping a tear away.

An incessant mosquito buzzes around my head. Mosquitoes pester me whenever Daniel thinks I should rise.

"At least," I think with relief, "they have replaced the palmetto bug."

Music continues to play a big role in my life. I now listen to "Our Lives Are Shaped by What We Live" by Odyssey. It causes me to think about changing timeworn habits again so I email the DJ who led me to the song to thank him.

"Music is a wonderful, intangible force, which has immense powers, and hopefully some of it can see you though," Cosmo Baker writes back in an email. "Brighter days are ahead."

I'm looking forward to those brighter days for everyone in my family says, "Nana is crazy." The weekly email update from Religious Science Fort Lauderdale seems heaven sent for it helps me to stay positive. Treatments within it open a whole new world of consciousness. The thought of accepting myself, as the embodiment of wholeness, excites me. I so look forward to taking more classes.

My Divine Purpose, chosen before birth, is to help others realize this is a dream of our own making that can change to our liking. This Divine Purpose is truly my soul's gift to God, which enriches the greatness of Source and moves me one-step closer to our true Home.

Since Daniel's transition I have literally let go of relationships, jobs, my home, possessions, and other things, and as a result have taken back my God-given power to support a new, and much better, way of BEing. It was not easy. But the life I live now supports a higher level of consciousness and is much better than my old life of limitation. I have created my own heaven on earth, paving the way for others to follow.

Email holds "Democracy Now" headlines for July and political petitions to sign. They come amid personal, spiritual, and business emails asking for advice on various issues related to hiv/aids. I sign the petitions first.

To-do lists and reminders, taped to the large, brown, computer desk, hold messages from Daniel along with newsletter publication dates. Daniel's voice again rings inside my brain.

"Respect James, build his confidence and cook for him again."

The task goes on my list that ends with "decrease medications" and "deliver new memorial CDs to Daniels friends."

Vulgar expletives fill my ears upon leaving the serenity of my workroom. Trust, held for years, fades quickly as confusion increases. When I cook dinner, and leave food for James, it usually remains in the refrigerator until I throw it away. Yet, glimmers of hope surface when Daniel informs me James will soon get a job. The thought is welcome for things seem way beyond control.

Everyone see things differently based on beliefs. Looking to that time, it now makes sense that my ego attacked me, through James, for everything is just a projection of my own mind. A Course In Miracles notes, projection is confusion in motivation making trust impossible. The ego is the physical embodiment of its fundamental wish to replace God. That wish seems to surround the mind with a body, keeping it separate and alone; unable to reach other minds except through the body it was made to imprison. To recognize the light of truth within is to recognize ourselves, as we are in our natural state, without a body.

The more I tried to rid myself of ego, the more it raised its ugly head to fight back. James served as just one of a variety of methods to help me. If I had reacted to vulgar expletives with love, instead of meeting them with more projection, my path would have changed. I would most likely be doing my work under different circumstances. Life is just the way I dream it. Illusions of duality spurred me forward to change myself and move towards my true work.

After more than half a century, I'm finally beginning to believe that everyone, and everything, in my dream world is a part of me, all offering another opportunity to recognize the truth. I am a part of God who wrongly thinks it separated from the whole. The ego in this body is just as finite as the body. Only my connection to Source is infinite and real.

Confusion spills over into other areas of life. Momma's doctor visits increase, now sandwiched between monthly trips to the diner. After one visit, I carefully explain to Terry that Momma can no longer eat certain foods because of many medical conditions. She's happily munching on foods forbidden by doctors when I return to take her to the park the following week.

"I got sick from the restaurant food," Momma tells me in her defense between hearty chews, "and the soup you made for us made me sick too."

Terry offers a triumphant look as he nods his head vigorously in agreement.

We are in an ego power struggle once again. This time, instead of reacting with anger and trying to convince them, I chose not to join the game. My plan, to stop taking charge of Momma's medical care, begins, despite documents that legally designate me as her medical decision maker.

It's time to escalate plans to stop unconscious energy stealing by removing myself from its many forms. My nervous voice breaks into a high-pitched, quiet squeal.

"I can't," I say looking down at Momma with tender resignation, "I can't do this anymore. I have to let you go. Terry will take you to the doctors from now on."

A glimmer of hope sparks the thought that Terry will follow doctor's orders when he's the one who speaks with her many doctors.

I must step away and let destiny take its course. It's best to give up on close-minded, negative people, for it seems impossible to deal with them without causing more traumas. Now I will use my resources on people who love themselves and know the difference between Truth and lies.

It's a tough decision to make. I have always been the leader, the one who helps family wade through medical complications. Yet, something propels me forward, to change, even knowing the decision might result in detrimental circumstances. Intuition says, it's the right thing to do. The karma between Momma and I is complete.

Momma happily nods her head as she speaks.

"Terry doesn't make me do what the doctor says."

Her small brown eyes sparkle with glee as she continues to state her opinion.

"That doctor doesn't know what he's talking about anyway."

My arms slowly wrap around her after she gets up from the kitchen table.

"I love you Momma," I say, stunned by the revelation of her statement, "but I just can't do this any more."

After another tight hug, I am out the door and on my way home.

The Fourth of July presents another opportunity for us to gather at Ruth and Naomi's house. In the wee hours of the morning, I again ask to pass quietly into the night. It is

Independence Day, isn't it? Daniel's voice permeates my mind.

"No Mom, it's not your time. Things will improve, hang on."

I rise, much later than usual, to send an email to his website's list subscribers.

"Daniel always enjoyed the Fourth of July," I write smiling with many memories of setting off, and watching, fireworks together. "He liked to be with family and friends, to light the fireworks, to throw the popping snaps and to trick everyone with the direction of his firecrackers. He loved the bottle rockets and M-80's and the swirling bursts of colored light as they either moved on the ground or soared into the night sky.

"This year when you celebrate the Fourth of July, remember his love for the fun of life, his joy of friends, and family. Most importantly, know that when you light that sparkler, Daniel will be on its tip showing you how our energy flows out into the world. Have fun, enjoy friends, and family, and remember our lives are truly shaped by what we love."

The elation in the core of my heart is hard to describe while feeling Daniel's presence behind me stroking my hair.

James and I seem caught, in a spiral of negativity, making me happy to dress quickly and leave the house in my own car. My family cannot help but remember the many years Daniel herded us to the best fireworks in town, off of Fort Lauderdale's beach. And I know James feels his loss even if he remains silent.

James' gallant effort, to entertain everyone after the sun sets with a fireworks display, makes me wish I'd brought the video camera. My digital camera picks up many orbs as he stands alone in the middle of the street. Orbs cover Ruth's face as she and Naomi walk outside. They are too numerous to count as James sets off bottle rockets, M-80's, and other fireworks.

A smiley face, which seems etched into the window frame, appears out of nowhere as I sit in the bathroom later in the wee hours of the morning. Daniel's voice fills my head.

"You have to let me go Mom," he says brightly.

An image of his smiling face appears and for a fleeting second his eyes seem to sparkle.

"You have to let me go Mom," he says gently again.

"I thought I did let you go Daniel," I answer softly to the air.

"Mom, you have to stop counting on me so much," he replies.

Tears form as I realize the truth of his words.

"Alright," I tell him silently while wiping them away. "I'll let you finish your other work."

"It will be okay Mom," he says as I move on to put the pictures from my camera onto the computer. "You'll see. It will be okay."

My favorite picture shows me sitting on the cars hood, smiling while watching fireworks. James and Samuel stand in the background while grabbing fireworks piled on top of the car. Three white orbs lie to my left. Another tiny red orb rests inside the car in front of the headrest.

"Life is good," I allow myself to think.

The mid-week service boosts morale with uplifting Science of Mind messages. I so enjoy group meditations surrounded by people who appear to think as I do.

Hannah is back in the hospital, for the last time. She makes her transition on July 15, 2005. I learn about it in an unusual way, two days later, while repeating blessings at 3:00 AM. A clear flow of odd words effortlessly enters my head after saying the usual prayer. I quickly associate them with Hannah.

"Hannah passed slowly, into the light, ready to start life anew. Everyone watched her, as she slowly went, waiting to greet her with love."

"Wait, wait," I think excitedly, "am I supposed to remember these words?"

The words continue. If I'm to remember them, I will.

"No one was noisy. No one was loud. They respected her wisdom and knew. Do not be saddened. Don't be afraid. Always be open. Fill your heart with love and know she is happy again. Amen. May God fill your heart with Light and Love."

The key word for me is Amen. Hannah used that word to end a poem she wrote for Abigail about her daddy the year before. Clearly, these words are for Hannah's children. I am to be the messenger. The words repeat in my head as I quickly make my way into the office to get a pen and paper. I write them down, knowing there will be an opportunity to give them to their intended recipients.

In the morning, I watch the video of our trip to Florida's west coast and decide to make a slide show of Hannah. It takes several hours to extract pictures from the video and set them to music. I plan on giving the video and Hannah's message to her children.

Rebecca telephones two days later to tell me Hannah passed away, in the middle of the night, alone in her hospital bed. We attend Hannah's memorial together but she's skeptical when I tell her about the message.

"I don't think this is the time for your nonsense Mother," she states with a smirk.

I'm determined to deliver the message. The opportunity arises when we go to Lydia's home after the service. Everyone is surprised to see the slide show play on Lydia's DVD player as I quickly turn to Hannah's children.

"Your mother," I say excitedly looking from Lydia to her brother, "wanted you to know she didn't suffer. She wants you to know she is happy on the Otherside."

Their stares portray disbelief and apprehension as they ponder how to react. It's clear they do not believe "Crazy Nana."

"It doesn't matter to me what you think for my job is done," I announce, handing them copies of the message, before walking to the patio in search of my drink.

It's almost time for our cross-country drive from Florida to Michigan when I see my doctor days later. The thought of living without the prescription drugs he prescribes is still a foreign concept. Some medications seem to work better than others do but several require another prescription for side effects. Even though I take the thyroid pills, religiously, there still seems to be tiredness. The doctor calls later to tell me blood tests show a further decline in body thyroid levels.

The thyroid controls the whole endocrinal system, Spaulding reminds us in Volume Six of Life and Teaching of The Masters of the Far East, *bringing it into harmony with other glands and the glandular system. This development makes it possible for our spiritual faculties to be "brought into conscious use." The spiritual faculties are "brought out and correlated" through the stimulation of the thyroid. My soul chose to experience this condition, knowing it would "handicap" the body, making it more difficult to be spiritually aware.*

:-)

Chapter Seventeen

On the Road Again

Part of your life's purpose is to move beyond lack, scarcity, and limitation. Although the experience of lack can be valuable in terms of learning certain lessons at certain times, it is not required as a learning tool. Poverty, lack, and scarcity stem directly from your primal fear, the fear that you are separated from your Source. You are the source of your own abundance. Through uncovering your beliefs concerning lack and scarcity, you can begin to create abundance in every area of your life, including financial freedom. www.uplifthumanity.info.

A job opportunity for James arrives days before my scheduled visit with family back home. Projection, our common tool of communication, escalates as we struggle to make sense of our lives. Negative energy fills the house making me happy to leave.

"Remember our talk last December?" I cautiously ask looking into angry brown eyes. "Neither of us is pleased with our lives right now. I'm on a new path, which will not change, and plan to complete my destiny by taking classes to increase spirituality. You now have a week alone to decide what to do about your life and our marriage."

James stares at me in disbelief.

"I've always blazed my own path, to open the way for others, and have always known subconsciously that this is my destiny. There have been many clues along the way to show me what I must do."

I sense it's time for us to part, to attend to our own needs and stop depending on one another. We both need people to support our every endeavor with love, acceptance, belonging, and a feeling of harmony and peace. Neither of us have that now. "At least Daniel supports me," I silently affirm.

"Have you made a budget for your trip?" James inquires insistently, raising eyebrows to look at his crazed wife.

James doesn't know about the money tucked away from my cashed in tax-deferred annuity. He now manages household finances and is very determined to learn how I'll pay my way to Michigan. I'm secretly glad for it's a step toward independence. Over his ten-month course of unemployment, I have slowly limited household chores, knowing it's time for him to learn how to shop, cook, and clean.

Money is just something to keep a roof over our head and food in our belly. I have never needed, or wanted, glamorous extras. But vacations and conferences are nice when you can afford them. Thoughts of returning to Las Vegas, instead of Michigan, accompany my reply.

"It won't cost you a dime."

"Remember you said that," he retorts before returning to his den.

Daniel's essence changes songs on the CD player to boost morale days later.

"I thought I had to let you go," I announce filled with joy.

"That's the trick Mom," he replies happily. "I'm still able to be with you because you let me go."

I smile, not really understanding, but glad he's back before our Michigan road trip.

Rebecca and I leave before midnight to join Momma, Ruth, Naomi, and Samuel in Michigan. My right side still numbs, impairing driving skills, so Rebecca plans to drive. The skies turn cloudy before we enter Georgia. After many years of traveling between Florida and Michigan, I no longer have the desire to stop only for gas and bathrooms. We're glad to reach our halfway hotel stop on I-75.

The fifteen-hour break does us a world of good. We're raring to reach our goal and back on the road at two o'clock in the morning. Rebecca speeds down the highway as I videotape. My usual obnoxious self pops out, hoping to catch physical evidence of Daniel's essence. The drive is dream-like for we paid attention to weather reports. We travel between raindrops while other drivers spend hours stuck in storms. Rebecca begins to tire so I talk her into letting me drive. I keep the car at a steady 70 mph listening to Daniel's spirit. At one point, while driving through dense fog, we cannot see two feet ahead.

"It's okay," Daniel announces. "You are protected and no harm will come to you. Stay alert and you will be okay."

I have always loved to travel by car. There's a certain kind of beauty traveling in the dead of night through mountainous areas. A scared Rebecca insists she cannot sleep while I drive and tries to take control of the driving again. I adamantly tell her we will be okay. After minutes of arguing, she falls promptly asleep. Positive energy fills the car as I happily sing along to my favorite music.

Rebecca takes the wheel when we near Ohio. I videotape the sunset for Samuel. The beauty of sunrise and sunset remains one of our favorite discussions. And in all of them, I've maintained that sunset is best. The truth is, I'm rarely up before nine or ten o'clock in the morning.

We're elated to enter Michigan the next afternoon and thrilled to be home as "Miss You" by the Rolling Stones plays on the CD player.

"Won't you come home, come home," Mick Jagger sings.

"We're home, we're home," we sing in unison.

"Isn't it funny how when we cross the state line we feel we're at home," says Rebecca with a quick glance my way. "And when we go back to Florida we feel the same?"

"We can live anywhere and be happy."

"Yes, we're bicoastal," Rebecca replies gleefully.

Daniel's essence fills the air before several bikers pass the car. The video camera begins to malfunction, and then shows colored lights, as we drive happily along the highway singing.

The world has changed immensely since our big move to Florida twenty-three years ago. Now the AAA map lists Gregory, Stockbridge, and Pinckney. The words "get down on it" repeatedly play alerting us to Daniel's constant presence. Rebecca turns the CD player off.

"I know he's with us Mom but I just can't take the repetition," she announces, with an anxious grin while turning the radio on.

Solid static replaces usual video sounds when we arrive at the two-bedroom cottage. It could be due to Daniel's essence, Naomi's parents, who owned the cottage before their death there, or all three. Smells of mold, hostility, and a closed-in feeling greet me as we enter. After two days of driving and interrupting my daily schedule, I yearn for some kind of normalcy. Thankfully, Sara invites me sleep at her house several miles away. Her guest room seems much more desirable than sharing cluttered space within the small, overcrowded cottage.

Thoughts of limitation plague me throughout the day. Sara arrives for dinner and we're soon on our way. The balance I seek lies in the nurturing atmosphere of Sara's home. The guest room is very comfortable with the same homey touches my friends' homes feature.

Sara goes to work in the morning leaving me to relax in the quiet house. Copies of Daniel's memorial CD, made on the new laptop for Michigan family members, sit in my travel bag when we return to the red, wooden cottage for dinner.

The atmosphere in the cottage is rife with power games that I do not want to play anymore. I watch the power struggles of "interrogation," "poor me" and "intimidation," amused, and glad to have a bottle of Myer's rum. The video camera turns itself off as I try to video the show. By now, it's typical for my electronic equipment to malfunction. I'm not supposed to tape dysfunction so it doesn't bother me.

Rebecca picks me up in the morning for a walk down to the water's edge. The sky is clear and the air quite refreshing. Small fish jump by the public floating dock and the beauty amazes me.

"There's not much that beats Michigan in the summer," I say sincerely.

My view of the world will enlarge greatly in coming years as I travel more and realize there are many beautiful places on earth.

A large fly on the bathroom floor catches my attention the next morning. I now silently communicate with creatures. Numerous palmetto bugs have allowed me to pick them up and carry them outside to freedom. Now I sit on the toilet wondering if I'm learning another lesson or, just stark, raving insane.

Sara is remodeling her bathroom and most of the old wallpaper is off the walls. It looks like a piece of the floor molding separated from the wall as she removed the wallpaper. The fly drops out from behind the hanging floor molding before my eyes. Much to my amazement, it begins to show it's aura as I speak. A field of white mist emanates from the fly's small body. The white mist surrounds the fly and moves when it does.

Intuition prompts me to be open-minded and receptive to thoughts. I'm to sit and observe, and do so from my toilet perch for about fifteen minutes, watching the fly's aura in wonder. This fly is transitioning to the Otherside just like the one seen in the blue bathtub at home. A bright, white light encircles the fly. It moves slowly around it, wobbling from side to side. Sometimes the light covers the whole fly.

Feeling cramped, I move down to the floor beside the fly and watch it for another fifteen to twenty minutes, as it seems to die. The transition is similar to that of the first fly. But this one is taking longer. The fly is dead when the white light disappears. The energy around the fly then changes as a yellow-gold, scattered mist surrounds the area. This energy field disappears after a minute or so. A smaller fly suddenly appears about six inches away from the big fly. The tiny creature flies past my face and buzzes around for a short while. The mist is gone when I turn to look back at the big fly. The tiny fly disappears as well.

Sometimes confusing messages fill my brain and I'm unsure of who they are for. Now I recall a message received during nightly blessings.

"Come on Home you old spice drop."

I also recall the words, "cinnamon bun" and sense it's my duty to relay the message.

One must be discerning when it comes to hearing messages from the Otherside. Over the course of the last five years, since Daniel's transition, it has become clear to me that certain things occur simultaneously upon hearing messages of Truth. I can actually sense a certain vibration around my body along with a great feeling of heat that starts in the middle of my chest. The messages come in different forms, and always empower me, which is another sign that they are "true."

Wondering if the message is for Aunt Lois, who we will soon visit, I ponder how to relay it without the family locking me up for mental illness. Everyone thinks I'm crazy, perhaps with Momma's schizophrenia. The message might also be for Momma, or James' mother Martha. Martha has been in a nursing home for several years, very different from her usual self, since Zephaniah's passing years before.

I suddenly remember the rest of the message.

"All is forgiven. Everything is okay. We all have lessons to learn and there is nothing more you can do here."

Turning my attention back to the fly, I bless it with light and love before leaving to see my best friend Esther who lives an hour away. Her house holds the energy of love and it shows in every room. The well-kept, spotless house holds pictures of happy smiling faces and lots of little touches that make a house a home. We are soon like two just rescued castaways, continually interrupting one another. It's clear we're "on the same page" even after years of geographical separation.

Although she believes that our Creator is Jesus Christ, she is open to my beliefs that we have one Creator, referred to by many different names, through many different religions. Esther jumps up and gives me a hearty hug when I disclose plans to start Science of Mind classes, which could lead me to become a reverend.

We discuss sensing when people will transition from human form. Esther is a nurse with more than twenty years experience. She stood by when many people made their transition. She now reports there's a sense of their passing but she does not see anything unusual. Like me, she has given several people permission to pass from their current state. I remain silent about the spirits seen passing from the flies, or the pure energy, or my soul group, occasionally seen in pure energy form during nightly blessings.

Our deliciously rewarding visit restores me with a feeling of spiritual closeness. Her youngest daughter takes a picture of us accompanied by an orb, hovering by their small tiffany lamp. Before leaving, I tell Esther that upon my transition I will contact her and use a certain meaningful term. Laugher fills the room as I whisper the term. It reminds us of an early AM grocery store trip, taken when we were young and reckless. The ride back to Sara's is effortless for I'm happy to have seen my friend.

Family visits rule the week as Ruth drives us to Detroit the next afternoon. Struggling to cope, she's jobless after seventeen years and on Zoloft. My video starts with static, blocking all sound, as we drive the ninety minutes into town. A big orb sits by Rebecca, as she lies on the back seat of the van, trying to rest, while Samuel and I continually harass her.

Samuel proudly wears his "Nintendo Rehabilitation Clinic" shirt. I like it much better than the shirt that says, "Hello my name is Go Away." Every time we joke and laugh Daniel's presence is noticeable on the video, as the sound of static increases. The static again blocks out all sound when we arrive at Aaron and Matilda's house.

Aaron and Matilda's house is different from the year before because Aaron painted the inside with lighter colors. I smile at the smiley faces on the refrigerator but feel a sense of loss in, and around, the house. The grave stone business is still across the street and Matilda remains in a wheelchair.

Aaron now knows the meaning of unconditional love as he caters to Matilda. Both he and Matilda say Daddy talks to them all the time. Daddy's ashes are still in their closet for they're not ready to let him go, yet. I'm the only one who seems to understand. Several familiar, see-through, whitish orbs grace our pictures. The visit is short for we do not want to keep Aunt Lois waiting.

Aunt Lois is still unable to talk because of her last stroke. We prefer to visit her with a family translator but do not know how long they can stay to be with her. Lois is visibly happy to see us, jumping up and down in her doorway, waiting for us to get out of the van. A white and black blouse hangs loosely from her now thin frame. She welcomes us warmly with a wide smile, several grunts, and hugs.

Our visit offers opportunities to hone the traits of patience, and tolerance, as we try to communicate effectively. The static is deafening when I put the video camera on top of the television while recording. Lois' household experienced three transitions, over the past ten years, so it's impossible to determine what energy affects the recorder. We excitedly talk for more than thirty minutes. The video camera sits on top of a working television but records only the sound of static.

Samuel demands that we all pose for photos before leaving to play outside with the boys. I sense Daniel's spirit at work as Samuel takes several nice pictures. My always-malfunctioning camera does not act up this time.

An unexplainable video camera phenomenon occurs, three times, over the next thirty minutes. The word "VOLUME" comes up on the video screen as if someone is physically checking the volume. Amid the sound of static, it first displays the sound level, set to above mid-point. Several minutes later, it again looks as if someone is checking the volume, and now, turning it from zero all the way up. Our chatter breaks through amid slight static and the sound of the television.

While Ruth and I sit next to one another on the couch, "VOLUME" again shows up on the video screen. Now it looks like someone is pressing the volume levels down to zero. The conversation records perfectly even with the volume level set on zero.

I think this physical display occurred so I would know spirits do things like this with our electronics. Orbs are also in many pictures. Several orbs, including a small, denser, white one, sit above our cousin's head as she holds her baby up for us to see.

Rebecca, Samuel, and I drive through Chelsea the following day. It reminders us that nothing stays the same. The small sleepy town turned into a trendy tourist attraction after actor Jeff Daniels opened his restaurant there. Musicians and singers line up along narrow streets as in San Francisco, New York, and other places. My video camera records with minimal static, allowing us to hear, as we cruise down the street.

The next day Ruth and the rest of the family pick me up from Sara's house to go to hell, Hell Michigan. The town is only a block long and consists of two small buildings and a place to fish. Ruth and I remember, Daddy used to take us fishing there when we were small. Hell changed just like the rest of the small cities around it. A tall devil mannequin, whose head turns as we walk by, greets us at the door of the town's shop.

We browse through Halloween things while I wonder why they're there. Souvenirs of hell are sparse and I know it will be my last visit. Fond memories, of fishing at the dam and eating a meal at the old cafeteria, surface as we enter the other building to find a small grocer. Momma makes the trip worthwhile

when she allows us to take her picture. She stands behind the short devil picture, propped up on the lawn, to stick her head through the hole. "I'm a LiL' Devil in Hell!" the lettering states as she defiantly thrusts her tongue out.

Ruth hands me an envelope of cash when we reach Sara's house.

"This is for the cabin you reserved for me," she says with a smile. "I know you need the cash."

I always reserve the family cabins, eleven months before vacation, by putting the cost on my charge card. This is the first year that Ruth repays me for her cabin many months in advance. The money is more than enough to pay for the expenses of this trip so I hide a one-hundred bill in Sara's dresser. I know she will be thrilled to find it. Two-hundred dollars goes into an envelope for James to pay for the gas charges on my credit card. I decide to hang on to the rest as long as I can.

Rebecca, Samuel, and I leave for home the next night at 9:00 PM. My daughter drives, singing like an angel, as I video the dark night. The video camera acts up for miles, pausing for no reason, amid the sound of static and her singing. Rebecca attributes the malfunction to the changes in altitude as we drive through the mountains. I know otherwise, Daniel is with us, assuring our safety.

:-)

Chapter Eighteen

A New Life

Do not be afraid of terror. Do not react
violently to violence. Do not feel pain about
pain. By doing so, you perpetuate what you
are seeking to avoid. When you pass
judgment, on such things, you are limiting
God's reality to your human understanding.
You can only bless, and pray, and open, and
trust. Who you are is a necessary step to being
who you will be, and so it goes through
eternity. Pat Rodegast - Emmanuel's Book

Thoughts of Heaven arise during the mid-week service for people of like mind surround me. Innovative ideas come easily to make Daniel's website better, while inspired (in-spirit) during meditation. Intuition offers useful advice. Words flow easily, from head to hand, as I type them into my desktop computer. It doesn't take long to complete the new Web page. People will take the time to read "Suggestions for the 21st Century" and that is all that matters. [3]

The wall calendar notes numerous doctor and dentist appointments, amid publication deadlines, mid-week services, calls to Rachel, and reminders to mail Abigail's greeting cards. After uploading the Web page, I leave to see my usual doctor about prescription refills.

James is anxious upon my return. His new job starts next week. He shows me a picture of Abigail standing proudly with a wide smile on her pretty, heart-shaped face in front of a large, green chalkboard. The chalkboard holds a handwritten list of the alphabet. Numerous dots of white light energize the air around her. I smile thinking she senses her daddy nearby.

The second book about Daniel's life, from age three to four, is almost complete. I plan to give it to Abigail on her fourth birthday. Designing the book allows me to grieve in a different way, unaware that ego clings to his memory, by pointing out how special he was.

James' sour mood escalates as I download email determined to avoid contact with him. Email offers a multitude of spam. There are 8,000 messages to weed through for I have not checked it in a week. It's a small wonder that my eye catches a very timely message. In *Eight Mindful Steps to Happiness,* Bhante Henepola Gunaratana notes:

"It is very important that you do not compare your actions to your partner's or judge your partner's behavior as unskillful. Rather, focus on your own actions and take responsibility for them. Recall those times when you looked into your partner's eyes and saw the pain you caused this person you love to suffer. If you can admit your own faults, if you can see how hurtful your actions were and tap into a sense of concern for your partner's well-being, then compassion and loving-friendliness will flow."

"What good advice," I tell myself, without considering that James may have missed me during our time apart.

Another email, from my publisher friend, announces the demise of a drug interactions book we co-authored. All the books sold but she will not publish more. They are not as popular as the other books and, therefore, not cost-effective to publish. I will miss the steady monthly income even though the amount is very small. The changes in my life continue to surprise me even though I know life is a lesson.

"Opportunities will find you," I hear inside my head. "Just be aware of them when they do and choose wisely."

James sneaks a quick look into the door of my home office.

"By the way," he announces quietly, "Rachel invited the family to visit on Saturday. You should call her."

I forget everything else to check with the family before telephoning Rachel.

Rebecca, Samuel, Terry, and I make the ninety minute drive to see Rachel and Abigail in the early afternoon. They meet us at the door looking tanned and healthy. Abigail looks more like her mother now. The gold necklace Daniel bought on the Valentine's Day before his transition fits her perfectly.

"Want to see my pony?" Abigail asks as she shows us her cats.

It's clear the animals keep them busy. Rachel and Abigail feed the pony, chickens, cats, the dog, and fish every morning and night. Memorial posters catch my attention as we head outside.

"It's time," I say softly with a hand on Rachel's arm, "to move on and let go."

She looks at me with a smile.

"Are you ready to go into the pool? I just put the new liner in and filled it with water."

It's important for me to stay dry because ointment covers a mysterious rash. I videotape as the family swims in the above ground, four-foot deep pool.

Rachel amazes me, throughout the day, as she teaches Abigail how to swim and leads her on the little, brown pony. Abigail loves to ride and Rachel loves seeing her do it. She rides in horse shows wearing long, black boots and tan riding pants. A tiny, blue helmet sits on her head while she proudly gallops around the neighborhood as we walk nearby.

Later in the afternoon, Abigail puts on my large, straw sunhat and looks up with pretty, blue eyes. Something about her gaze tells me she's clairvoyant. The feelings I hold inside fill her mind as she carefully pulls long strings, on each side of the hat, into small hands.

The visit is thoroughly enjoyable. We leave promising to return whenever Rachel has time to fit us into their busy schedule.

Things would be very different now if I realized then the power of words. It's interesting to watch the video of our time together. Many pictures hold orbs in places where they are easy to see, including one of Abigail with her dog Bear, the pony in its stall with Rachel holding the reins, and Samuel and Abigail.

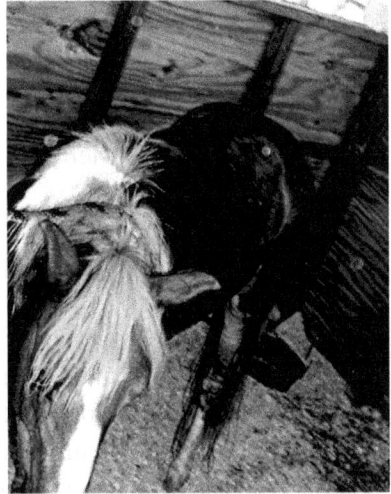

Days later, I volunteer as hospitality person after the mid-week service. It does not seem odd that the scheduled volunteer cannot attend Rev. Ernie Chu's new, three-week class on Soul Currency. The class shares ways to convert spiritual wealth into material abundance.

Rebecca telephones with news of a job interview to feed the fires of hope. I smile remembering Daniel's message of three weeks ago. He said both she and James would soon have new jobs. Intuition tells me her job is a gift and it's where she's meant to be. I know Daniel has somehow made it possible for her to have this desk job. It will be much easier than many years of sixty-hour weeks as a general restaurant manager.

Changes are opportunities for growth and struggles can be great lessons. My plan to take classes at the Center and help others, through the tough times we seem to be having, is underway. I'm grateful to continue to learn because of Daniel's guidance as I cut all old volunteer ties. It's easy to remove myself from unpaid positions that no longer fit changing energy.

Messages from Beliefnet seem to come just when I need them. Another quote from Bhante Henepola Gunaratana catches my attention after a long, heated discussion with James.

"Skillful speech not only means that we pay attention to the words we speak and to their tone but also requires that our words reflect compassion and concern for others and that they help and heal, rather than wound and destroy."

Things happen the way they need to. It's all about human evolution and spiritual growth. People with struggles and hardships learn the most, if we allow ourselves. Support for my business disappears from every avenue. I close the checking account because of new monthly fees.

"There's opportunity to learn a lesson in everything that happens to us," I announce to one of Daniel's dearest friends via email. "Yet, it is easier to ignore the opportunities like I have for too many years, no more, for I'm finally aware of the need, and desire, to grow spiritually."

The 2005 Atlantic hurricane season was the most active Atlantic hurricane season to date, in recorded history, with twenty-eight storms and fifteen hurricanes. We were luckier than most in South Florida. Hurricane Dennis made landfall far away from us, on the Florida Panhandle, a day after the Fourth of July. Hurricane Katrina hit several states in late August, propelling many people into the throes of awakening as they waded though very personal losses of homes, family, and friends.

Tropical Depression Twelve forms over the Bahamas on August 23, 2005. It sits off our coast and churns over open waters. The first area rains, and wind, start early the next morning with the approach of newly named Tropical Storm Katrina. Katrina becomes a hurricane, a mere two hours before making landfall several miles away, with gusts up to 98 miles an hour, on Ruth's fifty-third birthday.

Ruth is still in Michigan, more than 1,000 miles away, when the depression begins to form. James and Rebecca secure her home while I video the beginning of the storm. James then clears a few things from our yard while I secure house windows. A box on the back porch offers sanctuary for stray cats. James gasses up his van but forgets to fill the gas container for the new generator.

After several hours of intermittent wind and rain, intuition tells me the storm will soon knock out our power. It will reach Category 2 status but the timing is uncertain. Someone else will bear the brunt of the storm.

The electricity goes out several times. It stays out after the fourth time when a power line falls in the back yard. I remain calm for the toy Furby says "Okay, luck," new words no one trained it to say. James shakes his head in disbelief when I tell him Furby said not to worry for we are lucky. He begins to set up the new generator outside so we can keep the refrigerator and television on.

The atmosphere has become increasingly hostile. We barely speak to one another, when alone, and now I'm concerned about the effects of our Virginia Woof episodes in front of Rebecca. She reverts to her usual codependency mode when the insults start. I often find myself in the core of the storm even though I'm adamant about not participating in power plays. My concern is well founded when Rebecca calls from her cell phone.

"Have a beer ready for me Mom," she says sounding worn-out. "I'm on my way with Samuel and the dog. Our power just went out."

"Join the crowd," I reply with a laugh.

"Well at least you have a generator," she states matter-of-factly. "I've got to concentrate on my driving now because there are a lot of tree limbs in the street."

She quickly ends the call.

Rebecca and Samuel arrive amid intermittent rainsqualls and wind gusts of up to 35 miles an hour. It's three o'clock in the afternoon and just a few hours before Katrina hits our shore. The newscasters tell us to expect the core of a Category 1 storm, with mainly rain, and wind gusts up to 75 mph, in Broward County. James leaves for the gas station after joking that we will have to take turns sucking the gas out of his van to keep the generator going. The core of the hurricane is a mere fifteen miles away.

"We're going to go home tonight if you two are going to fight," Rebecca says with an apprehensive look at the driveway.

"It's going to be okay," I tell her. "I've stocked up on hurricane supplies and ice. And there is a roast beef with potatoes and carrots all ready for dinner. I'm going to take care of some precious things," I announce while walking out of the room. "I want to store the business files away, from the top of my desk, for there's a big crack in one of the windows. I'm not sure it will withstand the storm."

"Nana you have too many precious things," Samuel shouts loudly. "Some things need to be destroyed so you can get new things."

James returns from the gas station. We soon settle in to watch one of the movies Rebecca brought.

The storm hits land at the Broward, Dade County line, closer to Rebecca's house than ours, at about seven o'clock in the evening. I try to remain positive, ignoring snide remarks, as the power plays began. Rebecca, visibly upset, asks James and me to please, stop bickering. Samuel copes by eating more food than usual. He wants ice cream after dinner. I talk him into having a small can of oranges hoping his hunger will go away. We watch the second movie as he eats ice cream.

Katrina slows in forward motion to six mph. When it's clear that she is hanging around, throughout the night, I tell Samuel he can sleep with Papa. He's already tired from helping the adults prepare houses before the storm and lies on the living room floor. We pull out the sofa bed, so his mommy and I can sleep, before he goes quietly to bed. I'm prepared to sleep in the comfortable, large, brown, rocker recliner but keep the information to myself.

Rebecca moves from the small love seat to the sleeper sofa and sits watching news of the storm with James and me. After listening to several negative remarks, she announces a morning departure, regardless of the storm. I try my best to keep silent. James retreats to the bedroom when Rebecca falls asleep.

Winds whip through the back yard as I sit on the dining room floor at three o'clock in the morning to repeat blessings. Rain drops from the ceiling, into containers on the back porch, as I thank God for our safety. It looks like the hurricane is slowing down and will be over us for a number of hours, more than originally expected. It's headed west, directly toward us. Newscasters soon report Katrina seems to be making an unexpected turn, south toward Miami. The move will spare us of greater harm.

I sleep peacefully for a few hours on the rocker recliner as Rebecca sprawls out on the sofa bed. At seven o'clock in the morning, James gets up complaining that Samuel took over the king-sized bed. Rebecca wakes to say she must check on her cat and assess any damage to his mother's house. Although the hurricane's core is past us, the wind and rain remain fairly strong. Tree limbs are all over the yard and street. Everyone's power is still off.

Samuel wakes hours later so I rise from the chair to sleep in the king-sized bed. Right before I drift off to sleep, I vaguely think there may be issues between James and

Samuel if Rebecca leaves. She cut his ADHD medication in half due to her poor finances. Rebecca is still unemployed but being with him a lot more helps a great deal.

I wake around eleven o'clock in the morning to breathe a sign of relief. Rebecca is back from checking on the house. She reports that aside from tree limbs scattered about the yard, and the cat mess on her bedroom floor, all is well. She picked up Terry, on her way to the house, and they cleared a number of tree limbs and debris. There are black circles under her eyes. She's physically and mentally exhausted and lies down on the king-sized bed.

"I just need a few hours of sleep," she announces before closing her eyes.

James raises his voice as I head into the kitchen to make coffee. Samuel rushes in. He seems upset and wants a snack. James tells him to get some tamarinds from the tree instead. Samuel storms back into the kitchen, several minutes later, with the tamarinds.

"I know Papa likes his tamarinds pureed," he says angrily.

James' voice booms into the kitchen.

"I'm only trying to protect you from getting fatter."

Instead of washing the brown seeds, and opening the pods so they can suck on the fruit like sour candy, Samuel crushes the tamarinds in his bare hands. He starts to put them in a bowl for Papa. When he does, James begins to yell loudly asking why he would do such a thing.

"Either peel them or go outside and get some more from the tree," he tells Samuel sternly.

Samuel brings the tamarinds back into the kitchen, complaining loudly, and throws them in the garbage.

The storm is now in the house as James gets up. He begins to walk through the dining room talking forcefully. I stand, between Samuel and James as they yell back and forth, knowing the noise will soon wake Rebecca. She enters the kitchen just as James grabs his two-foot long, heavy-duty flashlight.

"I know what you need," says James looking at Samuel's face. "You just need a little discipline."

He begins to bring the flashlight down to hit Samuel but I forcefully take a hold of each of James' wrists, surprised at the power within me. I'm suddenly able to force his long and powerful arms down as Rebecca grabs Samuel and backs away. The strength it takes for me to hold his arms down comes from another place. Between sentences of agreeing with James, Rebecca instructs Samuel to get his things together so they can return home. I distract hypoglycemic James by asking if he ate breakfast.

Rains and wind continue as I ask Rebecca to stay until the storm clears. She asks if I have any pills for Samuel. I hand over pieces of saved pills then quietly ask her not to feed James power by agreeing with him. Rebecca becomes angry. She's in her panic mode, reacting as usual during conflict situations, by leaving the scene. I feel distanced from my family once again.

Things change in a short amount of time. Knee-jerk reactions of the past fade away, when I still my mind to connect with Higher Self, before considering whether to respond to events. I learn to offer loving energy during potentially harmful situations. It will be clear that experiences led me to do exactly what I do now, help others to realize the divinity within themselves and all living things.

Rebecca hurries out the door with Samuel as James loudly reminds them of the several things left behind. Samuel returns a couple of times to get their things. James is quiet when they finally pull out of the drive. He won the power game. I stand in my workroom to watch as they drive away into the hurricane rain and 25 mph wind. James puts the sofa bed back up and sits smugly in the rocker recliner to watch a fishing show.

This is the last straw. I decide to remind him of the three choices we already discussed.

"I'm tired of all the bickering," I announce with resignation. "Let me remind you of the choices we discussed in December. You can file for the divorce, I can, or we can finish the counseling we started twelve years ago to see where it leads us."

James ignores me. His eyes remain on the television.

"This time I am putting a deadline date of one month on the choices," I advise him.

I am relatively certain that I will file for divorce.

"Why don't you just leave," he asks quietly with an angry glare. "You know I'm Catholic."

I turn and walk back to my workroom adamant that he face his disassociation with reality. He must face up to his responsibilities as an adult family member. "Things are not perfect here, but they are not supposed to be," I silently tell myself.

It's time for me to fully wake-up, face Reality, and weather the process of dismantling the life I think is mine. The soul's plan to dismantle darker aspects of myself, in order to purify and release negative energy, continues as opportunities to adjust perceptions and beliefs increase. My willingness to change how I live slowly inches closer to aligning with new, and higher, ways of being and living.

The rain and wind continue throughout the day as outer bands of Katrina blow through Fort Lauderdale. Broken tree branches scatter across our yard and there are a few more porch leaks to deal with. I lay on the futon in my home office as Daniel's 2005 memorial CD skips erratically on the battery-operated CD player. It's a bit more than 80 degrees inside the house so I put an ice-packed washcloth on top of my head.

"Just be still," Daniel announces. "Think of the artic, the penguins' house we saw at the Detroit Zoo, the cool seven-mile bridge snorkel trip we had, and you'll be okay."

Other voices join Daniel's after I fall asleep. Members of my spirit group tell me it's indeed time to grow again. I get up, go to the bathroom, and look for the smiley face etched into the window frame. The words, "Smile, be happy, it will be okay," enter my mind when I spot it. A bug crawls up the screen to avert my attention. When I look back for the smiley face, it's gone.

Rebecca returns with Samuel and two pizza's around seven o'clock in the evening. I ignore the knocks on my workroom door so she enters and touches me.

"Are you sleeping Mom?" she quietly asks.

"Kind of," I reply still thinking about what my spirit family said.

"I've brought some pizzas for dinner so come out before they get cold," she advises before quickly leaving the room.

Pizza always seems to present a diet challenge for me. I join them in the living room, minutes later, to scrape grease and tomato sauce off of the pizza, before eating, so my stomach will not complain.

Rebecca asks if she can use my car as we eat. I always fill my gas tank before a storm. The power is still off at the gas stations and her car is out of gas. She takes my car keys after dinner. I know Rebecca feels the negativity around James and me as she quickly leaves with Samuel.

"There's a lot of yard work for us to do in the morning," she announces while walking out the den door.

Rebecca calls to report that her power is on the next afternoon; ours is still out. It's 85 degrees in the house and I still have a washcloth filled with ice cubes on top of my head. James tells me to get my clothes together because I am going over to her house to cool off. Discussions with James, about our house, and thoughts of two previous divorces where I walked away with nothing just to be free, lead me to stay where I am.

"Just be still, think of the artic, the penguins, the seven-mile snorkel trip we had, and you'll be okay," I hear again.

Rebecca arrives minutes later. James told her I agreed to visit. I tell her that's not the case and fill her in on our divorce discussion.

"I'm not going to leave my home," I insistently announce.

She immediately screams at Samuel to get up from the couch.

"This is a power struggle and I'm not going to get involved," she retorts heading back to the den door. "Let's go, NOW Samuel."

A negative energy field appears to surround James. I quickly return to my workroom believing he's beyond my help. I sit on the futon to read after grabbing a spiritual book from the black bookcase. Positive energy flows within me while reading about many things that I intuitively know. It feels good to be in a place of white light, with windows open and blinds up, while dozing off and on throughout the day. I replace melted ice cubes within the washcloth as necessary.

House power returns at eight o'clock in the evening. I make my first conscious move to 'higher ground' when James leaves. Air seems empty and cold in other parts of the house. It's an easy decision to shift my favorite clothes, across the small hall into the bedroom office, and to sleep on the futon. The permanent move affords me with a new sense of awareness as positive energy increases.

Life has a strange way of shoving things into your face and giving you another opportunity to deal with them. The weather report announces that Hurricane Katrina is on her way to Louisiana. I email my friend in New Orleans upon hearing the storm will soon be a Category 5 hurricane.

"Get out of there if you haven't already," I cautiously advise. "I'll continue to send everyone in Katrina's path white light."

A mandatory evacuation goes into effect for New Orleans as Hurricane Katrina approaches. I send another blessing of white light, love, and safe harbor to the people in her path. My pal evacuates to her friend's house in Northeast Mississippi but her partner, a nursing supervisor, has to stay behind at the hospital.

The storm spares Kenner Regional Hospital, in the New Orleans area, but the area around it is devastated. Tulane Hospital evacuates as floodwaters advance. I continue to send love and light to keep friends and their loved ones safe amidst the fury of wind and storm surge. The earth is cleansing and purifying itself to make way for higher vibrating energies. My friends and their families' in New Orleans bear the brunt of her wrath as we get what I hope is the last of Katrina's rain.

Katrina hits New Orleans, as a Category 5 hurricane, to change the world. Millions of people lose electricity. Many more bear much worse pain as reports of deaths, in seven states, become well known. The storm leaves years of wide and devastating effects. I cannot imagine the loss felt by my friend but replying to her emails comes easily as fingers move over the computer keyboard.

"I think in times like these we are prompted to help out those in need. Some people will wait in vain to be saved. It is too sad for words to convey adequately.

"Since my son Daniel passed on 4/4/04, I have come to many realizations. The belief that we live more than one life, and that our spirits travel with the same group of people throughout eternity, helps me a lot.

"The evidence of Daniel's spirit (life-force, energy), after passing, is clearly noticeable in my daily life. At this time, I can only begin to relate some of the many things I have seen, or heard, or that have happened to me that are out of the ordinary since 4/4/4. Of course, I do have photos and videos, and documentation of strange occurrences, but my family believes I am crazy. Well, it is not the first time they have called me nuts, and I have been called much worse things, in immature years of course.

"I believe we each live as many lives as we need to learn the lesson of what it is to be human. To be human is to care for humankind and have faith that we will evolve in order to survive. Everything that happens to us has a lesson in it. Everything we ignore just repeatedly returns until we 'get it'. I know this is extremely difficult for everyone affected by Katrina. At this point, it is important to value the life we have now and hope that those who passed were ready to do so.

"I lost all of my belongings, twice, when I was very young and going through two different divorces. I thought it was okay as long as I had my kids. Well, I cannot see Daniel in his human form now. But quite honestly, he communicates with me more than he has for many years. I am blessed to feel that somehow I got him back from the dark side of life.

"Help is coming, be patient and grateful that you, and your family, have survived and that you have one another to count on. I believe that love is the key, along with peace and harmony for all living things. That is our goal. Help less fortunate people and you will begin to feel better. Helping others helps us to take our mind off of our sorrows and helps to rack up 'spiritual credits'. Corny, but I think, true. And yes, I know, I am talking to the band but like when I go to the Religious Science Center, hearing someone else speak what I have thought helps me big time."

I sum up thoughts on a more personal note.

"Keep writing because that helps too. And especially keep writing me because I care for you deeply and will always be with you."

Emails from spiritual groups cause me to pause and wonder what is missing. Mindfulness, being totally present in each moment, continues to be a foreign concept for I spend my time still wrapped up in dream-world dramas.

"Trials only help us to grow," I email to another friend. "Daniel's spirit is with me very often to help and I am grateful. Love is the key."

Abigail's card, letting her and Rachel know that all is well, sits in the mail moments later.

The ascension process involves the earth for we move, into higher states of being, through the earth herself. All geographical areas hold their own unique energies and vibrations. Natural disasters such as hurricanes and floods are ways that the earth uses to cleanse, and purify, itself of negative energy. Areas attract a much higher vibration after these earth changes occur. Geographical areas, which support our growth, draw us to help balance the area's energies. We are edging closer to a New Earth. It makes sense that areas vibrating at a lower level, using old reality ways, will cleanse themselves to make way for higher vibrating energies.

:-)

Chapter Nineteen

A New Mission

Through the hologram of consciousness, a little change in our lives is mirrored everywhere in our world. Gregg Braden - The Divine Matrix

Increased visits to the Center, coupled with new sleeping arrangements, support spiritual growth. Visits with Michael help me to decrease medication doses. The opinions of others, pegging me as "Crazy Nana" no longer matter. A stronger urge, to care for personal needs, surfaces while working on the computer and getting Samuel from school several days a week. There's so much to write about but I keep hearing, "This ain't no dog and pony show." Sometimes energy seems to move about the room but I cannot be sure. As the atmosphere quickly changes, I sense that we, as humans, are losing time.

An early September journal entry voices feelings that rise like fireworks in a black night. The urgency to end my ten-year mission, of hiv/aids awareness and nutrition education, escalates. But who will carry on the work? It's time to begin an even greater mission with many more challenges. Several months ago, I started signing emails with the word "Blessings." It just happened. Now, I think I know why. September 11, 2001 was a 'call to arms' for many of us. The stakes are high and I fear that the survival of humanity depends greatly on a steadfast feeling of love, harmony, and peace, for all living things. We must evolve into the forms I see so frequently now, especially at sunset and later in the evening.

Many changes occurred since the Twin Towers incident. It's easy to blame others. But I have to admit, there might be a more valid reason for these life changes, beyond my current comprehension. There has to be a greater reason for my uneasiness. Why do I now sit isolated in the only place in the house where I feel light, and love, and sense only positive energy?

Fear of hell on earth rises. Television images, of the aftermath of massive Katrina, flash through my mind, along with bits and pieces of the news followed so religiously for years. Intuition warns, another storm is already on its way as I pack boxes of clothes, pocket game toys, books, CDs, and other things for my New Orleans friend. She's staying in Mississippi.

Eighteen months of reviewing pictures, videos, and voice tapes of Daniel hinder spiritual growth. The long Labor Day weekend unfolds as I dwell on the past. After spending the last nine years of Labor Days with convention friends, I cancel my trip when funds fail to materialize. A new realm awaits me. So many wonderful, and unexplainable, things have occurred that I have no choice but to believe they offer yet another opportunity for spiritual growth.

Meditation, prayer, reading spiritual books, and singing is now habitual. The quietness of the neighborhood, as I offer free concerts, even after eleven o'clock at night, amazes me because no one complains. I often heartily sing "Breath of Heaven" pouring my heart out. "Be with me. Breath of Heaven, hold me together. Be forever near me Breath of Heaven."

My plan to help from the Otherside never wavers. Although the increasing awareness of God permeates me more each day, I still intend to transition when my essence will be most useful to those lost in the maze on earth. At 7:05 PM, when I again adamantly state my intention, the clock above me stops ticking. I have no idea why since the battery is brand new.

I see, and sense, my soul group daily. They give me hope and faith in a better and more purposeful future. It's becoming very clear, things are revealed as I'm ready to accept them. A need for more supportive people surfaces in my lonely life so I join the monthly "Sisters in Spirit" group. Dr. Arleen Bump's title for the evening's talk, "Beginning Anew," seems appropriate in many ways. She informs us that our thought process has a great deal to do with how life unfolds.

An immediate connection with Rev. Peck surfaces when she rises to speak. Goose bumps fill my arms as she discusses her goal, of building a center in North Carolina within three years. At least twice before his transition, Daniel discussed buying property in North Carolina. He asked if James and I would be interested in a joint venture, with his friend Job, months before his transition. Upon arriving home, I quickly look up Lake Lure on the Internet and find it quite appealing.

A sorrowful human thought shocks me. I must let go of all things that bind me here, in order to continue upon my path. The thought causes an unexplainable glimmer of delight. Daniel tried hard to keep close to his earth family, but apparently, that was not his destiny. Perhaps we share the same destiny. His destiny, in my opinion, is to lead the way to greater realities.

My own destiny remains uncertain. For now, it's seems best to focus on spirituality and avoiding the pain of loss (that continues to spring forth with thoughts of Daniel). Humanity, I know, must evolve into another form in order to survive. Continuing to feel odd within my human frame, I capture my image on film expecting to see visible changes. But nothing about my physical appearance looks any different.

The family's closed-mindedness urges me to concentrate on people more likely to accept help towards the white light of our Creator. Center attendance increases during the second week of the month, which subsequently leads to greater spiritual growth. I cannot get enough of the Center's loving energy and now attend two services a week. Just as the theme of the Center's magazine, my life is in a state of change. An article on transformation by Dr. Charles D. Geddes entices me.

"I believe we can not *transform* without *healing* and remembering our innate *wholeness*," he writes.

Dr. Geddes notes time spent with a dear friend who was making his transition. I sense he knows the pain of losing someone dear.

His *Bible* quote, "Be ye transformed by the renewing of your mind," serves to spur questions in my own mind. Can I really heal my body by transforming my inner mind? Time will indeed tell as I progress in New Thought studies.

It's Sunday, September 11, 2005 when I join others of like mind for a special celebration of Oneness and Unity. The title of the morning's service, "I Stand For Love," with its five speakers, draws me like a moth to a flame. A special event held in the afternoon calls to me as well. Curiosity about a sacred healing process seems to fit right into my new spiritual growth plan.

Rev. Penny Macek, Pastor of the Religious Science Church in Lake Tahoe, offers the healing and revealing event. The multi-page handout calls for revealing newness through group healing. It's clear that I've talked myself into a whole new growth experience after quickly skimming through sheets of white paper beyond a purple cover.

I've never considered my own intentions for I am a "do it now because it's time to do it" sort of gal. Thinking before acting, even about intentions and feelings, seems like a time-consuming luxury. Intentions are something for other people to figure out. Why should I change the way I conduct my life?

Ego fights me all the way, while listening to Rev. Macek, coloring worksheets, and filling empty boxes with words. Rev. Macek speaks of hope and faith, newness and oldness. Am I not "enough" already? Ego reins during the first half of the workshop, until we discuss beliefs.

As I rack up the offenses ego attributes to others, it's clearly time to let go of guilt, and shame, and to stop projecting it onto others. My finished "Co-dependence Worksheet" reveals that the natures of their offenses are mine. I must recognize the power within and stop trying to control others. It's clearly time to return to love.

The "Fear to Faith Worksheet" is an eye-opener as words of error and resistance flow through my mind like a quickly moving muddy river. A flash of understanding notes it's time for a much overdue change in beliefs. The dismantling and rebuilding process begins when I take the handout home to practice "The 7 X 70 Forgiveness Process."

James works at his new job leaving me grateful to have the house to myself. My Higher Self wants to dispel the illusion of the mind but ego fights me all the way.

"This is really stupid," I hear myself say, as I forcefully thrust out my left arm to release my belief in illness. "I release my need to control," my voice booms loudly as I whip out my right arm to accidentally hit the kitchen cabinet.

I continue the process, ignoring my throbbing right hand, by raising both arms to the sky.

"I am grateful God is the health I AM!" I announce forcefully to the empty room.

It feels very good to shout the words.

The process of changing my conscious mind, to bring it into alignment with the Principles of Truth, continues as the voice of ego lessens. Of course, ego, with it's cornucopia of excuses, puts up a fight during the next step, for changing my subconscious mind is a totally different matter. I forge ahead determined to align physical, mental, and spiritual energies. It's not easy but the week ends after successfully repeating my three-sentence affirmation seventy times a day.

The daily practice session serves a three-fold purpose. In addition to helping with the spiritual purification process, it makes me feel better and immediately increases the amount of exercise I get. There's a mass change in both arm muscles. The journey back to wholeness continues, as I persist for the rest of the month with a renewed sense of self, to work with words of error, and qualities of God, identifying my Greater Truth.

*We exist in a matrix of energy, a soup of possibilities that connects everything. We take a quantum leap to wholeness by feeling healing in our hearts, as if it has already happened. We are part of **All That Is**, perfect, whole and complete. And we recognize this truth once we feel that in the core of our being.*

Our bodies DNA gives us access to the matrix, which we tap into through emotion. Scientists consider ninety percent of DNA as useless "junk" but they are learning that this type of DNA is active during psychic activities and with intuition. This DNA appears linked to group consciousness. It may explain such phenomena as psychic ability, body healing, and the power of one's spoken word.

As noted by Gregg Braden author of The Divine Matrix, "We're tuned to our world, and the world shows us physically the energy of what we experience emotionally." We change the reality of our world with a shift in focus. In other words, thoughts are things that manifest into our reality. Seeing ourselves as empowered makes all the difference in healing for our beliefs are the only things that limit us.

The Global Peace Project, founded by James Redfield (www.celestinevision.com), is one example of people coming together to heal and change the world with the power of thought.

Commitments lessen as Ruth, or Terry, takes Momma to the doctor while I concentrate on myself. Another workshop compliments my spiritual growth resume after they leave to attend a funeral back home. This time I take on the role of hospitality person for Dr. Bump's introductory class, "History of New Thought and the Basic Principles of Science of Mind." I plan to join the class that starts the following week.

The east windows in my new sanctuary offer a better view of the skies. I gaze upward the next morning at 3:00 AM. A strange feeling of excitement fills me while trying to determine why. I'm not a fan of astronomy but find myself videoing the full moon and what looks like a very bright star. The star, with its purple core, jogs around in the sky like a Mitch Miller bouncing ball every time I zoom in on it. I soon subscribe to updates about space online (www.swpc.noaa.gov), read them, but remain unaware of how the sun, moon, and planets affect humans.

Forecasters expected 2005 to be a quiet year but the number of geomagnetic storms, and x-ray solar flares (X-flare), from the sun, exceeded expectations. Solar activity increased on New Year's Day when a sunspot exploded producing an X-flare. Sunspots, magnetic fields that become unstable and explode, are the main sources of solar activity. These explosions produce flashes of electromagnetic radiation (solar flares) and can hurl hot magnetized gas into space causing geomagnetic storms that result in auroras.

In September 2005, a sunspot exploded producing one of the brightest X-flares of the Space Age. The growing spot exploded eight more times in the days that followed. Each X-flare caused a shortwave radio blackout on earth and pumped new energy into a radiation storm around our planet. The blasts hurled magnetic clouds toward earth, creating ruby-red auroras seen as far south as Arizona, on Sept 10 and 11. Almost every day for two weeks, solar flares issued from the giant sunspot and protons peppered the Moon.

*It is now well known that solar activity affects humans. We are integrating all of our selves, through our current personality, moving beyond the third dimension and returning to the light body, eternal life of which we truly are. This integration requires a change in all aspects of our being mentally, emotionally, within our auric field, and at the cellular level. We are the ones we have been waiting for. Our souls chose to become enlightened, en masse, prior to this lifetime. Eternal life is ours as we end separation and unify in the oneness of light, of unconditional love, as an integrated soul dedicated to total acceptance of **All That Is**.*

In her book <u>The Ascension Primer</u>, Karen Bishop notes our bodies experience energy shifts when solar flares occur. Solar flares bring in very strong blasts of higher crystalline energy. Only crystalline substances can exist on higher dimensional levels. Our bodies are evolving into this new structure. Crystal makes it possible to resonate to a higher level of divine consciousness. This fiber creates a new internal foundation and is necessary to help us adapt to the New World.

Surges of crystalline energy are the most forceful, dramatic, and powerful forms of energy shifts, creating the most immediate change within us, pushing the older and denser energies out. These phenomenal energy surges can cause symptoms such as flu-like signs, exhaustion, anxiety, heart palpitations, severe bloating, and indigestion.

Hurricane Rita forms as a tropical storm over the Turks and Calicos Islands on September 18 and moves south of the Florida Keys as a Category 2 storm. The center postpones my first Science of Mind class due to wind and rain. I follow a link in the *Celestine Prophecy* book, while waiting out the storm, and marvel over the website.

James Redfield, the author, carefully explains the spiritual vision of the Celestine Insights in his books and on the website. I ask myself with wide-eyed wonder, "Am I part of this critical mass experiencing a new spiritual awakening?" I have consciously started to change my mission and do seem led by mysterious coincidences. I'm also clearing the past by recognizing my particular way of stealing energy from others. Most of my brothers and sisters use the same methods of "intimidation," "interrogation" and "poor me" as I. It's up to me to stop the game.

Is this my spiritual mission? Or is there more to it? An increasing flow of mysterious coincidences does seem to occur. Since news of Daniels passing, I've enjoyed a potpourri of resources, books, music, Internet articles, classes, etc., to spur me forward into the vast land of open-minds. It's a whole new world immeasurably different from life led in the past.

Answers to frequent Cosmic questions often come in the dead of night. For months after that dreaded phone call, I woke several times during the night crying for Daniel. The deep dream-state of past years is now history as I wake frequently to recall words or bits of dreams. In waking hours, intuition often leads me synchronistically towards people at the Center who answer my many questions.

Could I, as noted on the Celestine Prophecy website, increase the frequency of guiding coincidences by uplifting every person who enters my life? Is it really that easy? And if so, can I do it? Is it possible to feel another's energy rather than judge it by body movement and voice? Can I train myself to see the beauty in everyone and increase the chances of hearing a synchronistic message? After all I've been through, I am willing to try.

Delicious curiosity fills me with the thought that I might be able to evolve into a higher energy state, as Daniel, by transforming my current body while staying alive. Can I indeed unite this dimension of existence with others and end the cycle of birth and death? My mind is in a daze considering the possibilities.

Energized while reading the *Tenth Insight*, I know, without a doubt, I am here on assignment. It's time to remember what I've come to offer the world. The Universe has indeed guided me to the perfect place for it's time to change my vision of reality. I'm finally feeling more connected to people at the Center even though I rarely speak of personal things.

The more I learn of the Center's common spiritual vision, the more energized I become. A sense of common passion permeates awareness whilst joining others to create a new spiritual culture. My faith in the power of prayer is restored. The latent power of Mind beckons me to continue learning so I can positively affect life.

The voice of my new mission roars while contemplating losses spurred by weather and illness. The world is changing drastically. "Suggestions for the 21st Century" become my mantra as I aim to boost the spirits of friends, affected by great loss, with blessings of peace, love, harmony, hope, and faith.

"Count your blessings," I advise. "I know if you think about it, things could always be worst. Be grateful for what you have."

Several hours at the Center, helping office staff label magazines for mailing, helps to fill the day after repeating morning prayers. The mid-week service inspires me as usual. I now look forward to volunteering in hospitality, every Tuesday, to attend Dr. Bump's classes without charge. The Religious Science Center 101 series consists of eight beginning classes teaching the Science of Mind by Ernest Holmes.

"I'm on to my spiritual quest for peace, love, and harmony for all living things," I confide happily to friends via email.

Science of Mind teaches the primary Law of Love. Classes help me to accept others and myself. I slowly learn to think more consciously and draw better things into my life while focusing on the Law of Attraction. It's shocking to learn that I'm solely responsible for my own experience. But upon understanding the Law of Attraction, I begin to direct attention to totally new experiences.

Knowledge of the Law of Attraction helps me to shift my energy into abundance, instead of lack, as I think more and more positively. The thought that rebirth is the knowing of what is already in our mind spurs me forward to a life of wonder and awe. I soon stop seeing myself as a victim of my own limited and fearful thinking. And now, truly celebrate because I have all the power needed to create what I want.

:-)

Chapter Twenty

Friends on the Otherside

Each of us has many souls in the hereafter…who are working to help us to carry out the plan that is to be our life's work on the earth. …the tools we need to survive, both before and after tragedy, are sent to us by those souls who truly care for our well-being. George Anderson - Walking in the Garden of Souls

Life remains a contrast of old beliefs, wavering between degrees of limitation, and new thinking that wears off soon after leaving the Center. Daniel's presence continues to appear, especially whenever I prepare to pass quietly into the night.

"You still have work to do," he warns, "and remember you're not alone Mom. We are with you."

I envision my soul group hovering nearby.

Daniel's energy turns the portable CD player on, or off, or lowers or raises the volume. Sometimes it turns itself on and plays a song to start my day. Tracks change haphazardly, to form sentences of hope, from words of five or more songs. Love and gratitude overflow every time he reassures me by manipulating music on his memorial CD. The music disk always switches to just the right words of comfort when I need them.

"Dry your eyes, don't you cry," I hear, before the CD quickly skims to words in another song. "Hang on baby, hang on, cause it's closer than you think and we're standing on the brink." It then plays "keep the faith," from yet another track. Filled with joy, I wipe tears away for now it's impossible to remember what upsets me.

Daniel knows my workaholic ways. The computer malfunctions often to prompt a change in actions. Frequent computer backups consume the time. Computers shut down whenever I ignore Daniel's advice, "Enough Mom, go to bed." Countless files disappear so I begin to halt work as soon as he tells me to stop.

Daily reminders, to repeat affirmations, help to rid myself of the need to hide or be unhealthy. Journal entries document opinions and sensations I'm unable to share otherwise. Daniel and other soul group members accompany me daily by the end of September. Along with the guidance from our Creator (or whatever you prefer to name *It*), they rule all actions.

The "dog and pony show," as Daniel calls it, always encourages me. Yet, I still feel odd about being on the toilet when the smiley face appears etched into the window frame. Various sizes of slow-moving bugs find freedom as I carry them out to thrive in their own environment. I actively seek butterflies, and cocoons, to replace them. A number of butterflies appear but, alas, no cocoons.

James now works in the same field but in a less demanding position than director/manager, which pays half of what he made before. I don't know who his employer is. So much has happened over the past few years to change our relationship, it seems hopeless to try and repair the damage. The best I can do is to take Daniel's advice as I again take on the responsibilities of grocery shopping, cooking, and household chores.

An old friend greets me one sunny day while grocery shopping. Our friendship started when Daniel was an infant after her mother gave me a full-time job at their French restaurant. The family continued to play an instrumental role in our life. We never would have moved to Florida without them.

Devastated to learn of Daniel's transition, and not knowing what to say, most of them avoided the funeral and memorial service. Tattie came with one of her daughters. Now she admits to frequent thoughts of Daniel and wonders if she's crazy. She hears him along with her departed dad, aunt, and grandmother. They speak to her in dreams and she often wakes up in cold sweats.

"I look at him," she says in a whisper with her eyes on the floor, "at Daniel's picture all the time."

Tears well in her large, brown eyes as I whip out the picture taken of him at his last birthday party.

"Do you mean this one?" I ask, breaking out with a wide grin.

"Yes, yes, that's the one," she notes vigorously nodding her head in agreement.

Supermarket shoppers stare disapprovingly as they move around the block we create in the air-conditioned doorway.

I do my best to assure her she is not going crazy as we walk to her car.

"They hear you Tattie," I announce adamantly touching her arm, "they hear you. Don't be afraid. They are only trying to let you know they're okay and they are here for you."

She shakes her head slowly and looks down at the pavement.

"There's another one," she says smiling to reach down for a shiny penny.

We speak of pennies found on the ground and memories of the "good old days" (when we were blissfully ignorant and happily drunk) and then part delighted to have connected.

James seems much less threatening as I unload the groceries. He begins to clear away his personal things, which have been scattered throughout the house for months. I wonder if Daniel communicates with him. When he leaves for the nursing home, to visit his mother, I spend three hours dusting and polishing uncluttered surfaces.

Martha, my mother-in-law, is now confined to a wheelchair and sometimes unable to recognize James. I know that preys on his mind. I also know we all have hurdles to jump, and it's okay even though he might never be on the path beside me. We each have our own lessons and our own purpose(s) in life. I feel strongly that our business together is complete. Only time will tell which one of us will be the first to move on.

Many changes have occurred since James started his new job. It looks like things are getter better. Since I have an extensive medical history, he asks me to look through the health insurance information so we can pick an adequate health care plan. Many of the eight prescriptions I take are free. James now decides it's unfair to continue with patient assistance programs or to let doctors see me without charge. This step toward responsibility pleases me. Yet, the dreamed of solid, healthy marriage still seems elusive.

A sudden flash of realization makes it clear that James insisted on handling our financial affairs because he had to learn how to do it. James seems resigned when I begin to take money out of the checking account, instead of going without. I now allow myself the pleasure of an occasional bunch of flowers, from the 99 Cent store, which I display prominently in the living room.

An overwhelming sense that I've somehow bargained with others before birth rules the night. Did I make a contract and promptly forget its stipulations after coming into this physical reality? There has to be a reason why I keep hearing the late Zephaniah's voice in my head. Why, I question myself honestly, would my husband's father be talking to me as Daniel does? The closest I ever felt to him was when we hugged less than a month before he passed.

Although our last time together was far from pleasurable, the hug between Zephaniah and me stands out as a happy dream fulfilled for the first time. I remember the occasion as if it was yesterday. James and I were on our way to celebrate his fortieth birthday in the Bahamas.

No one in my husband's family seemed anxious to hug anyone else, especially people not exactly like them. Zephaniah seemed different. We connected on the very first day we met, a year after James and I married. Over the years, my bond with Zephaniah grew as he went through the motions of devastating illness. I often stopped to visit during frequent hospital rounds while checking patients' meal satisfaction. He was barely alive when I stood next to his bed and tried my best to bring him back to life.

Our time together ended, after several weeks, when he returned home from the hospital. A new relationship formed between us after that. For the next five years, I watched as his family seemingly ignored his next diagnosis. It was clear to me that his time with us was limited. I had no idea how ill Zephaniah would be by the time we left for our trip when I planned the surprise birthday gift for James.

"No, no," Zephaniah told us insistently, with that knowing look of assurance and slow nod of the head, "you kids go on and have a good time."

There was not a doubt in my mind that his time was very short as I looked into his now glassy eyes. Yet I knew I had to follow through with our plans.

"I don't know what Ma is going to do when I do finally go," said Zephaniah wistfully as we stood outside the front door saying goodbye.

"We'll take care of her Pops," I told him wrapping my arms around his gaunt frame.

Although hugs were rare in his family, he gripped me tightly and squeezed before his arms fell slowly to his side.

The show of affection took me by surprise. I quickly sensed he would not be in the same state when we returned the following week. Two days later, as James and I stood drunk from Bahama Mama's, in the rain at a phone booth, we learned he was back in the hospital. Zephaniah made his transition a few days after we returned, while lying in a hospital bed at home, watching his beloved birds in the backyard.

Now, I sit trying to make sense of it all wondering if I'm indeed crazy as family speculates. A sense of the future controls thoughts while considering Zephaniah's words from the Otherside.

"You will be taken care of after you let James go to grow on his own."

I carefully ponder the words. Am I going to reap the fruits of my father-in-law's labor? Why would that be so? It is an exhilarating thought to think I will soon live a new life, with unlimited freedom to do as I please, even if I do not know exactly how or why.

Returning thoughts to the present, I look around what is now my bedroom. Is my marriage to James really over after eighteen years? I sense it truly is. It's time for both of us to fulfill our soul's obligations. James is a younger soul and we bargained, as souls, before birth. Perhaps I agreed to propel him forward, by encouraging his spiritual growth, in exchange for the financial assistance that allows my soul to accomplish its growth through community service.

The time to begin repairing relationships is here but I have no idea how to start. Rebecca and Samuel choose to avoid James because of the Hurricane Katrina "incident." I continue to get Samuel after school but now take him to his own home rather than have Rebecca fetch him after work from ours.

Rebecca's new job seems like a dream come true but she remains mired in debt accumulated during months of unemployment. She filed for bankruptcy but still has personal debts to pay. My ambitious, beautiful daughter is struggling to catch up but I can no longer help her. The savings account from years of back child support, which arrived after my kids became adults, is gone.

I wonder why James is not as compassionate as Daniel was. Yet, as Rebecca and Samuel deal with their poverty, I begin to realize that they have lessons to learn as well as James and me. They continue to live rent-free in Martha's house while James and his sister decide if their mother will ever return home. Several weeks of house repair to make it livable paid off, and now, aside from a leaking roof, it's a safe and affordable haven.

It encourages me to think we all lived together before and will live together again after this life ends. Sometimes in the dead of night, when I allow myself to cry over the loss of Daniel's physical body, it's my only comfort. All things happen as they should and I no longer believe in coincidences. It's up to us to see the opportunities and learn the lessons. It's up to us to reach out and take the offer to grow spiritually or stay in our cocoon of lack and ignorance.

Many books and other things at the Center verify thoughts. Family remains leery of my interests despite efforts to open their minds with invitations to the Center. It's difficult to see them seemingly suffer through trauma after trauma. But I'm unwilling to change my new perspective to join them again in the land of severe limitation. I'm still making my own way to the open field of freedom, and abundance, while experiencing visits from departed relatives.

Daily affirmations, nightly blessings, singing, meditations, spiritual growth reading, and time spent at the Center serves me well. I begin to consciously monitor thoughts, words, and actions. Most of the time I meditate when upset and remain calm, without taking the prescribed high blood pressure medicine. It's so much easier to do when alone in my little, sun-lit, white light room with the shades up.

Perception changes, just as it did in the seventies, after re-evaluating my life. I know where I've been and have a general idea of where I want to go. I'm a facilitator; and although I usually do not get recognized, or rewarded for starting a new path or wandering into unknown territory to lead the way for others, I'm okay with that. It's a big step to admit that I no longer need to be recognized for my efforts.

A greater awareness of our different belief systems comes more into focus as I listen to James discuss his new 401K. Material possessions are not as precious as human connections and spiritual growth. Spending money on living, now, and having fun with family, sounds much better than waiting until retirement to reap the fruits of labor. I sense Social Security will not be there for those who need it in later years. I stopped paying into the 'system' when my employment ended at the hospital in 1993. And it's unlikely that I'll live long enough to collect retirement funds.

"I believe this next mission," my voice announces wistfully to the empty room, "to be my last before I get to peacefully pass into the night."

It's now vital to let family learn their own lessons as I try to limit co-dependant ways. Conflicts lessen when I stop feeding others by withdrawing from the power grabbing game. Recognizing the age-old "intimidation," "aloofness," "poor me" or "interrogation" ploys becomes easier. Intuition guides me to leave the premises, usually after letting the responsible party know that the "game" is over.

Journals document the wonder of a new life. I sometimes see orbs and often feel soul group members. They hug me, or say encouraging words, as I drive to, enter, or participate, in Center activities. I now shake my head joyfully hoping for their company while leaving for the Center again. New, delightful words fill my brain.

"You are where you need to be for now."

Ernest Holmes and I have things in common, I learn during my first "The Spiritual Path" class. We never failed to speak our mind and dropped out of formal education.

Thoughts of spending six years to become a practitioner do not bother me because completion of the classes remains uncertain. My soul group takes turns hugging me, encouraging me to go forward, as I sit at the back table listening to Dr. Arleen. It's difficult to concentrate upon hearing Daniel's encouraging remarks and seeing orbs in front and to the side of me.

Knowing that we live, move, and have our BEing in a Universe governed by Love, and powered by Law, thrills me beyond belief. Perhaps, it's possible to consciously direct the flow of Universal Mind into form and improve my life. My new journey to reach a greater understanding, of the nature of life and God's relationship to me, begins in earnest as I consider what type of project to design for the final class. Pictures of orbs in my room, and family photos with what appear to be angels, fill my mind.

My new friend, Sylvia, is ready the next night when I arrive to drive her to the Center's mid-week-service. I passed her last week as she laboriously departed from a bus nearby. Upon recalling my own short-lived bus days, I gladly offered a quick, and less demanding, ride to future services.

Daniel's voice fills my head as we meditate during the brief Wednesday service.

"You're the Baum Ma," he says.

Rev. Hooks soon speaks about how very special we are.

"We all," he announces confidently, with a smile that melts my heart, "have everything we need already inside of us so there's no need to seek for things outside of ourselves."

I love to hear him speak, and when my new friend David offers Sylvia a ride home, grab the chance to ask Rev. Hooks for my first 'treatment.'

Rev. Hooks listens intently as I confidently note that a twenty-year hiv/aids mission seems to be over. I now sense a new mission, one of being a practitioner. I mention a letter, mailed to the Magic Johnson Foundation, in hopes of finding someone else to nurture HIV ReSources, support it, and keep the information available, without exploitation. Rev. Hooks repeats an impromptu treatment, with self-assured calmness, looks deeply into my hazel eyes with his baby blues, and kisses both cheeks. Fighting tears, before quickly turning to scurry away into the dark night, I announce, it's like losing a baby.

Tears flow as I walk to the door of my car. I wipe them away while mumbling hello to someone coming into the Center. Cheyenne calls to me from his car two aisles away.

"Hey, Sam," he asks softly, "is everything okay?"

I know he left the building before anyone else and sense he's been waiting for me. But I'm in no mood to talk.

"Yes, yes, I'm fine," I lie reaching for my car door.

How strange that he senses something amiss for I have only known him for two weeks! Yet, he seemed familiar when we first met at the mid-week service. It's odd to feel a familiar closeness with a mysterious man. He dresses as most black men at Sunday services, in a black suit with a crisp, white, dress shirt and tie.

A strong familiarity prevailed when we first held hands while in the treatment circle. His strong faith and spirit flowed through his hand to mine and I noticed he bought a book about prosperity before leaving. I quickly encouraged him to return to the Center but had no idea why he seemed so familiar. This Wednesday, I admitted to sensing he was a man of faith, the week before, when we were in the circle. He nodded and agreed.

Tears flow down my face while leaving the parking lot. They are still flowing when I reach the house. James is home and I do not want to get out of my car. Maybe I just do not want to discuss it with him, thinking he will never understand. Perhaps, I'm afraid he will ignore my distress. Ruth and Naomi's anniversary card lies on the seat beside me. It's an easy decision to mail it at the post office. I back out of my lawn parking spot, still crying, to drive there.

The CD player plays songs I'm accustomed to hearing in times of despair. I sit in the post office lot crying, blowing my nose, and wiping tears. The stamped envelope goes into a mail slot ten minutes later before I head for home.

Minutes later when I ask, James says the chicken I made before leaving for the service was great. He does not notice my despair. It shakes me to the bone to realize that a man I have lived with for twenty years does not sense my despair, yet, a man who I met two weeks ago, and spent less than five minutes alone with, does. Perhaps there's another door for me to open…

:-)

Chapter Twenty-One

Manifesting Change

Oh! I have slipped the surly bonds of Earth
And danced the skies on laughter-silvered wings;
Sunward I've climbed, and joined the tumbling mirth
Of sun-split clouds, - and done a hundred things
You have not dreamed of – wheeled and soared and swung
High in the sunlit silence. Hov'ring there,
I've chased the shouting wind along, and flung
My eager craft through footless halls of air...

Up, up the long, delirious, burning blue
I've topped the wind-swept heights with easy grace
Where never lark, or even eagle flew –
And, while with silent, lifting mind I've trod
The high, untrespassed sanctity of space,
Put out my hand, and touched the face of God.
John Gillespie Magee, Jr., RCAF - High Flight

October comes too soon filled with calendar reminders of Center activities, family responsibilities, and cards to send. Abigail's card includes a CD with fun animal songs, smiley faces, and pictures of the family's vacation in Michigan. Since I attend the Center on Tuesday and Wednesday nights, now I pick Samuel up from school on Mondays and Fridays.

Ruth picks him up the rest of the week, leaving more time for my new mission.

Life continues to change while reconsidering the mission started after Luke transitioned by the 1985 avenue of aids. Friends met during years of conferences email and phone to ask why I no longer attend. Newborn spirituality and the classes that nurture it take center stage.

"There's no 'I'm better than you' attitude at the Center, or people trying to make others feel small; no stealing of each others energy," I tell them, with delicious delight. "Everyone gets their energy from what most people call God. I refer to It as the Maker of us all, the Source, the Universal Consciousness. It takes a bit of learning but we can all connect to this energy, to give and take, in times of need."

"So, how's that working for you?" asks one of my oldest friends during a quick telephone conversation.

"I've successfully decreased the number of medications I take through meditation, affirmations, and other positive means," I calmly reply. "And I'm pleased with myself and feel blessed."

"What kind of a reaction are you getting from James," she inquires with a worried voice.

"My husband is going through his mid-life change and doesn't seem to find value in what I do," I answer honestly. "Although we live in the same house, we sleep in different rooms and basically ignore each other. I think he's growing in other ways as he works his new job and learns how to manage the checkbook." I take a deep breath before adding, "One of the reasons I stopped my volunteer work is because he's refusing to support my efforts but there's hope for now he seems interested in marriage counseling again."

I sense her concern as she pauses before asking the next question.

"Are you getting the support you need from the rest of your family?"

"Wow, that's a loaded question," I tell her laughing heartily. "The rest of my family is mainly close-minded and were talking about putting me in an institution because I don't think as they do. I see things like raw energy and orbs, hear odd noises, meant to get my attention so I'll listen to messages, and I follow the flow of Spirit."

"I see," Amanda replies with a nervous chuckle.

"It's okay Amanda," I quickly announce while changing the CD playing in the background, "for there's no need to worry. I know that just as an unseen force led and supported hiv/aids efforts, it supports new missions as well. It's time for a big change and I'm ready for it. My spirit son still communicates with me in many ways, and the more I learn, the more convinced I am that Love is the key to everything."

"How does Daniel communicate with you?"

"He changes songs that play on my portable CD player or talks to me in dreams. Sometimes he waits until I say my blessings, at two o'clock in the morning, or talks while I'm driving."

The line is silent as I sense Amanda has her fill of metaphysical talk.

"Well, it's getting late and I've got to hang up and get to bed," she says, ending our conversation.

Unconcerned, I start nightly blessings with the usual words of peace, love, and harmony. The words comfort me in times of stress, as well as at night, before crawling onto the uncomfortable futon to sleep. I picture peace, love and harmony, among all living things, even whilst hoping to end the parade of bugs warranting attention. Various bugs find freedom after I carry them outside. I consider it one of my tests.

Spiritual growth remains my top priority. Intuition tells me more people will begin to seek help, while trying to determine why they feel so lost and confused. They'll wonder why the world seems to have suddenly gone wrong. I plan to lend a hand, when allowed, even knowing people with closed minds, like my family, are not ready to accept help.

Classes prompt a change in beliefs, I never dreamed possible, upon recalling my view of God as a child and now as an adult. Words such as Mind and consciousness quickly become common while designing positive affirmations to improve life in general. Affirmations become my saving grace. If repeating an affirmation leads my mind to a state of consciousness, where it accepts what I want to believe, then I'm all for repeating affirmations throughout the day. The words, "I AM God in health," energize me. Daily meditation is a vital part of class work as well.

Time so freely spent on business newsletters, electronic lists, and websites becomes scarce as I focus more intently on spirituality. Guilt, over limiting the old hiv/aids nutrition business, consumes me as I send out a heartfelt message to friends, subscribers, and colleagues.

"As many people, 9/11/01 prompted me to think of how fragile human life is. I have felt an increasing urgency to help my fellow human beings differently, in this ever-changing and chaotic world, since that life-changing tragedy.

"For the past almost ten years, my business has not met expenses even without paid employees. Volunteers, articles, and other resources just seemed to appear at the right time to keep the mission alive. In the past year, business support has literally disappeared.

"Since the passing of my 37-year-old son, I have sensed that my mission is to now broaden efforts, toward a more comprehensive goal, serving humanity in a different way. Recent events confirm my beliefs. For this reason, I am striving to become a Licensed Practitioner through Religious Science. I must let go of the past to make room in my life for this new humanitarian mission. I must find a way for the business to continue, and for me to care for myself, and cover the costs of my new mission.

- 226 -

"I have had offers to exploit the business, for monetary gain, by advertising various products used for hiv/aids, mainly drug companies. I would like to avoid the exploitation of the business while still assuring that the information already developed, and published, remains accessible to the general public. I am now in the process of finding a way to do this."

Days later, on our eighteenth wedding anniversary, I go with James to see Martha. Intuition guides me to buy her a popular talking doll for her birthday, which is in a few days. Our joint visit is my present to him. It's the best present I can imagine knowing the quick, infrequent visits to see Martha's deteriorating form, on his way to fish in the Everglades, are not pleasant. The three-hour round trip is always tiring. There is no way to tell if traffic will allow us to return to the big city in time for dinner at a reasonable hour. We plan on having dinner nearby after the visit.

We sign in at the front desk and walk slowly to her room. Martha greets James, with a cheery hello, while glancing behind him to look at me.

"Who's your new friend?" she asks, with wide-eyed innocence while clasping hands in her lap.

Martha does not remember me. I step forward and hand her the loosely wrapped present.

"Mom," I explain while helping her tear off the gift-wrap from the doll, "I know it's been a while since you've seen me but it hasn't been that long."

Her face lights up when I lift the doll from its shiny box and push on its stomach.

"I love you," says the doll enthusiastically.

Martha claps her hands with delight as I place the toy on her lap.

"She'll talk to you whenever you hold her," I tell Martha lightly pressing the dolls hand to make sure the computer chip engages.

LightworkersLog.com

"What fun will we have today?" the doll asks brightly.

Martha's hand flies to her mouth in surprise.

"Oh, my, where did this come from?" she asks with glee.

The toy doll is a hit. It now causes squeals of delight and thanks from Martha when we repeatedly answer her question and announce that it is hers. It is the first, and last, time I see her ecstatically happy. I'm jealous of her new ability to live in the Now moment, even if it is the result of Alzheimer's.

Some souls choose the experience of Alzheimer's or other memory disorders before birth. Being present in the "Now" is a doorway into inter-dimensional consciousness. Living in the "Now" affords the opportunity to connect deeper to our Self, all life forms, and the Creative Energy surrounding us. This enables us to reach our full potential as a multi-dimensional being.

The present moment offers us many valuable qualities such as no history from the past or agenda for the future. Filled with peace, and stillness of heart and mind, we rely on our inner strength rather than relying on logic. It is a state of true centeredness, being seen, and known, for who we are now and accepting everything as a moment of gratitude. We become more open to the potential for magic and transformations, and being one with the experience, reduce unwanted energy loss through power games, emotional tricks, or the adrenaline instinct to drive our actions.

James and I retreat to separate bedrooms, after a quiet dinner, eager to end the day. The forgotten pieces of our Selves slowly incorporate back into the fold of our being, and although we do not realize it yet, once all the pieces are back in place we will part for the final time.

We compromise parts of whom we are in order to survive. The vague feeling of being incomplete often drives us to fill the void by partnering with someone who demonstrates the qualities we no longer recognize in ourselves. I spent many years working excessively, often two jobs at a time to care for two children, missing the luxury of spending time with them, or my thoughts.

When James entered the scene, I felt complete, for he possessed all the things I gave away while struggling to survive. He was my opposite, my perfect other half, the soul mate that made me 'whole' again. I needed to learn how to enjoy myself and take time out for the simple pleasures in life. I needed to stop restricting myself so much and let go with wild abandon. James held all the characteristics, and traits, that I buried long ago and now subconsciously recognized the need to integrate back into my life.

The years served us well as we slowly welcomed back the dismembered parts of ourselves. We would no longer feel the need for one another after realizing the inherent wholeness within ourselves.

Time-consuming email updates and newsletters on hiv nutrition decrease, while slowly gravitating toward a new mission. Lorna Owens discusses "Turning Our Dreams into Reality" at the monthly Sister's in Spirit dinner. Family members decide a free dinner is not worth their time so I forge ahead alone. All is well as I advance towards a new, unknown assignment. But another test lies on the horizon.

:-)

Chapter Twenty-Two

Family Fun

You are here to manifest God's love in all that you do. Many times it will feel easier to go along with the desires of the lower self, but be patient. Don't succumb to the waves of mass consciousness. Seek truth even when many attempt to fill your head and your heart with falsehoods. Never compromise your spiritual ideals, because that hinders your progress. Never forget that you are an eternal child of God. James Van Praagh - Reaching to Heaven

Most family weekends discourage me. They serve as a way to clash while sharing power play techniques. I agree to a family outing during a moment of loving compassion. Momma misses her youngest daughter and Ruth prefers to have me along.

Sarah lives nearly four hours away. I'm not looking forward to the trip but decide to make the best of it by driving Momma so we can avoid much of the struggle for human energy. We leave earlier than Ruth to assure that frequent bathroom stops do not set us too far behind. A new affirmation, to keep me centered, sits safely in my pocket.

Momma stares blankly, with legally blind eyes, as I point to numerous things during our leisurely drive. She talks until it seems there's nothing left to say and then I play music CDs for her. They're not very good so I resort to cassette tapes before singing along to Daniel's memorial CD. Momentary glances assure that Momma likes my singing. Her face repeatedly morphs to form smiles.

We stop at every turnpike rest area to use the bathroom. Momma continues to note she's full from a lunch of fruited yogurt but agrees to an ice cream sandwich after two hours. She eats very quickly but denies being hungry. Chocolate cake mixed with ice cream melts down cheeks and chin after her first bite. I pass the wet naps as she settles comfortably back into her seat when the treat disappears.

"Dinner will probably be the ham and potato salad I left at your house last night for Ruth and Terry to bring in the vans cooler," I announce loudly so she can hear.

"Terry warmed it up," she informs me with a chuckle, "last night when he got home from dinner and drinking with his buddies."

I shake my head in disbelief and silently repeat the affirmation.

The beautiful, orange, setting sun is such a treasure to see that I miss the turn to our rented three-bedroom villa. After an hour, of being hopelessly lost and asking for directions several times, we reach the complex an hour after everyone else.

They have left the big bedroom, with the private bath, for me. But I point out the wisdom of giving it to Momma while talking about respect for elders. Rebecca and I discussed the decision days ago. Momma seems to enjoy having her own room and promptly takes a nap.

Rebecca and Terry smirk and talk about who "won the bet" minutes later. Apparently, they bet I would say something and I met their hope. They act as two "birds of a feather," concerned with only what they can do to make themselves happy. There's no opportunity for meditation so I resign myself to repeating affirmations as Spirit helps me through the weekend.

Family discussions of schedules progress while I unpack food brought from home.

"I thought," I announce while storing snacks, "that we could just chill out, watch movies, hang around the pool, and use the whirlpool."

"Boring," Rebecca and Terry say in unison, nodding their heads at one another.

"That doesn't sound like much fun to me," says Ruth.

I silently repeat my one-sentence affirmation.

"I do not react to outside forces as Spirit freely guides every aspect of my life."

Rebecca and Terry leave with a grocery list to complement the food we have. It's four hours after Momma's usual dinnertime when they return with bags from a fast-food restaurant. At nine o'clock in the evening, I scowl watching Momma wolf down a greasy hamburger and fried onion rings, forbidden by physicians. She immediately gets sick. Terry takes her into the bathroom to clean up and get ready for bed. I wolf down food from home while he does.

Sarah's husband drops her off an hour later. Momma rises to kiss her before promptly returning to bed. When Terry goes outside to smoke, I decide we need to talk.

"You know," I say, gently touching his arm, "even with my degree in nutrition; I don't know how to feed Momma."

I hint at what might be best for her diet because doctors diagnosed me with the same diseases (irritable bowel, gastrointestinal reflux disease, and gastritis). "Perhaps," I silently hope, "he will give her the prescribed diet of six, small, low-fat meals with whole grains, instead of their much-loved white flour and fatty junk food."

Family discussion centers on a fun-filled weekend when we rejoin them. As Ruth, Terry, and Rebecca think of fun things to do, Sarah quietly arranges personal things in our bedroom. I think about medication schedules (Momma's, Sarah's, and my own), and bathroom habits, wondering how the focus of our trip got changed to a frantic, fun-packed weekend. Terry and Rebecca still cannot afford to pitch in for the villa but they can afford fun times. Sarah's husband has given her one-hundred dollars to spend yet, she tells us they cannot afford one of her medicines.

It seems that everything Ruth, Terry, and Rebecca desire will be difficult to do for Momma, Sarah, and I. Feeling the need to step away from drama, I joke around while unpacking Sarah's forbidden ice chest of wine coolers. Samuel takes several pictures as I pretend to drink from small, colorful bottles and get drunk. I know Daniel's spirit directs as he works the camera. Photos reveal several transparent orbs.

My determination to remain centered and thereby avoid power plays disappoints everyone when I turn down a drink. The week's homework, another positive affirmation, sits in my pocket. Adults talk and drink around the table as I retire to say my blessings. It's early for me but they plan to wake early so I decide to do the same.

I so look forward to sleeping in a real bed for now the futon at home is very uncomfortable. Iron bars dig into my back despite new foam pads placed under the thin, black cushion. How heavenly it feels to plop down, smile, and quickly drop off to sleep!

Sarah and I take turns, all night long, getting up to use the bathroom. At one point, I jostle her out of a semi-comatose state, as she stands looking confused, in the middle of the bedroom. I can tell her diabetes is not under control. She gets up shortly after nine o'clock in the morning but I decide to sleep for a few more minutes.

Rebecca soon sits upon my comfortable bed.

"Time to get up Mom," she says smiling while holding a large cup of coffee. "We're trying to plan our day."

A nice, restful visit, which does not disrupt medication schedules or daily activities of living, seems practical, but I do not voice my opinion. I silently repeat my affirmation instead and feel calmer.

Several attraction flyers sit on the living room table. I shuffle through them minutes later while watching the main players decide what everyone will do.

"Here's a dinner show for half-off," I announce loudly.

Everyone agrees to go to the "Al Capone Dinner Show."

It cost more than we usually pay for dinner but Ruth, Terry, and Rebecca search for something else to do. After grumbling over the cost of Disney and Universal Studios, the discussion turns to "Captain Kidd's Adventure," a mini-golf course that I adamantly oppose. Momma does not care what we do as long as she sees Sarah. I think of the heat of the day and Momma, with her cane, trying to walk through a maze of fake grass.

The "get me through this family weekend affirmation" silently repeats in my head while deciding to play mini-golf. I'm still working on my big cup of coffee when it's time to go. It's a familiar practice, during family outings, for me to forego the daily bathroom elimination, breakfast, and medications schedule, even knowing I will later suffer physically and mentally. I now wish for the freedom "to fly" after the weekend.

One look at the up and down course tells me Momma cannot walk through it. Everyone ignores me and walks away when I ask to take a picture of our group at the entrance. I quickly lose my center. Rebecca hears me curse.

"F**k you all, I don't need people in my pictures anymore."

I return to the entrance, to snap a picture of lilac flowers, as the others head for the first hole, after leading Momma to a table in the shade. A constant parade of butterflies encourages me greatly. I'm amazed at how quickly one appears when I ask to see a purple one. A border

of light brown encloses the pale lilac butterfly. It has darker purple spots, and small, black circles within the spots.

As we walk through the course, I take pictures of the landscape whenever there's a good shot or Daniel's spirit is near. Thoughts of his decision to deal with addiction issues, by reincarnating, prompt sadness. Current beliefs do not allow the luxury of frequent visits from spirits who chose rebirth. I'll miss hearing him so often; for I believe, spirits only communicate with those on earth if they chose to remain behind the veil of the Otherside.

The decision is best for him so I wish him well and vow to help, by staying near Abigail upon my own transition, if blessed to be that advanced. A vast amount of work to help my spirit advance stands before me, before returning with loved ones for the "last war." The small voice within adamantly promises to carry on, for Daniel, to blaze through the trail he made so that everyone knows there really is an afterlife.

Constant reminders irk family members.

"I'll be bugging you after I pass because we don't die, we only change form," I repeatedly announce.

Of course, they still call me crazy. They may not yet realize minds must be open for it to happen. My major wish, to get out of this body as soon as possible, remains while trying to live each day as if it's the last.

Momma roasts in 90-degree heat, with her sweater on, at a table partly under an umbrella, while Sarah and I help each other up slopes to eighteen holes of mini-golf. Our group takes a long time to play. Sarah's knee, and all my joints, cry for relief as Ruth allows several players ahead of us.

It really is a beautiful, and fun, mini-golf course but I cannot enjoy it knowing that Momma sits alone. It's unfair and ill-suited with the original reason for our trip. My digital camera continues to monitor pictures by occasionally refusing to work. Sensing Daniel's spirit, I ask Samuel to pose. A small white orb sits near his nose when the photo appears on camera.

Sarah and I sweat profusely, and are out of breath and exhausted, after eighteen holes of mini-golf. My joints remind me that the Celebrex, prescribed for osteoarthritis, sits in its plastic bottle at the villa. Momma found a nearby bathroom, during the two hours we played, but missed seeing the table next to her that sprayed a steady, cool mist of water from its umbrella. She's also hot and tired. We join Ruth for a short nap back at the villa while everyone else walks over to the swimming pool.

The world seems a better place when I climb out of my lovely bed and agree to be designated driver for the evening.

Momma enjoys the actor cop trying to rile her up while we wait outside in line. The food buffet offers a variety of choices. I try to stick to my diet while eating during the 1920's style gangster show. Momma seems to like the music. The evening ends with a spray of balloons. Some of them hold slips of paper designating prizes. Both Samuel and Sarah are thrilled to win plastic gangster hats.

Our exhausted Momma retires as soon as we return to the villa. I hear prayers while using her bathroom and kiss her goodnight. It occurs to me we were lucky to get last-minute seats in the front so she could see the show. Many people, who reserved tickets weeks, or months, earlier had to sit in the back of the room.

Ruth, Rebecca, and Terry are ready to play pinochle with me thinking Sarah can watch. It's important to me that Sarah does not feel ignored. I quickly announce that my schedule includes watching a movie brought from home but I will help Sarah play cards while doing so. Sarah is very slow as I periodically help her play through a couple of hands. She has a hard time sorting, and holding, the cards.

Terry decides to wash and dry clothes. It's difficult to hear the movie playing on my computer so I decide to retire at one o'clock in the morning. As the rest of my family heads to their rooms, I lay in bed wondering when the noisy dryer will stop. It sits directly across from our bedroom and continues to disrupt the entire villa. Terry finally turns it off, after about an hour, cussing that it's not drying the clothes.

Sarah and I again do our bathroom runs throughout the night.

Everyone, except Momma, still seems asleep when I get up at nine o'clock in the morning. I consider calling for a late checkout and sneak back into bed. The rush of scurrying feet soon fills the air, as everyone runs about trying to get their things together so Ruth, as usual, will not yell at them for not being ready when she is.

I rise quickly to pack and store things in the car while silently repeating my affirmation. Everyone seems surprised when I'm ready to go by 10:00 AM. As the rest of the family drinks coffee, makes their bathroom trips, and puts things into Ruth's van, I sit next to Momma on the couch while she pretends to watch television.

We leave the villa forty-five minutes later. Sarah drives with Ruth while Momma sits in my car. Ruth's trip will be longer than our drive for Sarah's house is more than an hour out of our way.

Numerous, amazing butterflies fly past Momma and I as we motor down the turnpike. They swoop down from above, on Momma's side of the car, to drift past my eyes before swooping back up to the sky. I lose count of them, for within the first two hours of driving, one or two glides past us every few miles. It's the most amazing thing I've ever seen, besides the lilac butterfly. An empty parking spot sits, just about directly in front of the entrance to the turnpike bathroom, every time we stop to relieve ourselves. We arrive at Terry and Momma's place before three o'clock in the afternoon. Momma is happy to take a nap after taking her lunch pill.

An overwhelming feeling of tiredness fills me while driving home. Life seems so different from how it was in the past. The hectic trip cost me two days of scheduled medications, missed breakfasts, and bowel movements so I happily drink a pot of coffee upon arriving home. Hours later, I lay down for a nap and again pray not to wake up.

Images flash through closed-eye vision less than an hour later. One of them is Daniel with his endearing smile. I jolt myself awake.

"I'm still alive so what is it I need to do?" I ask.

"No one knows the exact time that they will be allowed to pass," is the reply.

"Stay the course Mom, stay the course," Daniel announces.

I rise smiling to finish the laundry before James returns from his fishing trip.

The years have served me well. It is now easy to realize that absolutely everything that troubled me about our family weekend, was either something I needed to change, or some outdated action finally removed from my life, which was trying to squirm its way back in to suit the ego.

:-)

Chapter Twenty-Three

Riding Out the Storm

All matter is just a mass of stable light.
Sri Aurobindo

Possibilities looming on the horizon in mid-October present overwhelming challenges. Thoughts of a rich, political agenda that robs America in every conceivable way concern me greatly. My mind views the increase in public monitoring devices, and the people they watch, as if worlds apart from me. Online banking and the use of plastic money will change the world less to my liking. Will a perceived future of disastrous earth changes, affecting scores of people, a bankrupt Social Security system, and lost pension plans really affect humanity? It's almost unbearable to watch the power plays unfold.

"People who have saved hard-earned money, and funneled it into stocks and bonds or government held accounts, will lose it all," I hurriedly write in a journal.

Yet, a glimmer of hope breaks though gloomy thoughts. It's my task, and the task of other old souls, to try and save humanity before we become as extinct as the Wooly Mammoth.

Each day I dread waking. Twelve-year-old Samuel takes on the attitude of family, to become more vocal, so our savored relationship changes. Torn between ego and the mission that looms before me, I stop recording political news when Samuel announces he will never watch the tapes. My mind stays open upon remembering that close-minded people end up alone, resentful, and bitter.

I finally announce publication of the last hiv nutrition newsletter for it stems spiritual growth. The doctor seems amazed by my normal blood pressure but warns me to continue the hypertension medication, which I now take only on rare occasions.

Three days later, on a glorious Monday evening, I meet the man who becomes my metaphysical mentor and friend. Dr. Charles D. Geddes prefers that we call him by his first name. I immediately love him knowing questions asked will reap honest and informative answers. His seminar at the Center rejuvenates me. Upon leaving for home, hope overflows more than any other time since Daniel's transition.

Daniel's spirit warns of an upcoming storm and Wilma soon forms southwest of Jamaica. Two days later, it becomes the strongest tropical cyclone on record in the Atlantic basin with 185 mph winds. The storm moves slowly, causing heavy damage to Cancun and Cozumel, as we all wait to see where it will head next.

As Wilma moves towards the Gulf of Mexico, and the people around me stay complacent, Daniel confides it will be a surprise Category 3 storm in South Florida.

"Don't worry Mom," he assures, "you will all be okay. I'll ride out the storm with you but then I need to go."

There's no reason to doubt him so I promptly withdraw cash from the checking account and began storm preparations. Within days, Wilma sharply changes directions, passes north of Cuba, and heads for southern Florida.

Wilma's outside feeder bands pass us on Thursday night as I video the action. The wind is very slight as she heads for the Gulf of Mexico but rains trigger flooding all around Fort Lauderdale. I decide to ride out the rest of the storm with Rebecca, and Samuel, as waters flood the lot behind our house and begin to fill the yard.

Everyone believes the worst is over. No one in my family considers putting up storm shutters until Wilma sharply changes directions to head back our way. Forecasters predict a mild Category 1 storm. Unsure if the leaking roof will withstand the storm, I spend several hours carefully packing precious things from my china cabinets into boxes the next morning. The greeting cards, with their colored envelopes for Abigail, sit on top of my desk. Twelve months of cards are ready to mail in case something happens to me. I want to make sure they stay safe.

Several boxes and my external hard drives are safely stored in the trunk of my car by nightfall. The talking Furby sits in the passenger seat as I drive to Rebecca's house.

"Be okay," it squawks, as I drive quickly through light traffic.

Although obviously tired of hearing talk of the Otherside, and adamant about not being videoed, it's clear that Rebecca and Samuel are glad to have me there. Rebecca shares her king-size bed with the cat, Princess the dog, and me.

Forecasters still expect a mild hurricane by morning, but within hours, they have their doubts. South Florida is now under a tornado watch as water sprouts erupt near Key West. Rebecca and Samuel begin to put up shutters. I videotape the action. The rain and wind that affected our area the night before is gone. We now enjoy a beautiful day full of sunshine and the familiar Florida heat. Science of Mind classes strongly affect the way I look at things. I point out safe animal harbors, in many trees surrounding the property, while manifesting butterflies. And I laugh with delight as the butterflies fly around me.

It still seems extraordinary that Rebecca lives in the home bought so many years ago by Zephaniah and Martha. Built in 1955, it has withstood numerous hurricanes but this year I have my doubts. Rotting wood, and small plants growing out of the leaking roof, are the source of my concern. Yet I know the land is sacred, for Indians lived upon it many years ago, and Daniel assures our safety.

The three-bedroom house stands less than a block from the Davie Boulevard Bridge next to an empty house on Middle River. The energy of the land invigorates me every time I walk Princess through the large lot next door. I know that spirits protect it. Sometimes while walking though the tall grass, I bless the land with love, light, and protection using the same blessing for my own home.

Rebecca and Samuel reenter the house after placing shutters over windows that James thinks will bear the brunt of the storm. Even though they do not shutter all the windows, I still feel protected in the hammock of sacred land.

"Trees will fall," Daniel confides.

I quickly move my car, away from the trees, behind Samuel's shuttered bedroom.

Rebecca's empty hope chest holds my packed boxes after dinner. The external hard drives fit in Samuel's closet. Wilma has a 400-mile diameter, and features tropical winds reaching 230 miles outside of her core, by the time I finish my homework on the back porch. There's no rain and very little wind. Forecasters in Key West now report the possibility of a Category 1, Category 2, or Category 3 storm. No one seems sure of anything, not even the expert, Max Mayfield.

The anorexic cat and Princess dance nervously throughout the house as I video their indecision. Kitty searches for safe harbor as my camera picks up blue streams of energy. More than twenty spirit orbs hover in a picture of Samuel. I finally admit to a nervous Rebecca that Daniel warned me about the storm.

"Your brother is protecting us," I calmly note.

She stares in disbelief before venturing onto the back porch to smoke. Orbs are too numerous to count in another digital picture of Samuel.

Rebecca reenters the house with a frown so I take her place on the back porch. The newly, honed down, storm treatment flows from my lips while sitting in a chair facing the water. Instead of the usual, "please God keep us safe" prayer of youth, the treatment acknowledges this peaceful, and harmonious, God of all living things. Although I have doubts as to whether it successfully incorporates Science of Mind principles, we'll be safe throughout the storm.

"God is in all things and always in the Light that flows within us," I note to the increasing wind. "This Divine Spirit made us in Perfect Love and Safety. We are filled with Harmony and Peace," my voice booms as a gust of wind blows through the screens.

Feeling the spirits of my protective soul group, I continue.

"God guides us as we experience this storm. Spirit's flow of Divine Love, Safety, Harmony, and Peace is unstoppable within our experience."

My voice does not waver and no one interrupts this new form of prayer.

"We are thankful that Spirit surrounds us with Love, Safety, Harmony, and Peace," I declare loudly to the night air. "As the Law of God accepts these words, they flow out into the Universal Consciousness. And so it is."

The Tibetan Art of Living offers a respite from ego's constant worry. I'm pleased with myself for bringing it from home. Wind whips quickly past a neighbor's noisy flagpole while I sense something in the darkness beyond Rebecca's yard. The book now becomes secondary. A yellow bookmark notes the page as I rise to investigate.

Intuition tells me to bless the land again. I walk to the middle of the neighbor's yard and stand under a huge ancient tree. Both arms rise to the midnight sky as blessings, filled with Love and Light, pour forth. The frequent sound of the bridge, as it rises to allow boat traffic in from the sea, is suddenly missing. There's only the sound of an occasional car by the time I walk back to the house.

Colored porch lights barely sway amid the increasing howling wind but the flagpole noise increases. By three o'clock in the morning on October 23, 2005, Wilma's eye wall is on the west coast near Naples. Its outer rain bands reach our east coast with hurricane winds. Madonna's hit song "Live to Tell" flows from my lips while flipping through a 1963 dictionary noting the many times Peter plus SAM appears. All is well. I quickly fall asleep but rise after two hours to finish storm preparations.

Both houses hold cash, batteries, hurricane food, and other necessities. I have cooked a meal for dinner, frozen jugs of ice, and filled the tub with water. It's time to pop Sunday night's popcorn while I make my coffee.

"Make it now Mom," Daniel's voice echoes inside my head.

Egos soar when the lights flicker and I begin my treatment out loud in the kitchen.

"Can't you wait until I leave the room," Rebecca asks adamantly. "I don't try to force my religion down your throat."

"Just because she hasn't prepared is no reason to take it out on someone else," my ego counters out loud after she leaves the room. "Who does that remind you of?"

With a start, I realize it is I.

The electricity goes out for the last time as soon as the second pot of coffee fills the container. I am so very glad to have inside information, while packing the cooler with drinks and food for the next two days, before saying my treatment again. Key West is waterlogged as Samuel hums

- 244 -

the Jeopardy song. Forecasters expect the storm to stay over us for twelve hours. Ruth calls Rebecca to ask for a weather report. They have no batteries and their screened-in porch is gone.

A tree falls where my car was as Daniel's voice breaks through the sound of wind.

"A few more trees will fall but none will touch the house."

There are no shutters on the sliding glass doors so it's easy to see storm effects beyond the screened in porch. Rebecca and Samuel rest in the safety of Samuel's shuttered room while I sit near the doors repeating my treatment.

"You're scaring Rebecca by staying so close to the unshuttered windows," Daniel announces softly.

"I've never been so entirely at peace," I answer out loud while watching the tree branches fly majestically through the air. "This house is surrounded by good energy."

Rebecca calls James to report after emptying a pan of water that dripped from the kitchen ceiling. I videotape the wind, lifting the den windows open, while noting that Spirit protects the house. Leaves swirl around outside as I stare filled with wonder. The twenty-foot Royal Palm falls away from the house, smashes our chain link fence, and lands on the neighbor's new wooden fence and boat minutes later. Rebecca's portable radio keeps us up to date with listeners' calls and newscasters' updates as Samuel speaks with James.

Wilma's winds are 120 mph with gusts of 155 as I hear, "Storms will be more frequent, and worse, in the future. But things will change after the storms."

It's old news to me.

Rebecca, upset over not being adequately prepared for the storm, enters the dining room where I sit. Our ego's clash again.

"The days of me getting blamed for other people's inadequacies are over," I announce as she leaves the room. "How many years have I judged others?" I silently ask.

More trees fall in the neighbor's yard as I watch the tree on the east side of the house, split and close, wondering when it will finally part. I sense the danger without fear for Spirit flows through me and around the house. Firmly believing we are safe, I hear what sounds like a freight train a few times during the backside of the storm. Daniel's essence lingers as I sing words to "A Mother's Prayer." [4] A rainbow of blue, green, and purple light flashes across the video screen while I chant, "Teach us to love as you love."

The video camera continues to record the action as I watch the storm fascinated by the glory of Nature. Kitty runs under the bed to hide. A white orb passes in front of the camera when Rebecca asks me to look at her. Kitty follows it with her eyes.

"We are one with Nature," I affirm, watching the huge tree, a mere four yards away, finally split in two to fall away from the house.

A now bored Samuel sticks a pillow under his shirt and plumps up his shoulders, with push lights, to look like a football player. He scoots through the house in a comedic fashion to divert attention and make us laugh.

The storm rages a few more hours before moving on.

"You're all safe now," Daniel says inside my head. I am off to be reborn and work on my addiction issues. Are you sure you'll be okay without me Mom?"

An unforgettable feeling of love and gratefulness now overwhelms me.

"Yes," I say with a full heart, "yes, I'm sure honey. You go on and finish your business."

Rebecca, Samuel, and I watch in wonder as orange and black butterflies, and a bird with a yellow breast, flies onto the back porch past missing screens. Tree limbs and branches cover most of the large yard. Four trees lay on the ground. A large, rotted tree limb hangs in the neighbor's tree. Grass in several yard areas appears shifted, in five directions, leaving us with the impression of tornados. Glass from two broken workroom windows litters the gravel drive.

We're thankful for minor physical damage. Our entire family made it though the storm safely, as did most of Fort Lauderdale. Although I'm only able to speak with Rachel for a few minutes, she assures me they're safe before quickly hanging up the phone to assess yard damage.

Rebecca leaves for work the following day as Samuel and I continue to clear tree branches from the yard. A fat, three-foot iguana sits in the sun on the seawall beyond the neighbor's yard, filled with tree limbs and debris. Inner peace dissipates later in the day, while trying to get Samuel back into the house. I revert to my old self, threatening to call his mom, while missing my "white light room."

Two beautiful magenta colored orbs appear as the sun sets. A picture of Samuel, goofing around with the wheelbarrow, shows a magenta orb on his right eye as he pushes it through the missing screen onto the porch.

Magenta colored orbs amid a setting sun

After three days, Rebecca's house is the first in the family to have electric restored so Momma comes to stay. We help her into the bathtub in the evening. What a pleasant sight to see how lovingly my daughter attends to Grandma's needs! I happily return to the serenity of my room days later. The atmosphere in the rest of the house seems more negative so I'm glad my packed boxes remain at Rebecca's house.

Several months ago, repeated house blessings stopped nightly raccoon raids. Now I treat with added fervor to fill the house with indestructible love and light. Although I rarely leave the sanctuary of my room when James is home, I sit in the center of the house periodically throughout the day, to repeat a blessing, engulfing the house and grounds. It's a simple blessing said with calm assurance of newfound power.

"I fill this house, the houses on both sides, and the grounds on which they stand with never-ending love and white light." I announce confidently, while envisioning the area saturated with the protective substance of God. "Only love and light can enter this space."

The loving protective energy of God surrounds me to spread wherever I direct my attention.

Owen Waters, author and founder of Infinite Being (www.infinitebeing.com) notes disasters such as hurricanes, earthquakes, tornados, and floods are driven by the chaotic emotional energy of mankind. We can heal and prevent all of these things upon channeling enough spiritual energy to soothe the chaos.

Our thoughts make a difference. When we concentrate on sending healing energy into the world, instead of negative thoughts, the incidence of these occurrences will end. Many healers note changes occur as we practice a sense of gratitude and love for Mother Earth. Filling the world with peaceful thoughts, and seeing it enveloped in the white healing light of the Cosmic during meditative states, helps a great deal to rid Mother Earth of negative energy.

:-)

Chapter Twenty-Four

Comparisons

Everybody is unique. Compare not yourself with anybody else lest you spoil God's curriculum. Baal Shem Tov

Canceled Center classes prompt indecision. Am I to complete Science of Mind studies or just pave the way for someone else? Intuition leads me to believe that something BIG will happen soon, something of global importance. Increasing unrest rules due to Hurricane Wilma. A distracting sense of loss persists amid hopeful signs from the Otherside.

Wilma's wrath vastly changes the area around us, for many weeks, but aside from a few broken tree limbs, the temporary loss of electrical power, and more water on the porch from the already leaky roof, we suffer no damage. A thought fills me with gratitude for small inconveniences. How are the people of New Orleans dealing with extensive and devastating changes due to Hurricane Katrina?

After years of being strangers, neighbors suddenly find themselves together, moving debris from the street, to carry on activities of daily living. Terry has neighborhood barbeques while Ruth deals with a missing screened-in porch. The maze of rubble increases travel time considerably. Roads seem like a virtual wasteland requiring the coming together of all concerned. We dodge road debris and deal with unfixed traffic lights. Everyone remains courteous, following the driving rules for corners without streetlights, as I carefully maneuver my Nissan Sentra to get Samuel from school. Gratitude fills me when the Center reopens. I gladly walk the two-block distance to Tuesday's class and Wednesday's service.

A new avenue appears within the game of life when classwork focuses on treatments for workshop partners. My collaborator yearns for love and the ability to express through love. A treatment flows quickly from head to paper. Divine Love, I declare, flows through him as he expresses that love effectively in his primary relationship. Failing to express Divine Love toward James, I unknowingly design the treatment for myself.

Dr. Bump announces Saturday's memorial service before class ends. I'm inclined to attend even though I do not know who Jim is. Something prompts me to make a copy of Daniel's memorial CD after returning home.

All sorts of people fill "Religious Science Fort Lauderdale" when I take my seat, in the back of the sanctuary, on Saturday. The memorial card notes Jim was my age. His friends and family lovingly honor him during the service but my attention continually moves to a man who sits alone nearby. He also looks about my age and appears devastated. People soon approach him with condolences as I watch while rising to leave.

A force of positive energy propels me as he quickly tries to make his way out the door.

"I'm sorry," I say stepping into his path and stopping abruptly, "but I'd like to talk with you."

"Do I know you?" he asks politely, while looking down at me with loving eyes.

A wide smile covers my face.

"No, no. I don't think you do but I have something for you."

Daniel's memorial CD seems to quiver in my right hand.

"I know what it feels like to lose a loved one," I quietly announce.

"Yes," he confides in a whisper, with a wistful look. "Jim was special to me. We were close friends at one time. We lost touch with one another when I moved away.

"Well, the music on this CD, which my son guided me to make, helps immensely as I go through the grieving process," I confess, placing the disc in his outstretched hand. "Perhaps it will help you too."

"Thank you," he chokes out, taking a step back as if to steady himself. "I appreciate your kindness."

There's a bounce in his step as he walks away.

It feels good to be an angel of hope and love. Music always makes a difference. I sense he will listen to the CD in his car as I do. What a comfort to know that the memorial CD will help him connect with his friend, just as it helps me to communicate with Daniel!

A letter of thanks from Jim's mother, for attending the memorial service, appears a short while later. An invitation to bid on the remainder of Jim's estate accompanies the letter. It's clear that her son's geographical move, in younger years, served to separate them in many ways. I respond by sending a quick email with spiritual links. It's another communication from the Otherside to someone I barely know.

"Please know Jim is at rest now and free from all the demands of human life," I type quickly. "I have always believed that our Creator designed this plan of human life to help us spirits learn what it is to be human. Jim learned his lessons in this life and is now free to continue on as he chooses."

I explain how my view of death and the Otherside changed after my own son's passing.

"It was very difficult to let my son's spirit go," I confide, as a sigh escapes thin lips. "Now that I have, I've found much more evidence that we are all connected, all in the Spirit of Mind.

"Knowing that God dwells in us all, I know Jim is a part of you. He will always be a part of you, as you are a part of him, and God. Peace, Harmony, and Love surround you. Feel it, let it soothe you as you go about your tasks this week. I am thankful that I was able to be at Jim's service and that we were able to share a brief moment in time.

"I'm sure Jim's passing was peaceful and filled with loving thoughts of you. Know that Infinite Intelligence flows within and around you, creating a sense of peace and purpose. And I trust that the Law of Mind will forever fill your heart and mind with *All the Good There Is*."

In case she wants to talk, before heading back to her home state after settling Jim's estate, I note my times of Center attendance.

"I tell you this just in case there are any questions, or experiences, you may wish to share with another mother who has let her son fly free as a butterfly in the warm summer breeze."

Homework later prompts a great revelation upon remembering what Dr. Vendettuoli said in a world religions course. Religion, defined descriptively as life, is always about that which is human. I am spirit having a human experience! Perhaps my desire to separate from the usual study of religion surfaced with that unconscious thought. In any event, my parochial way of looking for God ended.

Dr. Bump encourages us to write more treatments. I quickly choose to design a treatment for Rebecca. She finally has the accounting job of her dreams at a fortune 500 company. The job is not physically stressful, and she gets to pick her working hours, but still seems plagued with health issues. In and out of the hospital for more than a year, she seems overloaded with physical, emotional, and financial upsets. I design the perfect treatment to help her. [5] Of course, I have to keep the treatment to myself, for Rebecca does not believe in my newfound spiritual awareness. But that does not make it any less powerful in my mind.

The greeting cards are gone when it's time to send Abigail her monthly message. I am devastated. Rebecca assures me they're not at her house and they're not here at James' house either. After years of our fighting, over my inability to help pay the mortgage, I've given the cluttered house to him, in my mind. The cards seem my only connection to Abigail. A few drinks help lessen concern as I work on the next Daniel book, while listening to Johnny Rivers' "Look to Your Soul." Unexplainable, hauntingly familiar longing accompanies the music.

"I nearly lost myself trying to be someone else," sang Johnny mournfully. "All of my life I've been playing the game. Gotta get out of myself it seems. Life's not real when you're in a dream…"

Daniel Book Three is part of my grieving process but I think it's for Abigail. Years ago, I listened to Johnny Rivers sing, consciously unaware of the meaning of his words, but still filled with a great sense of loss. Daniel's birth made life complete for I thought he was the missing piece. Now, upon looking to my soul for the answer, it's clear that I know much more than previously believed.

Work as a hospitality volunteer increases the next day before a movie at the Center. I now regularly set up the coffee station before Tuesday night class and feel comfortable in the small kitchen. *Behind the Scenes of the Celestine Prophecy* helps me to renew the promise to stop family power plays.

Huddled in my "white light room," I stare at pictures taped to the desk wondering what I could have done to avoid past trauma. My eyes rest on the picture of Abigail, taken in August, as she wore my wide-brimmed, straw hat. She appears older and wiser than her physical age of three as blue eyes stare into hazel.

"This is the last time I will see my nana again," I hear her say in my head.

I sincerely hope I am wrong.

So much has happened to draw me further away from my human self, the one that suffered so much by sensing another's pain, grief, and suffering. I still spend too much time watching news reports of hurricanes, earthquakes, tornados and floods, which sadden me beyond belief. On some days, I just do not think I can carry on. Can I survive as a human and help all the people that need comfort and love, empathy, and compassion?

Sometimes I give up and lay upon the futon begging *It* to let me come Home.

"At least," I sullenly plead to the air, "let me pass into 'the middle' where I may be of more use to humanity."

As usual, I end up encouraged by unexplained objects in the air, or the constant playing of certain songs on Daniel's memorial CD, or voices that speak softly in my head.

"Yeah, the voices in my head; it sounds nuts but it's not nuts," I swear to myself.

Encouragement always comes when I need it the most. But now I choose to get drunk because I cannot humanly bear the thought of any more loss.

Life continues to change as I experience more upsets and imaginary losses. James returns from a visit with Rachel and Abigail to relate that they are well. I quickly use his report as an excuse to email Rachel.

"Glad to hear from James that you and Abigail are doing well," I type before losing my resolve to connect with her and Abigail more fully. "I'm here for you when you need me and that will never change. Blessings."

The thought that I might not see them again consumes me but I do not call to ask if I can visit too.

It is a tough decision, to put the business up for sale, hoping someone will continue to offer the world a service my heart no longer feels bound to do. The power of my thought will provide a means to continue my new mission and the cash to prove it is a worthwhile venture.

My new laptop helps to go between work and personal projects as the desktop computer sits safely stored in the closet. When the laptop begins to malfunction, while uploading published newsletters in Adobe format to the business website, I decide to break and meet family for a trip to the 99 Cent store.

Momma is ready when I arrive after my spiritual reading. I feel strongly that another great human loss is in the wings as she turns off the television. The weather channel notes that storm number twenty-seven will most likely strengthen to be called gamma but I do not think that is the reason. We drive quickly to get Samuel from school.

The next three hours go badly from the time we meet Ruth and Naomi, at the store, until I carry Momma's groceries inside the house. The power plays and negativity wear me out. Three hours later, I'm thankful to be on the way home alone. I am uncentered and ready for a drink.

Ear-piercing noise from the car alarm fills the air before I reach my vehicle. Family now believes it's Daniel's way of saying hello but I know it is Spirit vying for attention. God, whom I refer to as Spirit, uses Daniel's voice and mannerisms to connect, for it makes me more receptive to communications. God's Voice speaks to me through a channel I love dearly and know well. However, Daniel must be reborn, to work on addiction issues, for I do not hear his voice. Perhaps, I'll take his place on the Otherside to guide Abigail, and the rest of our soul family, through tough times.

Terry's neighbor hears me tell the car alarm to stop as I acknowledge that Spirit has my full attention. His surprised grin tells me all I need to know. It's no big deal that one more person thinks I am nuts. I turn on the portable CD player after starting the car. Daniel's memorial CD begins to play. But blocks after leaving Terry's house it's erratic.

With hopeful recognition, I tell Daniel, if he has something to say he should do it quickly for I am going to break down and have a drink. It's not that I drink a lot but over the past year have found that drinking helps to get me through rough times, especially after being with family. I deserve the human release for I've successfully stayed in a spiritual state of mind in their presence.

When the message comes, I start to cry. Tears roll down my face as I sit at the traffic light less than a mile from Terry's house. My brain hears it is time to stop sending Abigail cards. Daniel assures me he will speak to Abigail about it so she will understand. Rachel will be moving out of town with her next year and I will not see her after that. I sense we will see them once more before they move. Stopping the steady flow of greeting cards will make the transition easier, for Abigail, and help her to learn the lessons she came to learn.

Abigail has lost so much for the material wealth she and her mother now seem to enjoy, my little mind tells me. People cannot, family cannot, be replaced by things. Two fish, two cats, two dogs, and a pony; ballet lessons and horse riding shows; still cannot replace a family. Abigail is such a bright, white light, full of love, caring, and tons of energy. She is very smart and loves both her ballet classes and her horseback riding.

It seems Rachel is beginning to listen to Daniel and do what he wants, at least some of the time. I ponder my actions toward her and wonder if they make a difference. Questions file through my mind like a snowball rolling downhill. Can I change the future with my actions? Have I not helped her to grow spiritually by letting her know she is not to blame for anything that happened? Have I not tried to nurture her and tell her she must always do what is best for her and Abigail? In a flash of sudden understanding I realize it's time to let Abigail go, just as I've let go of Daniel, for even such a tiny thing as sending her a card through the mail makes a difference. It is time for me to let go and trust God.

In my now drunken state at home, I still hope to transition, but agree, it's not fair to Momma. She suffered so many more losses than I did and it's just not right. I thought this new path would not be so difficult, says ego, searching for an excuse to continue drinking.

In the second series of Science of Mind classes, I will learn that a liquor habit is the desire to express life thinking it must be expressed through intoxication.

I now recognize the God within and document a vow into my computer journal.

"Throughout eternity I will remain dedicated to helping all humans grow spiritually. Throughout all eternity I will await the day that I will once again be reunited with the souls I am linked to, and love the most, all of them."

Because I still feel responsible for those souls who died in the fire, when I lived a past-life and failed to get them to follow me to freedom, I think it only right.

Rachel sounds depressed when I telephone the next day to see how she and Abigail are. A touch of sadness fills her voice.

"We lost a lot of trees. It might be time for me to move on," she confides softly, "get rid of all the material possessions I have and move to Tennessee where my old school friend lives."

I encourage her, even knowing it will never be the same if they move. Illinois, I note, might be a safer place to live. That is what intuition tells me. She responds differently than in the past and voices an urge to talk more when not in so much of a hurry.

:-)

Chapter Twenty-Five

Errands from Beyond

We are not bound by the laws of physics as we know them today. Gregg Braden - The Divine Matrix

Rebecca feels alone, she confides, upon thinking Daniel's soul chose rebirth. I'm never alone for spirit orbs, protons, electrons, and other Stuff of Matter follow me everywhere. An abundance of white and pinkish-colored orbs frequently covers my field of vision. I see green orbs as well. It's awesome, and not at all scary, as I try to identify the meaning of each colored orb.

Daniel's soul lives in a newly born body but his essence still communicates. The Universe discretely directs me to halt work when the computer malfunctions, changing beliefs yet again.

"Spirit allows me to do what it wants me to, so if someone reads this, it is because they are meant to," I write in a journal.

Spirits, I now believe, communicate from other planes and maybe from this one too. For instance, while the body sleeps. Daniel's now infrequent communications occur when his soul's host, the infant body, sleeps.

I have stopped listening to my portable CD player in the car. Copies of Daniel's last memorial CD sit, inside the glove box, waiting for opportunities to reach people who might want to hear it. Daniel guides me to take the CD player out to the car while doing errands days before Thanksgiving.

The player acts erratically as soon as the engine roars to life. It changes songs, skims across tracks, and makes the now familiar sound when a song switches to another. I head for the post office while trying to concentrate. A clear message silently enters my mind upon parking in the nearly empty lot. I am not to mail the letters or get out of the car.

Daniel directs me to drive out of the post office lot and head north, instead of west towards home. I intuitively sense directions unaware of tasks or destinations. It's now normal to travel easily through traffic, getting all green lights, since starting classes at the Center. I've also learned how to manifest beautiful butterflies to perk me up!

Green lights turn red before I reach them but butterflies soon catch my attention. The yellow or orange-gold butterflies drift across my windshield as I wait for traffic lights to turn green. It's nearly three-thirty in the afternoon when Daniel directs me through a detour off the main street. I come across a mail carrier getting out of his truck and kindly ask him to take my mail. He nods his head happily in agreement and sticks out a weathered hand as I wish him a good day before driving away.

The detour takes me east, closer towards the beach, and then west, back up Commercial Boulevard, where I wait for a slow freight train. I'm beginning to get annoyed, at all the stops, when I realize that Daniel is directing me to Jeremiah and Judith's house, again right before Thanksgiving.

I went there last year on a Daniel directed mission but cannot remember the exact house. Upon parking, I sense his friends are to get one of the CDs in my glove box. It's my task to announce that they must throw away the first memorial CD and listen only to this last one. This newer CD is more about never dying or losing anyone, just "keeping the faith."

Jeremiah pulls into his driveway while I ponder whether to get out of my car. He slowly opens the door to his dirty, white truck. I quickly get out of my little car, pleased with myself. As his big, black dog leaps out from the seat beside him, Jeremiah looks back with surprise to see me at the rear of the truck.

"Bet you didn't expect to see me did you Jeremiah?" I ask wrapping my arms around him for a quick hug.

"No, no," says Jeremiah as his eyes began to tear, "you were the last thing on my mind."

I quickly hand him the CD.

"Here, Daniel wants you to listen to this instead of the one I gave you last year. How are you?" I ask quietly.

"My Dad is much worse than he was last year and we don't know if he's going to pull though this time," Jeremiah replies with a tortured look. "How are Rebecca and Terry? I haven't heard a thing from them in a long time."

He wipes his eyes. Before I can reply, he looks deeply into my eyes and speaks.

"Tell Rebecca if there's anything, I mean anything at all, that I can do to help to please call me."

Tears fill his eyes once again making me feel strangely uncomfortable. I give him a kiss on the cheek and hug him tightly.

"I'll tell her," I say brightly. "Listen to the CD now for I'm sure there's a reason why Daniel directed me to give it to you today."

Jeremiah smiles his infectious smile as I walk quickly to my car.

I drive away wondering why I do not feel the need to wipe my mouth after kissing him. It's an odd practice recently started after kissing certain people on the cheek. I stopped kissing people on the mouth long ago. The CD player plays normally as Daniel thanks me for listening.

The next day I see my urologist so he will renew the costly prescription medicine for interstitial cystitis. It's been months since my last appointment and he's surprised to see me in such good spirits.

"Your urine is so clear it could be sold," says Dr. Fletcher with a grin. "What's changed in your life?"

His nurse answers quickly as she pulls out the sterilized patient kit.

"She's waited so long to see you that she's cured herself."

"Actually, I've started taking classes at the Religious Science Center," I tell them both excitedly, "and it's changed my life."

"Well, whatever you're doing keep it up," Dr. Fletcher replies as he lightly pushes my bare belly. "I'd be out of business if all my patients used the power of their mind."

Before leaving his office, I decide to cut the prescribed drug dose down from six to two pills a day.

Science of Mind classes continue to make a positive difference. I have not contemplated what I value, or what my most important goals are, for a long time. The "Hidden Belief Exercise" helps to uncover hidden beliefs while realizing it's possible to rediscover my Self. I finish homework, in class, by creating another treatment. [6]

We break into small groups to explore the evenings' questions. Workshop partners speak of things I've believed for years. They stare at me with awe as I excitedly relate experiences, such as seeing undifferentiated substance, Stuff of Matter, float before my eyes. A rich source of personal information on mental telepathy, and the power of love, I'm ready to allow Law to flow through me.

"Are you familiar with *A Course In Miracles*?" a young man asks with curiosity.

I answer no and quickly forget the question.

My personal observations of death garner attention after class. Based on the experiences of family, and close friends, I conclude that it's often five years from the time of a near-death experience until an actual passing. Both Daniel and Zephaniah spent many days in the hospital, hovering between life and death, five years before they made their transition. I try to determine how long one can stay in "the middle" before rebirth and conclude it could be eighteen months or more.

Thanksgiving Day is upon us. For the first time in years, I want to remain at home in my "white light room." Despite newfound spirituality, disruptions pull us apart, whenever I join family. Terry takes on the responsibility of cooking the family dinner that we often shared at Rachel and Daniel's house. I wonder how he's managing and call to ask at eight o'clock in the morning. When he tells me he will put the turkey in the oven at noon, for a 4:00 PM dinner, I cringe.

"You could have waited a few more hours to call me," Terry says tiredly. "I didn't get home from the bar with my friends until five o'clock this morning."

I offer to help, instead of taking the bait, and quickly end the call after agreeing to bring a fruit tray.

Last minute shoppers fill Albertson's when I pay for the fruit salad with money from my hidden stash. James sits outside at the patio table, talking to still unemployed Ruth when, I arrive. She's now profoundly depressed. Our younger brother Amos is in jail for drug use. It's cause for celebration because he'll eat and clean up once again. Hopefully, my dietitian friends in the correction system will remember him.

Terry glares angrily as I enter the house. I promptly ignore him while giving Momma a hug.

"What's wrong with your eyes Momma?" I question, backing away, upon seeing familiar fingernail marks.

We spend the next few minutes in high alert mode as Terry admits he refuses to fill her prescription, "because her insurance changed and now it cost too much money."

"I'm sure you know what you're doing," I tell him walking outside to join the others.

"Huh," says Terry with a nod of his head and hands on his hips.

Rebecca and Samuel pull into the drive just in time to help Terry with the mashed potatoes. I sigh with relief. Naomi arrives last and continues to intimidate, instigate, and separate family for the rest of the day. As the beer begins to flow, no one asks why she and Ruth drove separate cars just like James and I.

My camera refuses to work but dinner is surprisingly good. The savory meal settles into my stomach like a lead weight. I gladly leave after Naomi steps up her intimidation efforts using the "interrogation" power play. It's just too hard to keep my mouth shut.

More than ever before, I pay attention to things around me. Everything seems to work out when I follow the clues, or hear words, and do what I think is appropriate. James now takes care of his own laundry in addition to writing the checks. He also gives me small sums of money to pay for little things.

It is almost as if he knows he needs to learn how to live by himself. He lessens fishing activities to concentrate on house repairs and yard work. A new, two-day a week, evening job affords him with extra money and the fly-casting experience necessary to meet his goal of being a guide. And for the first time, he shops alone at his retail job to buy Samuel birthday presents.

Rebecca and I take Samuel and friends to a new Harry Potter movie the Saturday before his thirteenth birthday. It's a treat for me as well for money from my secret stash buys everyone's ticket. Boys act like little angels after I threaten them with a big hug, and kiss, for misbehavior.

Samuel becomes an official teenager the next day. Most family members celebrate the long awaited occasion at a local restaurant. We watch him open gifts full of the thoughtfulness that one has when missing a loved one now on the Otherside. No one actually says it, but we all still miss Daniel's playful attitude. His absence creates a somber mood.

Samuel's mood wavers, between a pubescent boy to a young man well aware that he's missed the luxury of a steady male role model. Family friends, unable to attend, sent gifts of money and electronic games via Rebecca. I watch him open gifts from me, purchased at the 99 Cent store, knowing he chose his souls' lessons before birth. James returns from a trip to his van as we wait for our server to bring birthday cake.

"I've got something for you from Rachel," he says, with a sly grin placing a bulky, wrapped present on the table in front of Samuel.

Everyone is now used to getting reports of Rachel and Abigail from James. Yet, they now stare at him with disbelief.

Samuel's mood brightens at the thought of an unexpected gift. We watch as he quickly tears the wrapping paper apart. The expression on his face changes when he sees the gift is his Uncle Daniel's Play Station 2. We watch speechless as he fights back tears remembering the many times they fooled around with the Play Station together.

"Uncle Daniel wants you to have it now Samuel," I tell him softly.

The server weaves though a crowd of people. Samuel's chocolate cake, with fourteen lit candles, glides above his head as a troop of singers follow.

"Happy birthday to you," sings the group in unison.

I watch proudly as Samuel goes through the motions of blowing out the candles without crying. He's beginning to control emotions, after years of emotional outbursts, and it makes me happy to see progress. The knife cuts through three layers of chocolate cake before I place a huge chunk of it in front of Samuel.

"Are you sure that's big enough?" says Rebecca sarcastically, with a look that would have shamed me years ago.

Samuel begins to eat, by mouthing cake like Daniel, with a lascivious grin on his face. A single tear clings to his brown, left eyelashes, the one eye that's visible to me. My only grandson is growing up too fast.

I'm anxious to print pictures upon arriving home. The video camera is no longer a part of family events so digital photos are all I have to physically document events and Daniel's presence. Pictures show undifferentiated energy, and numerous white orbs, all around us.

The next day I pick Samuel up from school ready to discuss the illusion of loss. He gets into the car quietly. We ride in silence for several minutes while I marvel at the beauty of the day.

"Mom and I cried for a long time when we got home," says Samuel from the back seat of my little car.

"Yes, I did a bit of crying too but it was because I'm so proud of you Samuel. You know, Uncle Daniel is still around. We just can't see him. But I can tell you one thing," I confide softly looking back at him in the rear view mirror, "he is very proud of you too."

"I can't believe Aunt Rachel gave me the Play Station," he says wistfully looking out the window. "Why didn't she save it for Abigail?"

"I'm certain she knows how special it is to turn thirteen years old and I know she believes Uncle Daniel wants you to have the game system," I reply without pause. "She could have been following his instructions just like I do."

"Nana," Samuel begins sounding like a disbelieving adult, "I don't believe he talks to you."

I stop for a red light, and turn back to reply, knowing that what I say will affect him deeply.

"Nobody dies Samuel. We just change forms when we leave our bodies."

He bites his lip while contemplating a response. I turn back toward the light. In a short time, we arrive at his house and all his attention goes to the game system.

Samuel plays as I sleep, sitting upright, in a chair on the back porch outside. I rise much more frequently during the night now and often find myself napping during the day. My odd sleeping habits do not bother me at all for I believe Universal Consciousness needs me, on other planes, at certain times. Knowing my essence connects to our Creator, I'm always responsive to giving and receiving.

I wake after an hour nap to contemplate my family's state of affairs while scanning the huge yard for butterflies. Butterflies do not seem as plentiful as before I decided not to pass quietly into the night. It's difficult to stand back and let people learn their own lessons. Sometimes it is hard to determine if interfering will stem their spiritual growth or support the process. I decide that raising teenagers is like nailing Jell-O to a tree.

:-)

Chapter Twenty-Six

Glimpsing The Past

Now he has departed from this strange world a little ahead of me. That means nothing. People like us, who believe in physics, know that the distinction between past, present and future is only a stubbornly persistent illusion.
Albert Einstein

The "Knots Landing Reunion" television show plays as I sit humanly alone. Rebecca and Daniel always stopped whatever they were doing on Thursday nights, sometimes much to the dismay of partners, to visit and watch "Knots Landing." It offered a way to catch up on life's affairs. We bemoaned our lot in life, sought advice when needed, cheered Val on and hissed at Abby. I so miss those days. Rebecca has come and gone, unable to stay and watch, as "Knots Landing" actors speak of an extended series run.

She arrived as I tearfully emailed notices of the last newsletter publication. The sound of an opening door went unheard while singing along to music by Lisa Marie Presley playing at full blast. Confusion ruled upon sensing a presence and feeling something lick my left ankle, so it seemed prudent to call out for Rebecca's small dog.

Princess ran into the room, frantically wagging her tail, seconds later. The part Terrier seemed preoccupied with looking up into empty space. "It's okay," I announced softly upon realizing she saw my spirit friends, "you're not in harm's way." Rebecca then entered to ask about using our dryer because Martha's ancient clothes dryer finally broke down.

When the telephone rings later, I let Rebecca answer it. Amos called from jail earlier and intuition says he's trying, once again, to get some cash. He's hoping that I'll feel sorry for him. I ponder our conversation and wonder why he still seems to project his problems onto everyone else, even after years of drug addiction. Amos wants me to go to his job and have his boss send a $40 money order.

"I need it within two days," he pleaded, "or I won't get it because they're moving me. I need the money for snacks."

He also wanted me to get his identification and license plate off of his car at the towing company.

"You know," Amos confided almost in a whisper, "the doc here said I've had two mini heart attacks and might be anemic."

Ah, the "poor me" power play, a favorite of mine for years.

"Well that's what happens when you use a lot of cocaine," I then smugly told him.

"Taking pills can do that too and you take handfuls of those every day," he snapped back.

Amos remains unaware that cash is harder for me to get and my marriage is in jeopardy. It does not occur to me that I might still be projecting my issues onto others. The time to learn souls' lessons is here but I remain oblivious, while deciding, right then, to stop taking any kind of medication.

Rebecca hung up the telephone to verify suspicions. We agreed. His boss paid him on his usual payday, the day he landed in jail. She returned from checking the dryer, with an open beer in her small manicured hand, minutes later. My latest preoccupation poured forth as she sat on the futon to drink and listen.

"You know, since your brother told me he was going to be reborn, I haven't felt him around half as much."

"I miss him too Mom," she said, before taking a long slug of beer, "but that's no reason to dwell on the past."

"Do you mean to say you've forgotten all the times he spoke, to both of us, after his funeral," I asked indignantly.

"No," said Rebecca taking another gulp of golden beer, "it's just not something people should talk about." She then looked boldly into my eyes. "Look Mom, I haven't turned off my psychic senses. I know he is no longer in 'the middle.' I know he is reborn but that doesn't make it any easier. Can we drop the subject? You know this futon is very uncomfortable and I don't know how you sleep on it."

She then rose quickly to head toward the living room.

When I entered the room minutes later, she laid snugly on the love seat, leaving the brown, leather, Lazy Boy empty for me.

"Rachel says it's okay if the rest of the family wants to come over on Sunday to see her and Abigail," she told me, looking up quickly during a television commercial break. "Abigail is going to ride her horse in the Christmas parade."

I remained silent but filled with joy as a "Ghost Whisperer" segment unfolded. Rebecca seemed extremely interested in the lead character that helped spirits finish earth business so they could move on.

"I didn't know you liked this show," I finally remarked, filled with excitement..

Rebecca became visibly upset and rose to fetch dry laundry.

"I don't see what difference it makes," she'd replied huffily, finishing a second beer.

She left minutes later. I'm not sure if was due to our discussion or that she could not bear to see the "Knots Landing Reunion." Rebecca thinks it's easier to quench psychic abilities. There's so much I see, hear, and listen to, so much I know, but cannot say. When I'm with Rebecca, or anyone else in the family, it seems as if I cannot be myself.

Now, I continue to work while thinking of our strained relationship. I try real hard not to be in my human self but sometimes it just hits me. After the show, I sit quietly, pounding away at the laptop keyboard trying to motor through feelings.

"I still lay on the black futon, in my 'white light room,' for hours, sleeping, waking, going to the bathroom, and then falling asleep again. When it's really tough, I always get pulled back into my spiritual mode. A voice from the past, or repeating numbers wake me.

"I am guided to not speak of these things, most of them at least. Still, I figure it's okay if someone is reading this. Whenever Spirit wants me to stop doing something, the computer freezes up, the television changes channels or turns off, or the DVD player malfunctions. Later, sometimes weeks or months later, I'm able to finish what I started.

"My old friend Mary Ann spoke to me a few mornings ago. I remember holding her infant Gene when I was nearly six months pregnant with Daniel. Encompassing love filled me with joy. He was such a good infant and felt so right in my arms. Gene died of SIDS, after I left the safe haven Mary Ann gave me for the days between juvenile court and living at Peter's parent's house.

"I now get the impression that Gene's spirit was reborn in Daniel because I was in a more conductive position to let destiny take its course. That is why it was important that we meet. The epiphany is alarmingly surprising but its truth settles calmly into my very being. It has been forty years since Mary Ann and I met. We only knew one another for a short time. She is a member of my soul family who helped me in an instant of need."

James returns from his night job and peeks into the room. He asks how long Rebecca stayed for Princess' water bowl lies forgotten on the floor.

"The whole family is going to see Abigail in the Christmas parade on Sunday," I announce with a smile.

"Well," James says, looking tired after a 12-hour workday. "I haven't had the chance to see them for a while and I'm going fishing tomorrow but I'll be free on Sunday."

"Will tonight be the night that freedom comes?" My brain silently wonders. "Or is there still something meaningful to do for humanity?"

The name "Bathsheba," and the word "stoned," rings through my head the next morning. When James returns from fishing, I ask if the word Bathsheba means anything to him. He remembers her as a prostitute.

"Samuel, you give me much comfort," lingers in my head the following morning.

Curiosity gets the best of me so I perform an Internet search using the words "Bathsheba," "Samuel," "stoned," and "life of." The *Bible* holds a clue. 2 Samuel 11 notes Bathsheba was the eighth wife of King David.

"The life of Bathsheba has the theme of waiting for deliverance," I read with interest, for deliverance is my goal as well.

King David sent messengers to request Bathsheba's presence while her father and husband were at war. They had not met but struck by her beauty, upon seeing her bathe in the twilight on her roof, asked about her. The scriptures say King David had seven wives but he "lay with her." There's no detail of how it exactly happened. Bathsheba, being a religious woman, followed the country's ritual of cleansing herself before returning to her own home the next evening.

She became pregnant and sent word to King David of her condition. The King summoned her husband, an officer in his army, to leave his men and return from the war to refresh. David thought Bathsheba's husband would sleep with his wife and no one would know of their indiscretion. Bathsheba's husband was a loyal soldier. He did not see his wife for he thought it wrong to take comfort at his home while his men continued to fight. King David then sent him back into battle. Bathsheba became King David's wife and birthed the next King of Israel, Solomon, after the enemy killed her husband.

It's quite humbling to think I was she so many years ago. Why else would I remember those words when waking? In those days, people who committed adultery were stoned to death but Bathsheba escaped that fate. Was Daniel Solomon reincarnated? What a heady thought!

Perhaps memory of a movie, seen thirty years ago, prompted the thought. Or perhaps I am, as the article says of Bathsheba, "waiting for deliverance." I must do as Bathsheba did. I must place the lives and destinies of loved ones in the hands of God. Now that I have tried my very best to teach them well, I must let them learn their lessons without interference. My life is now about correcting past life errors, making things right.

Several clues to improve behavior come while investigating the life of Bathsheba. But I ignore them. Bathsheba respected her husband, I read. A Christian author reports that until we respect our husbands, our approaches to them will not be with the wisdom of Bathsheba. My respect for James disappeared; therefore, I do not respect myself. Neither of us feels treated the way we should be. Daniel told me to respect James six months ago but I missed this subtle clue from Spirit.

Eventually, I'll believe it necessary to make things "right" to end the cycle of birth and death. As I bask in a period of grace in 2006, where everything is surreal, I will follow instructions to bathe three times on a single day. The New International Version Archaeological Study Bible will inform me about information on 'ritual purity' and bathing rituals, of ancient times, that correlate to the life and time of Bathsheba.

Will a past life regression make sense of it all and help me to determine why I'm now with James? It is such an intriguing thought that I have to try and find out. After reading *Through Time into Healing*, by Dr. Brian Weiss, I make my own regression tape. The following day, after taking a nap, I wake to document the time when our relationship first arose by regressing myself to a past life.

A beautiful woman, wearing a white, flowing gown with gold trim, walks down a staircase in my closed eye vision. It is I. Upon entering an iron gate in front of me, I notice old, dusty, leather sandals on slender feet. A long, red, loosely fitting dress that accentuates my wavy, long, brown hair now covers me. I am Bathsheba answering the door to find three footmen sent by King David.

All three footmen are men who I now know. James is one of them. He appears jealous of King David's ability to fetch me. Alfred, the man who I shared time with in my current life before meeting James, is King David. In this ancient life, he promises to return my husband from the war in return for a night with me. The other footman is the best friend distanced from Daniel before his transition, Horace.

Images flash past my closed eyes quickly. I see James, with his jealous stare, watch me leave the palace, and myself, vomiting while my mother tells me to see King David to report I am with child. I then see myself as an old woman dying of natural causes while several people stand at my bedside. When the regression ends, I strongly feel Rachel was King David's seventh wife.

I'm not sure about living as Bathsheba but the regression seems to link me with James, Rachel, and two other men in my current life. It seems that James is now in my life for he wished to be with me during King David's reign. Perhaps, our current relationship fulfills dreams of that time so long ago. In my mind, it's time to correct errors towards Rachel in a past life, for her son lost the opportunity to rule because the kingdom went to Bathsheba's son upon their father's death. I decide to continue with thoughts of getting James and Rachel together to make up for past behavior.

Lost in new thoughts, I consider ending the signing of various political petitions to concentrate more fully on spiritual and family matters. Christmas is approaching and money is still an issue. Shopping in the swarm of people during the holiday season fills me with dread. I quickly decide to give everyone a family video, of his or her choice, in the new DVD format. There are many years of videos to choose from so everyone will be happy with their gift.

Transferring family videos onto DVD's keeps me busy but old business still earns my time. I publish the last newsletter online but continue weekly subscriber email updates, even though my heart is no longer in tune with the work. Time spent answering emails, concerning hiv/aids, decreases dramatically. Editors now do much of the work. Spiritual matters and family take up more time.

On the first Sunday in December, everyone is excited to see Abigail ride her pony in the Christmas parade. The visit clearly shows Rachel and Abigail growing in every imaginable way. Abigail is the only child riding a horse and looks right at home with Rachel walking proudly beside her. I nearly fall over in surprise when they present me with an early birthday present. A large box of greeting cards sits under the intricate wrapping paper.

Thrilled to get them, I consider the gift a message from Source. It's a sign to maintain contact with Abigail. Rachel is surprised when I relate the saga of my lost greeting cards.

"Thank you both for the cards," I tell her and Abigail. "Now I know I lost them so you could give me new ones."

"Well," Rachel tells us with a loving look at Abigail, "it was her idea."

Indeed, we are part of Universal Mind, with one Absolute Divine Source, flowing through and connecting us all with love.

We head back to Ruth and Naomi's house to see their Christmas decorations after our visit. Ruth and Naomi again surpass their usual glitzy display by decorating the roof with twinkle lights. A talking Santa Claus greets us as we near the front door making us all laugh with glee. Numerous orbs appear as a drunken Terry yells at the talking Santa to shut up.

Later, I make out a thank you card for Rachel and Abigail and invite them to spend Christmas with us at Rebecca's house.

Schedules fill with the usual tasks of fetching Samuel from school, sandwiched between Science of Mind services, classes, and dinners. I avoid society, particularly family, feeling they do not relate to a new way of being. My quest to avoid society deepens while immersed in Science of Mind studies. Opportunities to influence me, for those who know nothing about the teachings of Ernest Holmes, are limited. Receptivity grows as I spend more time alone, away from television, news, and those not seeking a higher consciousness.

:-)

Chapter Twenty-Seven

Focusing the Host

The focus of our awareness becomes the reality of our world. Gregg Braden - The Divine Matrix

Music from the television fills the house while I check the usually overstuffed email box. Things that mattered so much before now slip away.

"Nowhere man, please listen," I sing loudly while weeding through more than 5,000 unread emails. "You don't know what you're missing. The world is at your command."

Nothing else seems important for I've happened upon the '70's movie that put the Beatles on the U.S. map. Vivid memories of "Sergeant Pepper's Lonely Hearts Club Band" rule the day. Daniel and I sang and danced to the album while trying to make our upstairs East Detroit flat into a home. Daniel was two years old and recovering from hernia surgery. It was a tough time. But now I look back and think how innocent it was, how pure, just a mother and her son trying to live a worthwhile life.

Peter eventually found us, found the rent money hidden in the blue, glass, light fixture, and left again, for another fix. I was so innocent then, so naïve, yet so determined to keep my son and raise him properly. We had fun times but mainly struggled trying to get used to life without Peter. It saddens me to recall taking out my frustration on Daniel, after seeing his messy bedroom, and finding the money gone. Daniel must have become accustomed to being alone as I slept after work in the early morning hours. It must have affected him in some way, perhaps it made him more self-sufficient, perhaps... it made him leery of trusting people, at the time.

Ego sucks me further into the illusion of this world by pointing out the "special relationship" designed to keep me in place. That relationship will slowly fade away while realizing it's another tool my soul planned to lead me back to the One.

Even though Daniel is reborn, fleeting signs from Spirit materialize. Our love continues throughout eternity. How comforting to know I am never alone! It fills my heart with joy when the CD player beeps, after silences of weeks or months, or when my car alarm erupts when leaving a family members house. I know we all miss Daniel but we are One, inseparable, no matter what family says.

My first 8-week Center course ends with gratitude for Daniel's guidance. Three more courses stand between the 100 series certificate and me. The role of Practitioner Intern looks good even if it may not come to fruition.

"Stay the course, Ma," Daniel continues to say, "Just stay the course."

Butterflies are not as abundant since agreeing that Momma should be next to go Home. Yet, I know it's not my decision to make. We must learn our lessons and have ample opportunities to do so. I'm more mindful than ever before, always looking for the lesson. And yes, it's still difficult to remain quiet for I continually tell family to be mindful too. Strange occurrences continue.

"The human skin is transparent," I hear upon waking on Friday.

The next night I watch an older ghost movie staring Sarah Jessica Parker and hear the very same words.

"The human skin is transparent and that's why you can't see them," a ghost says.

On Sunday, I hear someone is pregnant. Rebecca announces a friend's miscarriage later in the day.

A dream wakes me minutes after drifting off to sleep. Samuel, Rachel, a baby, and I were buying food.

"You've got to think about what it costs, money, to raise a baby," I tell them. "Think about what it costs the baby too. And that's why I say a treatment for the baby when I first awake."

The dream is so vivid that I decide to write a treatment for children to put on the Internet. It's my fifty-fifth birthday as I write while sitting in my sanctuary of a room. Words flow quickly from head to hands on the computer keyboard. [7] Isolation continues as I work on Daniel's third book, for I'm unwilling to tempt fate by celebrating with family. The book documents his life from age four to five.

What seems like unbearable pain in joints and bladder soon makes it too hard to concentrate. Sleep beckons earlier than usual. I wake frequently throughout the night, without pain, thinking I'm in heaven. It feels like an unseen entity is lovingly holding me. Their arms wrap snugly around my torso. A feeling of great love fills my heart. I know Daniel is doing the best he can to help me recognize that love never dies. The feeling is close to that sensation of unconditional love, first experienced during a near-death experience at age sixteen. It marks my first conscious awareness of being in another dimension.

In March of 2006, I will begin to study A Course In Miracles, *the popular teaching device that leads readers back to God. I will read the words that assure me my quest to find meaning in an unseen world is worthy.*

"The world about him shines with love because God placed him in Himself where pain is not, and love surrounds

him without end or flaw. Disturbance of his peace can never be. In perfect sanity he looks on love, for it is all about him and within him. He must deny the world of pain the instant he perceives the arms of love around him. And from this point of safety he looks quietly about him and recognizes that the world is one with him."

Another movie flashes past closed eyes during meditation two days later. Sara, another woman, and me are standing in a land of gold, with golden skies and golden fields. Stars appear, throughout the images, and a baby crawls, quickly morphing into a man with brown hair who briskly walks past. It's a side view of Daniel who is finding new ways to alert me of his presence without triggering much emotional response.

Daily meditation helps to lower blood pressure and I've cut down on many medications. Full use of my right hand returns days before Christmas. The need to peck at the computer keyboard, to assure that my right side does not numb, disappears. What a blessing to write longhand again! This is the best I've felt since Daniel's transition. A letter to long distance friends, written in longhand, marks the occasion. I sandwich judgment about others between updates on spiritual progress.

"I'm taking lessons to help others through these tough times and feel it's my last mission," I joyfully write. "My first semester of the Religious Science 100 series of classes is complete. There are four semesters over a period of three years and then another eighteen to twenty-four months of internship to be a practitioner.

"Thankfully, I get to be the "coffee lady" to pay for classes. Spirit finds a way for me, always. After the first of the year, I may take two classes a week as I seem to know so much of the teaching already. It comes easily to me."

My life story, I now decide, will be a best seller. Constantly following Science of Mind principles seems impossible to do as I waver between heaven and hell. Although James appears to secretly get anger management help, through his new job, our paths are different. We live very dissimilar lives. Our marriage is over because my path is to increase the humanitarian work James appears to dislike. James remains on the "fly-fishing track." His goal, to be a fly-casting guide, continues to spur him forward. I'm grateful for little things. He's much more responsible about doing his own laundry and managing the checkbook.

New words fill my mind upon waking on Christmas Eve. We canceled newspaper delivery, to save money, and I have not watched television news for many months so there's no reasonable explanation for the message.

"There was a bomb threat earlier today."

James visits with his mother and sister while I attend the candle lighting service at the Center. His pictures show that Martha lost more weight. She seems lost while looking down at the floor as family members smile for the camera.

Two days later, while cleaning a cluttered table in the living room on December 24, 2005, I find a section of newspaper that James brought home from work. A headline reports, "Bomb Scare Closes I-95, Guns Found." My psychic abilities are rising.

James and I drive to Rebecca's in the early afternoon on Christmas Day. Over the last several weeks, I have made DVD's for family members and copied statements from James' retirement accounts. Something prompts me to keep copies hidden in my room. Our marriage no longer feels good and I'm sure James feels the same by the way he acts.

When we are on our path, when we feel good about something, we are in alignment with our soul's intentions. James and I had a serious discussion in 2005. I told him my soul was no longer happy. We were both miserable and in a lower vibrating space no longer excited, or passionate, about our marriage. It's clear to me now that our souls hit a fork in the road and we were no longer in alignment with each other.

Rachel and Abigail surprise us with a visit in the late afternoon. Rachel wears a t-shirt that says "Reasonably Priced," two gold necklaces, two diamond earrings in each ear, five gold rings, a silver bracelet, and a watch. It's clear that she and James have a special relationship. I privately tell her she can have him for our marriage is over. James allows Abigail to paint his face with a beard, mustache, big eyelashes, and a flower in the middle of his forehead. He looks happy to see her and stays close.

Family DVD's or framed photos with pictures of family members are well received. James surprises us with gifts bought from the store he works at part-time. We have a ball singing karaoke with Naomi's talking Santa. An increase in energy surrounds Ruth and me as we sing. The family complains that my camera is broke so I stop taking pictures after six photos.

Several of the forty-three family Christmas photos show changing energy fields. Nineteen photos feature orbs and a white mist is prominent in several pictures. One picture shows Naomi looking wistfully at white mist with orbs behind her. Another orb blocks the camera from seeing Rebecca's left nostril. A whitish mist surrounds her in another as she holds Princess. A streak of white light is clear on the dog's right hindquarter as she lies on Samuel's bed. One orb looks like a smiley face. A tiny, bright, white orb, on the back of my head as I take presents out from under the tree, delights me.

I continually ask for guidance from the Otherside. The feeling that there's more to my marriage with James overwhelms me. It's easy to recall my horoscope for the week we started dating. It spurred me into investing in a relationship with someone totally different from previous loves or me.

"You will experience life as never before by opening yourself to this new relationship," it confided. "The riches that come to you as a result of this lifestyle change are beyond your wildest imagination."

It's time to make sense of it all by investigating a past life. Just as Dr. Weiss says in his book, I remember everything after a lengthy nap.

It is sometime around 960 A.D. I see myself as an old woman with brown eyes, long, brown hair, and olive colored skin. My leather sandals are brown, like the ragged, sack-like, cloth garment tied at my waist. The sandals have straps over the big toes. My legs are shapely and look well toned but my hands are old and wrinkled.

It is night as I walk past white, adobe houses with flat roofs in a small, sparsely lit village. A man calls out to me as I walk by.

"Hello Samantha," he says holding a lantern with a candle to light his way.

I pass him but stop to ask a richly dressed woman, who seems to be waiting for me, "Where do I go?"

"To the father's house," she tells me insistently pointing up to a big, white house, "do not tarry, he is waiting for you."

It is Samuel's father's house. Hills, or mountains, on three sides surround the desert area. I begin to walk quickly up a hill. The roadway is scattered with rocks and pebbles. I stumble past them for I do not have a lantern to light the way. Fear fills me as I walk looking at sandy, sparse land with small trees that have few limbs or leaves.

I am to talk with Rebekah about her son James who is in need. The war is over and soldiers are looking for him so he needs a safe place to hide. He is to stay the night at my little house so he can travel further the next day. James is to go to Smyrna to seek refuge from the new King who has decreed that he must die due to his belief in the Master Jesus. My house is near the border. There are no hills or mountains there but it is somehow hard for people to see it. I was chose to help James because my home is hard to find and I am not well known.

The door opens before me as I stand at the back entrance to the house. James, a big, burly man who smells of liquor, and who was my son in a previous life, is there. He subconsciously hates me for I was not a good mother in our previous life. In this life, he still holds resentment for me. I quickly realize he is the fiancé that my daughter left after seven years. The woman with him in the house is his mother now. She bids him goodbye. He follows me, carefully, so as not to be seen by others.

As we walk, he periodically stumbles and pushes me ahead saying, "Faster, walk faster old woman."

He is not a very intelligent man and takes advantage of me, using me as a servant, when we reach my one room home. Fear fills me as pain bloats my intestines, stomach, and bladder. James falls quickly asleep. I lay with my back to him, crying softly, praying he will leave when dawn comes.

James leaves quickly in the morning right before several soldiers of the King arrive on their horses. One of the soldiers is Zephaniah, my current husband's decreased father. Zephaniah is the one who stabs me for hiding the refugee. People from the village come and take my donkey and meager household items of pottery and cooking pots.

I take time to learn that my previous life lessons were to learn humility and to help others. It is clear that my propensity to use the acronym SAM relates to this past life. Have I met the soul contracts made with Zephaniah and Rebecca's past fiancé?

The regression ends and now I'm weary and freezing. My soul group comforts me in the safe, white room envisioned many times. Most of them surround my bed with the flowing mosquito netting. Daniel says he will meet me, beyond my room, on the beach that lies past the invisible door.

A sense of what is to come interrupts thoughts. Has my soul bargained before human birth to balance karma from the past life when Zephaniah killed me? It is exhilarating, and depressing, to think that the father James knew in this life was the King's solider responsible for taking my life in the past.

A few days later, before New Year's Eve, I decide to regress myself back to the first life lived with Daniel. I again see myself in a white, flowing gown with gold trim walking down a staircase. This time the staircase is made of lines of white light. An arched, wooden doorway covered with lush, green vines and pink and red flowers stands in front of me. When I step through the doorway, I become a young, unclothed, shapely, white girl with blonde hair and blue eyes.

It is early B.C. and I am in a lush garden in Nubia. A young boy in green, sack-like cloth approaches me. He is the master's son. I recognize the boy as Daniel even though it does not look like him.

"The master is in need of your services," he says without emotion.

I soon ask the master why I'm there. He announces that my birth mother gave me to him thinking I would be cared for and safe. I was four years old at the time and she could not afford to care for me properly. Another scene flashes before my eyes. A younger girl replaces me.

The master is Daniel's father in our current life. He tormented both Daniel and me in this past life. It is clear that Daniel and I shared the same life lessons. We were to know that pain, and suffering, teaches compassion and that we do not always have control over our life due to environmental and age issues.

Questions fill my mind for a long time. Did I meet my contract with Daniel's father this time around? Who was my mother in that life? Who was my father then?

"It doesn't matter who your parents were," I hear. "The lessons are all that matters."

Another life review fuels a greater interest in spiritual growth. If I could work a variety of twenty-three jobs, over the course of twenty-seven years, starting as a server when Daniel was one month old and progressing to a position that required a college degree, I can do anything. I am a quick learner and that courageous part of me is still within. The road has been long, and rough, but I can succeed. Now I ponder the sale of my company to propel me further down the path.

My first book begins to take form as I dedicate it to everyone who ever lost his, or her, way on the path of evolution. I sincerely hope it will help people to believe in themselves and recognize their ability to have a better life.

Prior to dawn on New Year's Eve, I rise and dress quickly before leaving the house to make coffee for the Center's World Healing Meditation. The event marks my first awareness of how the world comes together as One by joining in consciousness, at an appointed time, to repeat the Peace Prayer. I sign "My Contract with Myself" filled with excitement and anticipation of a New Year. [8] The "Releasing Ceremony" afterwards affects me greatly as I let go of the past using the Burning Bowl method.

The Universe is telling me to let go of the old to make room for the new. Back in my room, I am still trying to determine what is wrong. File uploads fail and weekly business updates are not going to subscribers. I now meditate regularly and reap the profits through messages that come as a flowing stream of thoughts, images, and ideas. It will be a while longer before I develop the skill of knowing it truly is all God. Yet, the renewing connection of meditation fosters an awareness and trust of the God within.

Fireworks light up the sky at midnight while I think about family enjoying the New Year's celebration. It did not take much convincing to get them to venture out without me for no one prefers my company. The fireworks lessen as I lay my tired body on the futon and, feeling the bar on my back, decide to buy another foam mattress.

A sense of loving companionship overwhelms me while staring at the empty space where my desktop computer used to be. The computer sits in the closet, along with many business tools, stored away before Hurricane Wilma. A magenta-colored orb hovers in mid-air. Its light reflects onto both sides of the large, wooden, work desk. Daniel's essence and a sense of indescribable love surround me. I smile and quickly drift off to sleep. The orb seems to remain there for the rest of the night.

It helps to see our guidance as though it comes from another level than our finite sense of self. And it helps to consciously ask for, and seek, help from "other" entities. I now realize those entities are part of my own consciousness.

*Everything we hear, even the inner voices that speak to us, comes from our own selves, our union with Omniscience (Consciousness that incubates creation). It may appear to us as other entities, guides from another dimension, or even angels. However, as there is only one infinite Self, in whatever form it appears, what we see is a projection of our own Oneness. Ultimately, we must allow our heart, our own inner wisdom, our own intuition, to be the final authority and trust that **we are God**.*

The Beginning :-)

Epilogue

Using the Law of Mind is not as hard as one might expect. It's all about monitoring thought patterns to create a perfect living environment. As Ernest Holmes wrote in 1926:

"One by one, people will investigate the Truth and put *It* into operation, and the time will come when disease and poverty will be swept from the face of the earth, for they were never intended to be. They are simply the by-products of ignorance and enlightenment alone will erase them."

I continue to recognize the unseen force that guides and ask for guidance knowing that more and more people seek *It*, the *One Thing*, every day. There is now a knowing that I must complete three more books within the next three years. It is the reason I remain here, currently enjoying a heaven undreamed of years ago.

Notes

1- "The Lord "is now" my Shepard, so even in chaos I will not want for anything. I have been created to lie down in green pastures, even in the face of chaos. In the midst of chaos, I am led to stillness. When chaos has affected me, the Spirit restores my soul. Even in chaos, it leads me in the right direction because God is the only power. Lo, though I walk through the valley of chaos, I will fear no evil because I can lean on the spirit, and it keeps me in line. It prepares a table before me in the presence of fear and doubt. My cup of life runneth over. Surely goodness and mercy shall follow me for the rest of my days, and I will live forever in the house of Spirit, where there is no chaos."
Starke W, *It's All God* (Boerne, Texas: The Guadalupe Press, 1998), 214.

2- It is February 23, 2009 as I continue to document life changes. Spirit continues to guide me much more than recognized. While looking for lost computer files, due to the haphazard operation of older computers, I find an old journal. The journal holds an explanation of my awakening process, from April 4, 2004 to January 2, 2007.

These things helped me to change the dis-ease within and to live life more fully as a healthy individual:

* A period of grieving that graduated from clinging to material things, unbridled singing, blessing, and helping others, to trusting in the unseen.

* Changing the focus of awareness from trying to improve others to improving myself; letting go of the past, negative feelings such as blame and guilt, objects of negativity (certain music, movies, thoughts, etc.) and detrimental relationships.

* A period of self-discovery, which resulted in recognition of an ever-lasting Oneness instead of a finite self.

* Spiritually guided purification process using candles, a bathing ritual, dietary changes (including a one-day fast drinking lots of water), elimination of caffeine, alcohol, drugs, and synthetic substances such as perfumes and deodorant.

* Concentration on spiritual growth through reading; classes; prayer; uplifting music; and positive affirmations to open the mind.

3- Suggestions for the 21st Century

* Make personal responsibility a necessity in your life; start by caring for yourself and your birth family.

* Always, put love of people, starting with you, before love of material possessions.

* Recognize that you have the power and knowledge within you to make your life better. Stop pride from limiting personal or spiritual growth.

* Always, ask questions, no matter how stupid you, or others, think they may be.

* Practice Mindfulness:

       Value love, peace, and harmony among all living things every day

       Think about the consequences to others, and yourself, before you speak. Choose your words carefully.

       Think about the consequences to yourself and the world, before you act. Know that your actions can affect people you do not even know.

* Always, love all living beings without remorse; act through love and not anger. Give more than you take; lend a hand to lift other people up.

* Help as many people as you can throughout your life to nourish the spirit in all people.

* In times of need, first help people who wish to help themselves; help all people if time and finances permit you to do so. Do not enable destructive people to hurt themselves and others by helping them repeatedly as they continue to destroy themselves and others.

* In times of loss or trouble always look for the lesson that can be learned.

* Be prepared to see opportunities for personal growth. Take them and put your fear aside. Opportunities for growth that create the most fear are the ones that offer the most positive growth. They always nourish your spirit the most.

* Assure that the world is a better place before you pass on.

* Remember, there are always spirit guides to help you choose the most positive ways to help yourself and others. To tap into this knowledge, focus on your heart with good intentions for all living beings. Offer love, peace, and harmony to everyone you meet.

4- "I know you're listening as I lay me down to sleep. It's not for me I ask but my children's souls to keep. It seems the world is going crazy and through I need to do my share could you please take them under wing, watch over them especially, keeping them safe from everything. This is a Mother's Prayer."
Manchester M, "A Mother's Prayer," (*Divas Simply Singing*, Trax Recording), 2000.

5- Treatment for Perfect Health #1

God is perfect health, perfect peace and limitless love, free of all dis-ease, discord or disharmony. This Divine Source flows through all things including me. Right where pain, dis-ease, discord, resentment, anger, or fear seems to operate the presence of Infinite Intelligence is.

Perfection flows through my blood, as I AM one with the Divine Mind. Spirit allows me to grow. There is no inner agitation or outward irritation in me. A warm sense of my oneness, in essence and experience with *All the Good There Is*, replaces inner agitation or outward irritation.

I give thanks to God that I AM guided by Infinite Intelligence, clearing all thought of limitation. I release this treatment to the Law of Mind knowing that perfection manifests itself within me forevermore throughout eternity. And so it is!

6- Treatment for Perfect Health #2

I recognize the nature of our Creator as being One Infinite Intelligence operating in effortless Perfection, ever expanding, growing, and nurturing the manifestations of the Divine Mind.

I know that I am a manifestation of the Mind of God operating in healthy and effortless perfection. Infinite Intelligence, free of any limitation, guides me. It is my nature to expand and grow, easily accepting that which nurtures my evolution. My life is a quest to nurture human evolution and serve our Creator with Love, Peace, and Harmony among all things. I welcome the knowledge I receive in achieving this honor.

I am grateful to Spirit as I recognize there is no limitation of any sort. I thank the Divine Source of *All the Good There Is* for the gifts I receive daily.

With effortless acceptance, I entrust these words to the Laws of the Universe, the Law of Mind, to flow eternally throughout all space. And so it is!

7- Treatment for Children

The One and Only Knowing Living Spirit surrounds and lives in all. This perfect being manifests itself without limitation through all children living on earth.

Harmony and spontaneous Unity, Positivity, Divine compassion, Complete satisfaction, and Perfect Health flow through all earth children, as they are one with God.

The Living Spirit Almighty freely guides every aspect of life for all earth children towards *All the Good There Is*. Fearless faith in the Creative Mind frees all thought of limitation.

I am grateful to the Divine Source of all-good for the gifts of Harmony, Unity, Positivity, Compassion, Complete satisfaction and Perfect Health that manifest within all earth children.

I release this treatment and entrust it to the Law of Mind secure in the Truth of One Mind manifesting the Spirit of the Universe within all things forever. And so it is!

8- Religious Science Fort Lauderdale's "My Contract with Myself"

"Right Now I feel great excitement and anticipation about my life and what is possible for me to express in 2006.

"I have felt like this before. This time I commit that it will be different. Because this time I will be different. I choose to take action and I choose to now follow through completely on my commitment to myself and my personal growth.

"I choose to create a fulfilling, rewarding and meaningful life in this year. By taking this sacred time for the Burning Bowl Ceremony, I have already taken the first step. I have gained the clarity and purpose necessary to expand this vision into my tangible experience.

"I know that it all starts with a greater idea about who and what I really am and the value I bring to the world.

"I know that it all starts with a greater idea about Life and all the new opportunities that I discover around me.

"I know that it all starts with a greater idea about God truly supporting me in all ways with this new identity of myself.

"I achieve this greater experience of Life by choosing to look for the good in myself and others, by choosing to believe something greater about myself and others and by choosing to expect the best for myself and others.

"I achieve this greater experience of Life by reminding myself that God is always ready, willing and able to respond to any greater idea in which I invest my time, energy and attention.

"I am so grateful for this new understanding, this sense of greater possibility and this decisiveness that I am now expressing.

"I will not waiver on this commitment to myself. Today I agree to do this, to identify myself in ever greater ways and to encourage others to do the same."

Center For Spiritual Living, Fort Lauderdale, FL., www.cslftl.org.

:-)

Bibliography

Books

* Allen, James. *As A Man Thinketh*, 1902. (www.AsAManThinketh.net).
* Anderson, George and Andrew Barone. *Walking in the Garden of Souls*, 2001.
* Atkinson, William W. *Thought Vibration*, 1906. (www.thoughtvibrations.com).
* Atwater, P.M.H. *Beyond the Indigo Children*, 2005.
* Baldwin, Sally. *Dying to Live Again*, 2001.
* "Bathsheba (A Woman who let's God Deliver)." (www.amarlis.net Accessed 12/1/05).
* Bishop, Karen. *Remembering Your Soul Purpose*, 2006.
* Bishop, Karen. *Staying in Alignment*, 2006.
* Bishop, Karen. *Stepping into the New Reality*, 2008.
* Bishop, Karen. *The Ascension Primer,* 2006.
* Braden, Gregg. *The Divine Matrix*, 2007. (www.greggbraden.net/).
* Chopra, Deepak. *Peace is the Way: Bringing War and Violence to an End*, 2005.
* Doner, Margaret. *Archangels Speak*, 2008.
* "Fear to Faith Worksheet," *A Sacred Healing Service Workbook*, 2003. (www.SacredDays.org).
* Foundation for Inner Peace, *A Course In Miracles*, 1976, 1992. (www.acim.org/).
* Freiberg, Richard. "Ba Gua Fa: Neurological & Vascular Decompression Method to Relieve Myofascial & Musculoskeletal Pain," HIV Nutrition Update, Winter 2005, HIV ReSources, Inc.
* Gunaratana, Henepola, *Eight Mindful Steps to Happiness: Walking the Buddha's Path*, 2001. (www.wisdompubs.org).
* "Hidden Belief Exercise," SOM-101 Study Guide, Class 7, Page 3, Rev. Sept 2003, Religious Science Fort Lauderdale.
* Holland, John. "Messages From the Other Side An Interview with John Holland," *Venture Inward Magazine,* March/April 2009, Vol. 25, No. 2, Association for Research and Enlightenment, Inc.
* Hollowell, Bud. *Watching Trains Go By.* (www.oneworldinsight.com).
* Holmes, Ernest. *The Science of Mind*, Original Text 1926, Rev. 1998.
* International Bible Society, *New International Version Archaeological Study Bible*, 2005.
* Keyes, Ken, Jr. "The Twelve Pathways," Living Your Authentic Life Class, Religious Science Fort Lauderdale, 2005.
* Lockard, Jim. "Letting Go," *One in Spirit Magazine*, July/August 2005, Vol. 9, Iss. 4, First Church of Religious Science.

* Lockard, Jim. "Personal Spiritual Practices Survey," Living Your Authentic Life Class, Religious Science Fort Lauderdale, 2005.
* MacLaine, Shirley. *Dancing in the Light*, 1985.
* Martin, Joel and Patricia Romanowski. *We Don't Die George Anderson's Conversations With The Other Side*, 1988.
* Newton, Michael. *Destiny of Souls*, 2004.
* NovaTech, "Spiritual Practice To Do List," Power of Spiritual Practice, Living Your Authentic Life Class, Religious Science Fort Lauderdale, 2005.
* Page, Christine. *Spiritual Alchemy*, 2003.
* Redfield, James. *Celestine Prophecy*, 1994.
* Religious Science Fort Lauderdale, "Declaration of Principles," 2005.
* Renard, Gary. *The Disappearance of the Universe*, 2002.
* Rinpoche, Sogyal and Patrick D. Gaffney (Editor), Andrew Harvey (Editor). *The Tibetan Book of Living and Dying*, 1994.
* Rodegast, Pat and Judith Stanton. *Emmanuel's Book*, 1985.
* Rodegast, Pat and Judith Stanton. *Emmanuel's Book II: The Choice for Love*, 1989.
* Spalding, Baird T. *Life and Teaching of The Masters of the Far East*, Volume 5, 1955.
* Starcke, Walter. *It's All God,* 1998.
* "The 7 X 70 Forgiveness Process," *A Sacred Healing Service Workbook*, 2003. (www.SacredDays.org).
* Van Praagh, James. *Reaching to Heaven*, 1999.
* Walsh, Neale D. "Healing with the Masters Webcast," April 30, 2009. (www.healingwiththemasters.com).
* Weiss, Brian L. *Through Time into Healing*, 1992.

Music

* Beatles. "Nowhere Man." *Yesterday and Today*. Capitol, 1966.
* Carole King. "Home Again." *Tapestry*. ODE/Epic/Legacy, 1971.
* CREED. "Higher." *Human Clay*. Wind-up Records, 1999.
* CREED. "Inside Us All." *Human Clay*. Wind-up Records, 1999.
* Dio. "I Speed At Night." *The Last in Line*. Rhino/Warner Bros, 1984.
* E. G. Daily. "Breath of Heaven." *Divas Simply Singing*. Trax Recording, 2000.
* Fleetwood Mac. "Go Your Own Way." *Rumours*. Warner Bros., 1977.
* Gloria Gaynor. "I Will Survive." *Love Tracks*. Polydor, 1978.
* Johnny Rivers. "Look to Your Soul." *Realization*. Soul City Records, 1968.
* Jon Bon Jovi. "Keep the Faith." *Keep the Faith*. Mercury, 1992.
* Journey. "Open Arms." *E5C4P3*. Columbia, 1981.

* Kansas. "Dust in the Wind." *The Best of Kansas*, CBS Associated, 1984.
* Kansas. "Hold On." *The Best Of Kansas*. Sony, 1999.
* Kansas. "On the Other Side." *The Kansas Boxed Set*. Sony, 1994.
* Kansas. "Portrait (He Knew)." *The Kansas Boxed Set*. Sony, 1994.
* Madonna. "Live to Tell." *Live to Tell*. Sire, Warner Bros, 1986.
* Melissa Manchester. "A Mother's Prayer." *Divas Simply Singing*. Trax Recording, 2000.
* Metallica. "Nothing Else Matters." *Metallica*. Elektra, Vertigo, 1991.
* Odyssey. "Our Lives Are Shaped By What We Love." Odyssey, MoWest, 1972.
* Queensrÿche. "Silent Lucidity." *Empire*. Capitol, 2003.
* Rolling Stones. "Miss You." *Some Girls*. Atlantic/Virgin, 1978.
* Sandra Pires. "I Miss You." *Divas Simply Singing*. Trax Recording, 2000.

Movies

* Biker Boyz, DreamWorks SKG, 2003.
* Easy Rider, Columbia Pictures Corporation, 1969.
* White Noise, Universal Pictures, 2005.
* Magical Mystery Tour, New Line Cinema, 1973.
* Somewhere, Tomorrow, Digiview Productions, 2004.

Websites

* Celestine Vision (www.celestinevision.com).
* Common Passion (www.commonpassion.org).
* Dolphin\Spirit of Hawaii (www.dolphinspiritofhawaii.com).
* Era of Peace (www.eraofpeace.org).
* Ernest Holmes (www.ernestholmes.wwwhubs.com).
* Foundation for Conscious Evolution (www.barbaramarxhubbard.com).
* Infinite Being (www.infinitebeing.com).
* InfinityAffinity (www.infinityaffinity.org).
* International Centers for Spiritual Living (www.rsintl.org).
* Joan Ocean Dolphin Connection (www.joanocean.com/Dolphins.html).
* Korotkov.org (www.korotkov.org).
* Life Paths Animal Totems & Earth Medicine (http://wolfs_moon.tripod.com/dolphintotem.html).
* Path to the Source (www.geohanover.com).
* Psychic Investigators (www.psychicinvestigators.net).
* Space Weather Prediction Center (www.swpc.noaa.gov).
* Uplift Humanity (http://uplifthumanity.info).

About the Author

SAM is a wayshower helping others to learn the truth of their being so humanity can return to Source. She is a lifelong believer in the power of love. Her inspiring life demonstrates the strength of Mind over matter. It is a story of progression from desperation to hope, poverty to riches, limitation to freedom and fear to love. *The End of My Soap Opera Life :-)* book series details this amazing journey of self-discovery and transformation.

The awareness that we are spirits in human form, having a physical experience, came after SAM's son transitioned on April 4, 2004. SAM's quest for self-mastery began the following year when his essence led her through the doors of an establishment teaching the Science of Mind. SAM turned her back on traditional medicine after decades of illness and multiple surgeries. Using Eastern medicine, and the teachings of Ernest Holmes, she successfully rid herself of many difficulties.

SAM's book series is a personal account highlighting the process of one Lightworker's awakening. Other books from this author include:

Book One: Death of the Sun

Transformation :-) Book Three

Prayer Treatments

Adventures in Greece and Turkey

Earth Angels

Return to Light :-) John of God Helps

Bits of Wisdom

Book of One, Volume 1

SAM is the administrator of the popular Lightworker's Log website (lightworkerslog.com) and currently concentrates on writing and spreading Spirit's message of Oneness. Guided by messages and synchronicities, SAM knows her most valuable asset is the ever-increasing awareness of our true BEing.